# One More Step

## Journey to Mt. Everest

## A Narrative Case-Study of a Successful Summit

### By Brendan T. Madden

B O U K E N
INTERNATIONAL PUBLISHING

One More Step

Editor: David Kellogg.

Foreword: Patrick McKnight.

Book Design and Cover by Richard Reay.

Photographs by Patrick McKnight, Brendan T. Madden, Martin Swzed, and Magnus Nerve.

ISBN: 978-0-9921623-8-2 (Paperback)
ISBN: 978-0-9921623-9-9 (E-Book)

Bouken International Publishing

For rights information and bulk book orders, please contact
Bouken.International@gmail.com

Printed in the United States of America.

*"A practical and inspiring guide which will be of great value to any aspiring Everest Summiteer. A perfect scene setter for anyone with a serious interest in joining a commercial team and a great read every step of the way."*
*- Matt Dickinson Author of 'The Death Zone'*

*After having watched some many grim stories about deaths on everest its weird to see a so uplifting video like yours.*
*- Edwards Mazukay*

*Without a doubt the best Everest Documentary I've seen.*
*-Juan McKelvey*

*This was one of the best Everest documentaries I have ever seen. It rivaled productions put together by discovery channel and National Geographic. Considering the large budgets and massive climbing crews they have your documentary is better. Top notch for sure. - David Daly*

*That was amazing. I have watched a lot of documentaries on Everest and this is by far the best. - Brandon Flickner*

*This has been an unbelievably motivating series. Thank you for putting in the time to record, edit, and publish your journey. Truly inspiring. - Andrew Wilikinson*

*I just climbed Everest and never left the house. I'm electric.*
*- SmartyThePants*

*Simply, one of the best accounts of an Everest journey. Congratulations and thank you! - Lamp man*

*Haven't been this excited to see a Mt Everest reality-doc since Everest: Beyond the Limit lol. - Terran Republic*

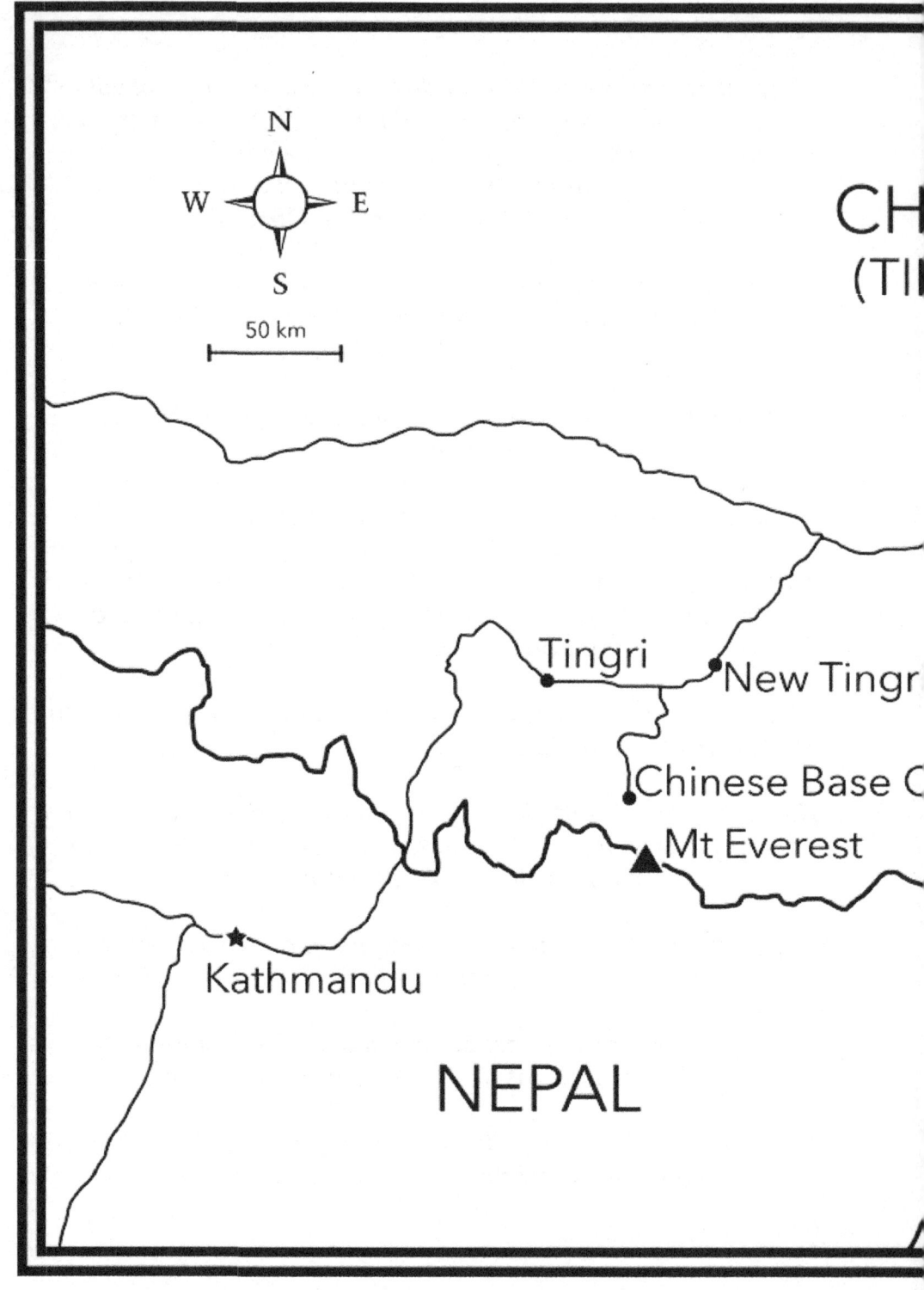

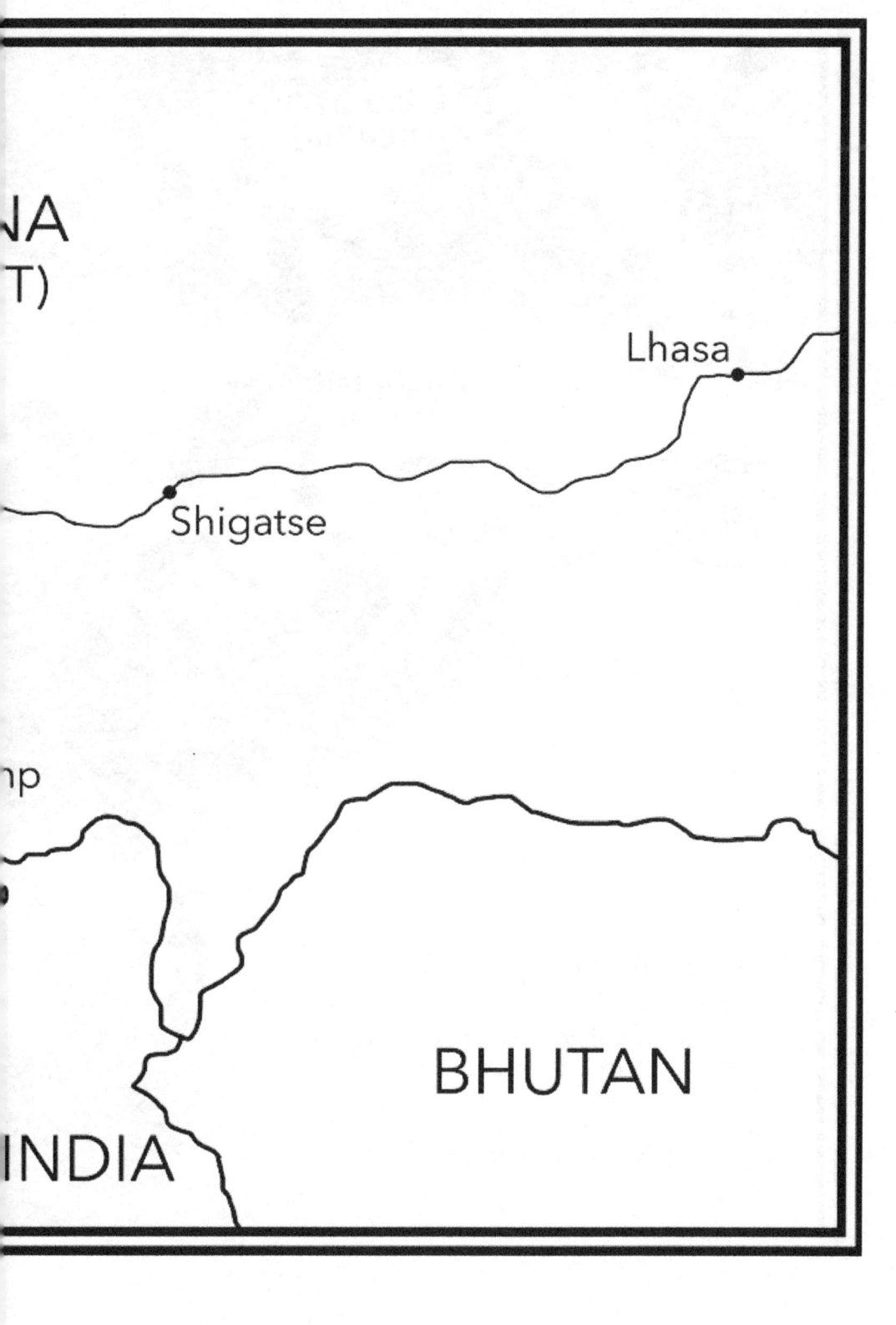

**Mt Everest**
(8848m)

3

2

1

**ABC**

**Changtse**
(7543m)

East Rongbuk Glacier

Rongbuk Glacier

IBC

## The North Face of Mt Everest

CBC - Chinese Base Camp (5182m)
IBC - Intermediate Base Camp (5742m)
ABC - Advanced Base Camp (6492m)
1 - Camp 1 - North Col (7020m)
2 - Camp 2 - Snow Slope (7700m)
3 - Camp 3 - Death Zone (8300m)

# ABBREVIATIONS

| | | | |
|---|---|---|---|
| CBC | Chinese Base Camp | SPO2 | Blood Saturated Oxygen Levels |
| IBC | Intermediate Base Camp | Os | Oxygen |
| ABC | Advanced Base Camp | PDM | Plaza de Mulas |
| C1 | Camp One | C2 | Camp Two |
| C3 | Camp Three | CTMA | Chinese Tibet Mountaineering Association |
| ALE | Antarctic Logistics & Expeditions | AMS | Acute Mountain Sickness |
| HAPE | High Altitude Pulmonary Edema | HACE | High Altitude Cerebral Edema |
| ASIJ | American School in Japan | QAIS | Qingdao Amerasia International School |

# TABLE OF CONTENTS

Foreword . . . . . . . . . . . . . . . . . . . . . . . . . . . . . . . . . . II
Preface . . . . . . . . . . . . . . . . . . . . . . . . . . . . . . . . . . VI
Acknowledgments . . . . . . . . . . . . . . . . . . . . . . . . . IX
Introduction . . . . . . . . . . . . . . . . . . . . . . . . . . . . . . XI

Chapter 1: Learning to Live. . . . . . . . . . . . . . . . . . . . 1
Chapter 2: The Ropes . . . . . . . . . . . . . . . . . . . . . . . 10
Chapter 3: Kiwi Crush . . . . . . . . . . . . . . . . . . . . . . . 35
Chapter 4: Committed. . . . . . . . . . . . . . . . . . . . . . . 52
Chapter 5: Training. . . . . . . . . . . . . . . . . . . . . . . . . 59
Chapter 6: The Tibetan Plateau . . . . . . . . . . . . . . . 75
Chapter 7: Settling In. . . . . . . . . . . . . . . . . . . . . . . 86
Chapter 8: Pinnacles and Puja . . . . . . . . . . . . . . . .106
Chapter 9: Failure on the North Col . . . . . . . . . . . .112
Chapter 10: A Second Chance. . . . . . . . . . . . . . . . .123
Chapter 11: Down Time . . . . . . . . . . . . . . . . . . . . .138
Chapter 12: Summit Push . . . . . . . . . . . . . . . . . . . .140
Chapter 13: Summit Night . . . . . . . . . . . . . . . . . . .168
Chapter 14: Halfway There . . . . . . . . . . . . . . . . . . .180
Chapter 15: Safety and Celebration . . . . . . . . . . . .193

Pictures. . . . . . . . . . . . . . . . . . . . . . . . . . . . . . . . .203
Postscript . . . . . . . . . . . . . . . . . . . . . . . . . . . . . . .224
About the Author . . . . . . . . . . . . . . . . . . . . . . . . . .231

Appendix
Everest Videos and Reference Links . . . . . . . . . . . . .232
Northeast Ridge Route: Timing and Distances . . . . . .233
Equipment List . . . . . . . . . . . . . . . . . . . . . . . . . . . .234

Note: All footnote links can be found at:
*http://www.indeepfilms.com/one-more-step.html*

# FOREWORD

After two treks to Everest base camp in 2014 and 2015, I decided one more go around to reach the top and then I would move on. Who better to share my third and final attempt with than my pal Brendan? We met while climbing Denali in 2011. He seemed to have the best time in the worst conditions. Me? I struggled with a team consisting of virtual strangers that could not get along. We had different situations and yet we both found the energy to laugh a ton together. Based upon a few hours on a mountain and roughly a day in a bar, we knew we could climb together. Flash forward to December 2014, we climbed together in Argentina and enjoyed the hell out of the adventure; the after-climb festivities were equally grand. Based upon these two exposures to Brendan, I knew I could place my trust in a strong climbing partner who would dedicate himself to preparing for Everest. I called him up...<recalled roughly>

Me: You want to climb Everest this Spring?
Brendan: Sure.
Me: Great. Let's do it.
Brendan: Hold on, let me make sure I don't lose my job.
Me: Ok.

I cannot recall the exact conversation, but I recall the theme. We briefly discussed climbing Everest together and he immediately jumped at the chance. I was actually blown away how quickly he pushed all his proverbial chips into the center of the table and said..." I'm in!" We were a team from that moment forward.

My training routine came from years of self-coached preparation for a variety of endurance activities. I painstakingly research the challenges of every event. Based upon my own critical self-evaluation and realized challenges, I begin a slow build-up of activities to mimic the stresses likely to be present. The build-up consists of a logical load progression with ample rest and ample stress. Basically, I impose a slow slogging approach to the slow slog ahead. My system works. It works for me at least. I tend to be in excellent shape and have sufficient preparation for any and all probable circumstances.

Brendan eagerly accepted my <insane> plan and readily adopted it. He was the first to ever train with me with incredible adherence - maybe better than my own. We checked in routinely and I found myself rarely surprised that he simply put his head down and did our agreed upon routine. Some of it was downright psychotic - at least according to those around us. We not only did the usual cardio and resistance training along with stretching for recovery as most others do (at least they report doing so) but we also added breathing, cold exposure and hypoxic sleep to the mix. Each of these require a little explanation.

**First, breathing.** We know we must breathe to live. Humans suffer without 3 minutes of air, 3 days without water, and 3 weeks without food. The problem with those rules of thumb is that people often die well before the 3 weeks, 3 days, or 3 minutes. Why? They give up. We were not going to be those people who gave up. The practice or rather the deliberate practice of breathing allows us to expand our tolerance (cognitively) for the lack of air. We cannot live long without air, but we can fight the temptation to breathe before we need that breath. Breathing helped us prepare for the uncomfortable.

**Second, cold.** There is little doubt that high altitude mountaineering exposes us to the cold. Many climbers die on Everest due to exposure. We needed to overcome our tendency to "feel" cold by appreciating the cold and our ability to overcome these feelings - much like we overcame the feeling of breathlessness by deliberate breathing. Brendan and I exposed ourselves to the cold for increasing periods of time. These exposures allowed our bodies to adapt by

developing more brown adipose tissue (BAT; a theory that now has more empirical evidence and likely will win the two who discovered the phenomenon a Nobel prize). We also became more tolerant of cold and better heat exchangers - all making us more efficient in these extremes.

**Finally, hypoxic sleep.** A growing body of evidence coming from decades of practice shows that sleeping in a normobaric (regular, sea-level pressure) but hypoxic (low oxygen or lower percentage than the 20.9% at sea level) environment allows the body to adapt to the hypoxic conditions while climbing. No large, randomized controlled trials exist to support this claim but I assure you that I am living proof (hardly convincing to the skeptic mind you) that the method works. I trained for Aconcagua by sleeping up to and above the simulated altitude of the mountain. Doing so allowed me to climb to 6000 meters in two days. Further, I trekked to Everest base camp in 24 hours with only one brief stop in Namche Bazaar to rest overnight. These two singular events were more than enough evidence that the method works for me and I knew it worked for Brendan. We climbed Aconcagua (via the normal route) without incident. Our efforts in preparation for Everest called for us to sleep at 6500 meters for at least two weeks before departing home; we did so gradually but without much interruption.

These three additions to the "normal" preparation meant we were physically, psychologically, and physiologically prepared. Our technical preparation came by way of doing what we both do well - be outdoors. Many folks who seek these big objectives fail to account for the daily hassles. We both spent many hours in tents, trudging through deep snow on skis, sweating profusely in cold, wet, and dark conditions. These exposures made us who we were before, during, and after the climb. Ed Viesturs was right - there are no shortcuts to the top.

The following book is almost completely Brendan's work. You will find his approach to the topic engaging and, I trust, educational. I was his compatriot for the climb - before, during, and after. We were a great team. I owe so much of my success on that mountain to him as I do to myself and to others who supported me. Take the time to listen to his sage advice.

- Patrick McKnight

# PREFACE

In September of 2012, I hit the jackpot of international school teaching. I was hired to teach high school science at the American School in Japan (ASIJ). Everything about the school was first class. The students were smart and cared about learning, the teachers were dedicated, and the decorum of life in Tokyo rubbed off on everyone. One of my colleagues Dan Stevens approached me because he heard that I played ice hockey. He said that he played for a hockey team in Tokyo called the Tokyo Canadians. After months of prodding me to play, I finally agreed. However, all my hockey equipment was at my Mom's house in Sonoma, California. I told him that when I went home for the summer, I would bring my hockey gear back.

I kept my promise and in September 2013 I showed up at my first Tokyo Canadians ice hockey practice. I hadn't been on my skates in five years. In fact, my gear had been getting stale in the garage for that entire time. I jumped out on the ice to play. A puck hit the chassis of my skates. The entire chassis crumbled like dry clay. I floundered on the ice trying to get over to the bench with one skate. Just as I did, the other skate started to disintegrate. That ended my Tokyo Canadian's tryout. I wasn't sure if the boys would have me back after that display. It took two months to get my skates fixed and back on the ice. When I came back, I found a great group of guys to slap the puck around with.

One of those guys was Richard Reay. He is a guide on Mt. Fuji. We got to talking about mountain climbing and hit it off right away. He told me he had climbed Mt. Fuji around 200 times and that was in 2013. I'm sure he has quadrupled that number now.

He also told me that he had written a *"Climbing Mt. Fuji Guidebook".* I was impressed and thankful, as I wanted to lead some new routes for my students in the ASIJ outdoor club. I used his book often for climbs and played ice hockey with him until I left Japan in 2017. Unfortunately, we never met to climb together.

When I got back from Everest, Richard saw my Everest for Mountaineers YouTube series and said,

"You should write a book about that trip."

Not one to turn down a challenge, I accepted. This book would have never been written without Richard pushing me to do so. Thank you, Richard, for your patience and help bringing this book to life. Hopefully, we will meet again soon on the flanks of Mt. Fuji or at an ice hockey tournament in Bangkok.

**Coronavirus:**
Due to the COVID-19 outbreak that started in early 2020, China and Nepal have cancelled the 2020 climbing season for both sides of Mt. Everest. This will be the first time that no one will climb the highest peak in the world since a huge earthquake closed the summit in 2015.

Likewise, many other peaks around the world including Mt. Fuji have also closed their 2020 climbing season due to this pandemic. We hope for the best and the reopening of all the mountain peaks in 2021.

**Note:** All footnote links can be found at:
http://www.indeepfilms.com/one-more-step.html

# ACKNOWLEDGMENTS

My adventures around the world would not have been possible without the support from my loving parents and hilarious brothers. My wife, Tatiana, for her support and dinners during my long training sessions.

Richard Reay for pushing me to write this book. David Kellogg, for teaching me to write well and pushing me to live outside of my comfort zone. In addition, Dave spent numerous hours helping me structure this book. He even missed a day of skiing PNW powder so that he could get the editing done. Dave, I will remember your kindness. The Qingdao Amerasia International School for believing that my climb would bring the school community together. Paco Monedero, the person that introduced me to the big mountains and seven summits challenge.

My climbing partner Patrick McKnight whose knowledge of Everest training, experience, and outlook on life had a huge impact on my own life. Our guide David O'Brien who negotiated a fine line of decision making and diplomacy that allowed for all of our team to come back alive. The superhuman Sherpas, the friendliest kitchen staff, and all other climbers on the 2018 Summit Climb team that made this such a positive, unforgettable, meaningful experience.

# INTRODUCTION

Living life without meaning, without goals, without ways of pushing your own limits and without an understanding of the world around you is no life for me. This ideology that I live by has led to this book. The WHY of this book is twofold:

**First,** for the prospective mountaineer: an unprecedented, detailed guide to climbing Mount Everest's Northeast Ridge Route with video accompaniment.

**Second,** for everyone else: inspiration to make decisions that allow you to live your life with meaning.

From the moment I committed to climbing Everest, the clock was ticking. I had exactly 230 days to get in the best shape of my life, confirm travel plans and climbing arrangements- which can be tricky in Tibet- and finally, acquire and test any climbing equipment I did not already have. I scoured the internet trying to be as prepared as possible. If there was a technique, nugget of information, or video that I could watch that would improve my chances of having a successful Everest adventure, I wanted to know about it.

On YouTube, the videos of Everest, especially the Northeast Ridge route, did not give the whole story of the climb. There were no videos that went deep into the training, the mindset, equipment, and the details of the acclimatization rounds. In the past, I have made incredibly informative adventure travel documentaries. In fact, with my friend Dave Kellogg, we established the adventure travel film company In Deep Films. I knew that with my video production experience and Dave's incredible writing skills, we could make hands down the most comprehensive video series on climbing Mt. Everest. I also realized that watching a couple of jackasses walking for a month and a half wasn't exactly mainstream entertainment.

However, while I was putting in long hours of training on an elliptical machine at the gym, that is exactly what I wanted. I wanted to know every corner, every crux, every section. Again, I wanted every advantage I could to accomplish my new goal.

Climbing and filming on Denali, there is a section called Denali Pass that I completely overlooked in my planning. It is a steep 1000m section of the climb that I had not planned on being there. Mentally, that unexpected section almost ended my climb. I did not want to repeat that on Everest. While Denali is expensive, Everest is monumentally so. I had one shot at this mountain and didn't want to leave any rock unturned when digging up information.

Another resource I used that inspired my climb, the videos, and this book is my climbing partner Patrick McKnight's blog www.climbingonpurpose.com. Patrick kept detailed records of his training, mindset, equipment, and his two attempted Everest climbs prior to our climb together. I wanted to bring this style of blog to life in video form.

With those goals in mind I created a seven-video series of my experience training for and climbing Mount Everest: Everest for Mountaineers[1]. From my range of background experience, to the training routine built by Patrick McKnight, to Chinese Base Camp and finally the Summit of Everest there is no one-stop resource that can give you written details and accompanying video for each step along the way to the top. This book can offer that.

In addition, I believe I inspire people and that you can be inspired by the accounts in this book. I came to this realization following countless conversations on Everest, developing the Everest for Mountaineers series, and interactions with thousands of K-12 students. I detail the process of my own inspiration and that of others in this book. I encourage you to be open to inspiration in your own life as you read.

---

One of my biggest honors was being chosen by the high school students to speak at the American School in Japan's 2017 Commencement[2]. Parents came up to me afterwards and asked, "Why are you teaching? You should take that presentation on the road!" Recently, I did a presentation at the American Community School in Amman, Jordan where I am currently a high school science teacher. The high school principal came up to me, he said that in his 30 years of being in schools around the globe my presentation was the second best he had ever seen. The first was Jane Goodall's.

Focused around my adventures with In Deep Films and the Everest Climb I have started the Seven Summits Leadership Workshops for middle and high school students. The aim of the workshops are to identify individual strengths and weaknesses, breakdown huge goals into easier to accomplish chunks, and learn fundamental communication skills critical for success as a leader. The workshop format follows the increasing difficulties at successive camps required for a summit of the north side of Mt. Everest. When it comes to the elementary crowd I have used assemblies called Ask a Mountaineer[3] to engage with the students on their level. The format is a brief introduction to mountaineering and then a panel of students ask questions that they have prepared in advance. My favorite question so far is "What do the clouds look like up there?" It is adorable.

This book is an extension of my vision that everyone can lead their lives with meaning. For most people this meaning isn't climbing Everest. Perhaps you will find it in having a family, creating a billion-dollar company, changing the lives of millions of refugees, or getting into the University of your choice. Whatever it is, I hope this book will inspire you.
**Find your mountain!**

---

2  YouTube. American School in Japan. June 3, 2017 - HS Commencement Ceremony.
3  YouTube. Ask a Mountaineer.

# CHAPTER 1

# LEARNING TO LIVE

Buried beneath a wool base layer, a polar fleece, a goose down summit suit, glove liners, and bulky outer mittens, accessing my watch was not an option. I'm guessing it was 2am. Gelje Sherpa, our guide, Patrick McKnight, my climbing partner, and I were surrounded by darkness. Our headlamp halos provided only a glimpse of the dangers directly in front of us and hid the 3,500-meter drop a single step to the right.

Getting here was difficult and dangerous. Every step higher increased the likelihood of staying on the mountain forever as a frozen landmark because a dead body at this altitude is too heavy to carry down. We had been on the move for three hours. The cold, wind, and lack of oxygen were taking their toll. Patrick's crampons were kicking out orange sparks as he was failing to gain purchase on the limestone face. Gelje's headlamp further up was my only indication of how steep this cliff was.

"Second step!" I yelled, trying to sound positive. However, with the hats, hoods, and hisses from our oxygen tanks, I doubt they heard. None of our headlamps revealed what I was hoping to see: the ladders. They are the telltale sign that we had made it to the second step.

I closed my eyes. "You've got to be kidding me," I thought. I realized we had only reached the first step, one of a series of three cliffs above 8,500m that you must surmount to reach the summit of Mt. Everest. This meant it would take more than an hour just to get to the second step and another six plus hours of struggle to reach the summit.

The reality of where I was, physically and mentally, sunk in. I chuckled to myself, a possible sign of dementia, about the foolishness of this climb. Something felt off. Maybe I had made a mistake. An odd thought circled in my head, "Maybe I should have stayed in my cubicle."

I was somewhere around Bellevue, Washington on the 405 South, crawling back to Kent, deep in traffic when the call came in. I mumbled something like, "Redmond Planning Office calling me, again?" I flipped the top section of the company-provided Motorola A760 and answered.

"Hello?"

"Is this Brendan, the project planner for the Willet Subdivision?"

"Yup, that's me," I said proudly.

It was good being a project planner at age 28. I was designing neighborhoods all over the greater Seattle region. Most days I was stuck in my cubicle with a ruler, the King County Code book for land use development, and an office coffee. I tried to get out of the office at least once a week to drop off applications for new subdivisions, new drive-through coffee stands, and new business parks. However, these days I was helping developers get around the very regulations I became versed in at school. It was OK. The money was way more than I thought I would be making at this age. I also had a girlfriend and played guitar in a rock band called the Cast of Characters. Things were going well as far as having the means to do what I wanted to do.

"Brendan, I'm one of the surveyors for the City of Redmond. This is the second time we have been out to this property and

the map you resubmitted still does not match this location," the voice said.

A wave of stress rushed through my body. I felt like throwing up. The million-dollar project that I had been in charge of was already behind schedule and over budget because of my own mismanagement. Looking over at the traffic on the 405 North, I knew I was doomed. Besides spending at least four more hours in the Northwest's famous bumper to bumper bliss today, this screw-up was going to cost me.

"OK, no problem, I'll head back over to you guys and see what is wrong with the location. Thanks." I hung up.

I verbally berated myself in the car for being such an idiot. "How am I continuing to screw these applications up?" I asked myself, looking for the nearest exit to crossover the highway.

A small mistake, transposing numbers, had sent the surveyor to the wrong parcel, again. Surveying teams are not cheap. In order to cover up my mistakes so that my boss wouldn't find out about it, I had to take this hit personally. I forked over $1,500 to the Redmond City Planning Office and begged the surveyors to get to the right property as soon as possible.

Hours later, I was back in my cubicle finishing emails to the developers, covering my mistakes. I ensured that even though the surveyors messed up again (a lie), they would be out to their property the following day.

It was 6pm, dreary and drizzling. If I headed home now, the 20-minute drive north on I-5 to Queen Anne, would be at least an hour and a half. I sat there with my head in my hands.

"This isn't me." I thought. I shut down my computer and grabbed my keys.

Driving in the drizzle, everything felt so meaningless.

Life plugged along. Work was not inspiring, and I continued screwing up, covering up, and coughing up cash to cover my mistakes. I just wasn't into this gig. I liked climbing mountains in the Pacific Northwest. "Maybe I could do that?" I questioned. But the pay would be a 10th of what I was making now.

I was sitting in my cubicle, updating my band's MySpace page, trying not to fall asleep when my colleague/skiing/mountaineering/drinking buddy Dave Kellogg called me. He was bailing on a plan to climb Mt. Baker in a couple of weeks. He said he was moving to China to help start an international school. They hired him to teach language arts.

Dave suggested there might be a need for a science teacher. "I'm in!" I exclaimed. We hung up the phone and I texted him immediately, "I'm in 100%."

Two weeks later I said goodbye to my girlfriend, band, and cubicle. I was on a flight to Qingdao China, to help start the Qingdao American International School. Climbing was put on hold.

I was having a blast teaching science, and everyday life in China was a shock to the senses. It was much like getting a whiff of smelling salt, although it was usually piles of trash, rotting fish, and/or burning plastic. Dave and I got deep into China. We learned the language, I started a popular band, we were best men at Chinese weddings, and ate anything they put in front of us. I don't mind a good fried scorpion every now and again. Dave and I even had a TV show that allowed us to travel from Shanghai's F1 Racetrack, to the farthest reaches of China's borders with Pakistan, Nepal, and Mongolia. We were so deep into China we started venturing off the beaten path, even accidentally strolling into places that we weren't supposed to be, like accidently climbing to a ridge that overlooked the main Chinese nuclear submarine base. We were both hooked on pushing our limits and were hungry for more epic adventures.

Dave and I had cunningly worked our way into the media department at Haier, one of the largest consumer electronic companies in the world. We had convinced them that leading up to the 2008 Summer Olympics, they needed a video web series about their mascots going Higher and Higher from Qingdao to Mt. Everest Base Camp. Their mascots are two boys in underwear - one dark skin with dark hair and one with white skin and blond hair holding an ice cream cone. We convinced them that that was us. We were the Haier Brothers and we were going to produce an eight-video web series about us, the Haier Brothers, making our way to Mt. Everest. Along the way, we would catalogue China's development for the games. They bought it. We were off.

The films started with an episode in Qingdao, our Chinese hometown, which was also Haier's home, and home to the Olympic sailing event. From there we put together three films in Beijing introducing tourist sites as well as the Olympic venues. In 2007, the 46-hour train ride from Beijing to Lhasa had just opened up. We were one of the first passengers on the train and filmed the ascent to Lhasa, the highest train ride in the world. Arriving in Lhasa, now we were in deep. Standing with our bikes and a couple bags of gear in front of the Potala Palace in Lhasa, Tibet, we were about to embark on a 700 km mountain bike ride, most of it above 4,000 meters through the Himalayas, to Mount Everest Base Camp. Once we reached the world's biggest roadblock, we would continue on the Friendship Highway down the longest mountain bike downhill in the world into Kathmandu, Nepal. But at that moment, standing in front of the Potala Palace, reality sunk in for the first time. I was jittery and nervous, like somebody punched me in the gut. This was a serious challenge. Perhaps I set my goals too high on this one. But we were committed and started to ride. The seventh movie documented our ride across Tibet.

Although extremely difficult, our bodies adapted quickly to being on bikes 6 to 10 hours a day and to the altitude. By the time we were nearing Mt. Everest Base Camp, we were in incredible shape. During the ride, the weather was clear, cool, and dry. However, at all the opportune viewing points, we or Everest were ensconced in clouds. Coming up the final straight away, we came around a corner and Mt. Everest finally came into view. We both stopped, pulled off to the side of the road and our jaws dropped. It was formidable, beautiful, and inviting. The final video of the Haier Brother series finished with us and our bikes at Everest base camp: 5,200 meters.

We could not believe we completed this feat. We were relieved and felt incredibly accomplished. We backtracked down to a small town on the Friendship Highway called Tingri. From there we completed a 3,800-meter downhill over three days into Kathmandu, Nepal.

We kept finding ourselves in situations that at the time were uncomfortable, nerve-wracking, and several times frightening. Especially when we really started to test international boundaries and attempted to ski from a snow-capped volcano in China, into North Korea.

I started to notice that these experiences - the coldest nights, the longest hikes, and political minefields - were addicting. It was addicting to see how I could adapt and thrive in extreme situations. With each goal I accomplished, my confidence grew, and I fell in love with traveling outside of my comfort zone.

In 2010, Dave and I were planning our next adventure. We were looking at countries that were politically "risky". We felt that we could go almost anywhere. We could go to a country considered an enemy of America and show that it wasn't as dangerous as the media portrayed. We could challenge our own prejudices and possibly those of others. Being American, of course, the Middle East came to mind.

We noticed on a map that in Iraq there was a spot of white. Is that snow? Could you ski there? With skis and a camera in hand, we went to find out.

Three connections and two days from Qingdao, we arrived in Diyarbakir, a city in eastern Turkey. Then it was a border run into Iraq via a hired taxi. A couple of perplexed looks and documentation checks and we were in Iraq. Each new city we went to we spoke with locals about where we could find skiing or at least some snow.

Our curiosity and persistence had brought us to Erbil and from there up windy mountain roads to a tiny village at the foot of snow-capped mountains. Villagers warned that there still were landmines up in the hills, remnants of the Iran-Iraq war in the 1980s, but that we should be OK if we stayed on the path. At least that is what we gathered from our game of charades before we departed from the village.

Four hours of trudging through brush, then slush, then corn snow, we finally got to a ridge. The sun was going down and we were required to check back in at Erbil that night or risk being arrested (per a warning by guards at a military checkpoint). So that ridge was as far as we were going. We turned on the camera, looked straight at it and I said,

"We've done some stupid things to get here." Dave chimed in, "But come on, ski Iraq. Can you believe it?"

It wasn't from a peak, nor was the skiing epic, but we had done it again. As I reflect on my statement, each step we took to get there wasn't stupid at all. The steps were risky but calculated, planned and executed with our vision. We were prepared and trusted that our preparations would carry us through difficult situations.

Our confidence grew and more adventures followed. We headed to Tehran, Iran during the 30th anniversary of the Islamic Revolution. We were deep in the crowd of President Mahmoud Ahmadinejad supporters when they started chanting, "Death to America!" We traveled to Mumbai weeks after the Mumbai terrorist attacks and then, despite Department of State warnings, skied in Kashmir located on the border of India and Pakistan with both nations at the brink of war. We even got out of our mountain comfort zones and headed to the jungles of Nicaragua. Our adventure there had political, natural, and physical dangers as we crossed the country on foot along the proposed and controversial Nicaragua Grand Canal.

I was addicted. Unbeknownst to me and definitely not premeditated, these adventures allowed me to live outside my comfort zone. They pushed me in ways that I wanted to be pushed. They became my passion. It became a way to challenge myself both mentally and physically. The adventures gave my life meaning.

It's not that I feared a life without meaning, I didn't have the capacity to think of it on that big of a scope. I had friends, I had a love life, I had a good life.

It's that I had come to fear time without meaning. I feared the tick, tick, tick - of a minute, an hour, a day, a week, a month, a YEAR - and how quickly they pile up without something really happening or changing. Anytime I didn't have an adventure to look toward, to be a part of, I felt adrift. Time itself, my personal raison d'etre, lost its "je ne sais quoi" (that concludes the French sayings, I promise).

Eventually, I took on Everest. Like so many of my adventures, I documented my climb.

Was it meaningful? Yes.

Let's see how some people responded to my video series of the preparation and climb:

(The following comments were taken from my YouTube series on the climb, Everest for Mountaineers).

**John Tiller** 2 months ago

No respect for any fool who climb mountain. They are a self centred idiots. And It NOT IMPRESSIVE

 👍 👎 REPLY

**maxjiro25** 1 week ago

take all these ego maniac, tell them they can go climb something amazing very similar to Everest, but no one has ever heard of this new spot and no one will cares on social media. 100% of them decline

**N**

**Norma Mimosa** 3 weeks ago

Pseudo climbers get the sherpas to carry their loads for them.

👍 16 👎 REPLY

**david garcia** 3 weeks ago

Sherpas are the ONLY athletes there. Everyone else is there for vain glory and arrogance.

👍 33 👎 REPLY

**Khaled Sid** 1 month ago

**and you think you're mountainers ....**

 👍 4 👎 REPLY

**Ronnie Civella** 3 weeks ago

Climbing Everest NOT impressive any longer. These guys are nothing more than tourists. What does it take MONEY

👍 👎 REPLY

No doubt, any climb is in the eye of the beholder. I do appreciate the middle finger emoji. That took some effort. Are they wrong? Not really. Am I wrong? Not really. This is a book that explores how I've come to understand why I climbed Everest and how I pulled it off.

# CHAPTER 2

# THE ROPES

Everest was on my radar about as much as going to the moon was. That is, until I was invited to climb Denali. Dave's friend Paco Monedero was on a mission to climb the Seven Summits, the highest mountains on each continent. Before him, I had never heard of the Seven-Summits objective. While there are several versions of this travelling mountaineer checklist, Paco was going for Messner's Seven Summits which include the following mountains in order of elevation:

1. Everest, Nepal 8,850m
2. Aconcagua, Argentina 6,960m
3. Denali, Alaska 6,194m
4. Kilimanjaro, Africa 5,896m
5. Elbrus, Russia 5,642m
6. Vinson, Antarctica 4,897m
7. Carstensz Pyramid, New Guinea 4,884m

Paco had climbed six of the seven summits but failed on Denali during his first attempt due to bad weather. Paco asked Dave if he wanted to join. Dave was interested. He asked if I wanted to go.

"No thanks," I replied.

I remembered reading a book on Denali called "In the Shadow of Denali: Life And Death On Alaska's Mt. Mckinley" by Jonathan Waterman. It sounded like the worst idea ever. Also known as Mt. McKinley, Denali is located in Alaska near the Arctic Circle and is known for its ferocious weather. At 6,194 meters, it is North America's highest peak. It would require multiple weeks living on snow, as well as climbing the same sections of the mountain several times to stash gear and food. The cost was more than I had paid for any adventure and with a success rate hovering around 60%, this didn't sound like something I wanted to take on.

I reiterated my, "No thanks," by adding, "Have fun."

Sure enough, a couple of days later Dave told me that he confirmed with Paco. My brain had just entered its competitive mode. I thought, "There is no way I am going to let Dave climb Denali while I'm sitting on my ass in China." I replied, "I'm in 100%." I had always wanted to go to Alaska. Never had I thought that I would attempt Denali, but it was to be another epic, yet risky adventure.

Our training began. At the time we were living in Beijing. The best way to get our mountain climbing preparation in was loading up our backpacks with bottles of water, starting at the bottom of our 16-floor apartment building and climbing the stairs up, elevator down, and repeat, for hours. Most Chinese apartment complexes have areas where the elders stretch, and the kiddos play. Ours had one with pull up and dip bars that we also put to use on a daily basis. We managed a solid four months of training before our flight to Anchorage, Alaska.

Dave and I met Paco in Anchorage. This was the first time I met Paco. He and Dave had met in Spain when Dave was studying there. Paco's first words to me were, "You want to go take a beer?" It was clear that Paco liked to party. We did as well. Possibly a little too much. I'm not sure if it was the hangover or the enormity of the task we were undertaking, but during the train ride from Anchorage to Talkeetna we had our first sighting of Denali, and I almost threw up.

Denali base camp cannot be accessed by roads. Instead you must be flown in on bush planes that have been specially designed to take off and land on snow. The entire plane is loaded up with your gear: food, fuel, equipment and plastic sleds that you use to drag all the necessities to keep you alive on the mountain. Many climbers snowshoe up the mountain, however, Dave and I pushed for skiing. Paco was not a great skier, but he picked it up quickly.

From the onset, I did everything I could to make sure I was worthy of this climb with Paco, a guy who had summited Everest. Every day, I was the first one awake and outside of the tent boiling water for all of us. As Paco was checking ropes for the day, Dave and I would be taking down the tent, stuffing sleeping bags and doing anything we could to make sure we were completely prepared for each daily push. On this climb, I felt like an apprentice to this world class mountain climber. Throughout the steepest hills and the windiest of corners, I made sure to keep up, stay positive, and film as much as I could. At Windy Corner I was filming Paco and Dave. It was amazing that that day there was no wind. Paco borrowed my water and gulped the rest down. We were still hours from Camp 4 and now the water that I had been saving was gone. This was incredibly annoying. However, we were becoming a team. I knew I was going to suck it up when Paco was doing things I didn't agree with. I also knew that he knew what he was doing and no matter what happened we were there for each other. I listened intently to Paco's advice and his stories as well as the stories from a handful of others who were traveling to climb mountains around the world.

When we made it to Camp 4, I heard the strumming of a guitar coming out of a tent and decided to investigate. The tent itself was not a mountaineering tent that I was familiar with. There were snow walls about half a meter off of the current snow level making a circle about 3 meters across. A mini nylon circus tent-like top was frozen into the top layer of the surrounding wall. The entrance was another piece of nylon that led to steps about one and a half meters down. Once you entered it felt like an igloo. Snow benches were carved out around the outside of the snow room. A large man with a white Stetson hat was sitting at the back strumming and singing with a heaping dose of big country Alaska in his voice,

> "Well some folks live here, and some folks don't,
> Some leave but you know I won't,
> I came here as a young man, it's been a few years ago
> Well I like these mountains and like these trees
> Sometimes at night I hear them calling me
> and with a song in my head, I grab my hat and go
> and after reaching the ridge at the end of the day,
> overcome by it all I just gotta say
> Odeleiiiheeeeeee whooooooooooo
>
> Strum it from the summit, oh yes, I will,
> If I can't strum it from the summit, I'll strum it from a hill
> Odeleiiiheeeeeee whooooooooooo"

He finished his song and welcomed Dave, Paco and I into his tent and offered us tea and snacks. His name is Marty Raney, an Alaskan if there ever was one. He told us tales of him and his friends climbing and working all over Alaska. Then he would put his teacup down, he called it a "chalmer," and would strum another song. While Marty had climbed Denali several times, once with a full-size guitar to the summit, this time he had brought his friend Brian Young along, fulfilling a 20-year promise that they would climb the mountain together.

Also, at Camp 4 we ran into a good friend of Marty's, Vern Tejas. Vern is an elite mountain guide, having completed the seven summits ten times over! His accomplishments on Denali are also superhuman. Vern was the first person to summit Denali in winter, has a total of 55 guided ascents of Denali, including the first paraglider descent, a 14 hour and 50-minute speed ascent[4] and even brought a violin to the top to jam with Marty. We asked him about the infamous Autobahn section of the mountain, named for German climbers that slid off the mountain on the section at high speeds to their deaths. We

---

4    "Vern Tejas." Alpine Ascents International.

hung on every one of his words:
"It's not intrinsically dangerous, but if a crampon comes off, if you trip, probably hundreds of mountaineers have died just tripping. Stupid thing, you catch a crampon and all of a sudden, you're on 45 degrees and you're going fast and you don't have your ice axe out. You're dead."

Much of the time at Camp 4 is spent looking for stuff to do. You stare at your tent walls, boil water, and try to meet people. Another gentleman we met was a university professor named Patrick McKnight. Patrick had planned a Denali trip with several of his friends but for various reasons the majority of them dropped out, and he joined a group with one of his friends and two random climbers. By the time he reached Camp 4, his team fell apart. He was fed up with dealing with one of his climbing partners and wandered into Marty's tent. We all hit it off, shared stories of past adventures, sang songs, and drank heaps of Marty's tea.

After being stuck at Camp 4 for over a week due to bad weather, our team made a push for Camp 5. For every climber on Denali, this is where the stakes are raised. The severity of the climb becomes tangible.

After 8 hours of climbing we arrived at 5,200m. It was around 11pm. The temperature was plummeting well below subzero. We were panicking. Our hands were becoming too cold to put our tent together. Each one of us was taking turns trying to get the damn tent poles to fit into their sleeve. Every second we were outside; we were a step closer to frostbite and hypothermia. We were on the verge of being too cold to put the tent together at all. And that would have been disastrous.

Once the tent was eventually together, we all fell into the tent. It was a miserable night. The tent was a two-person tent that none of us had ever put together before that night, nor did we test if we could all fit. We managed to fit with Paco and I at the bottom of the tent with Dave sleeping the opposite way in the middle. I was slammed up against the tent wall. My lofty sleeping bag and goose down jacket were no match for the pressure against the nylon sides. With no loft, there was no air to insulate me from the elements. My heat was being whisked away by the exterior wind and subzero temperatures. I thought that my left tricep was freezing to the side of the tent.

The next morning, we awoke to a spectacular day; in Paco's words, "It's no wind. It's sunny. It's incredible."

Paco was elated as he realized that the weather was perfect to secure his seven summits.

Departing from Camp 5 our team of three safely crossed the Autobahn. From there, I thought we would enter a flat expanse called the football field which leads to the final steep section, pig hill, then the summit. This was not the case. We turned the corner to Denali Pass, and the mountain punched me in the face. It looked like it went up to the stratosphere. I was getting frustrated, and the altitude was becoming more noticeable. I was moving slow, I had a headache, and started to become indifferent to summiting or not. Denali Pass was a beast. It took every ounce of my energy to keep going. Dave was right in front of me; his persistence to take step after step pushed me to do the same. He was figuratively dragging me up the mountain. Without him in front of me that day, I definitely would have turned around. On that section of the mountain I also developed a mantra that has helped me on every climb since.

When I was a kid and a practicing Catholic, I had to say prayers before bed. It wasn't the religious aspect of the prayer as much as remembering my family members: my grandparents, parents, and brothers. I wanted to be strong for them and use them to give me strength. After the sign of the cross, the prayer went "Godbless Papa, Grandma, Nana, Pa, Mom, Dad, Julian, and Stephen." I dropped the Godbless part and for each step I would say one of the names. Papa. Step. Grandma. Step. Nana.

Step. Pa. Step. Mom. Step. Dad. Step. Julian. Step. Stephen. Step. I would repeat this over and over until a couple of arduous hours passed and we finally reached the football field.

As a team we looked up to the summit. The altitude was putting us in a dreamlike state. I'm not sure if it was in my head, or if it was discussed as a group, but I was ready, and felt that we were all ready, to head back down the mountain.

Just then, a mountaineer shrouded in a black hat, black geek beak, sunglasses, and buff came bounding toward us.

"You guys! You got it! It's right there! Keep going! You are so close!"

It was Patrick. With his enthusiasm and encouragement, we cracked smiles, congratulated him on his summit and headed to our own summit.

With success on Denali, I became hooked on the challenge of big mountains, the views, and the bond you attain with these like-minded idiots.

My mountaineering curiosity was fueled and my interest in the Seven Summits became a way to satisfy that summit fever. Like being addicted to travel and adventures, this new hobby linked them both.

In August 2012, I moved to Tokyo. I had an incredibly busy year working as a high school science teacher at the American School in Japan (ASIJ). There, I started the outdoor club where I led camping trips, Mt. Fuji climbs, and ski weekends to some of Japan's most epic ski areas around Nagano. On the weekends that I wasn't guiding trips, I was climbing or skiing on my own. I was also trying to find people to climb Kilimanjaro with me. None of my friends or climbing partners were available so I took to the Internet. In a Yahoo chat group, I met a girl named Sarah from Washington D.C. who was planning a trip for July with another person she met online, Dimitri, from Russia. I had always climbed mountains with good friends. This would be my first climb where the team was made of strangers and porters. I was hesitant to sign up but the allure of the seven summits was too strong. I committed. The trip was set for the beginning of July. The school year finished in June. I had a month to go to my brother's wedding in Connecticut, meet friends in London, go see Victoria Falls in Zimbabwe, and then work my way on a dilapidated bus overland to Tanzania.

I have never been a fan of traveling with tours or climbing with a tour group. However, on Kilimanjaro it is required. The price tag was a little shocking to me at $3,660 USD, however, it did include a two-day safari afterwards to Safari Tarangire and the NGorongoro Crater. In addition, it is recommended that you tip the guides and porters an additional $100 USD per day. That is an extra $700 added to this trip. This Seven Summits checklist was going to be a lot more expensive than I thought it would be. The group we were going with was kili-worldbornsafaris. They are a local Tanzanian company and made me rethink my opinions on climbing with guides and porters.

At the start of the Machame route, a 7-day trek, the porters load up everything you have but your water bottle and a spare jacket on their backs. Most of the porters blasted ahead of us while two climbing guides stayed with Dimitri, Sarah, and I. Inspired by Marty Raney, I had brought a small acoustic guitar with me that I was planning on carrying on my backpack. But our climbing guide would not allow it. He wanted to carry it. For the rest of the trip, he held it in his hands.

The climb winds up through five climate zones, each with unique flora and fauna. For the three of us, Sarah, Dimitri and I, there were 13 porters. When we arrived at the first camp, they had our tents set up with sleeping bags and sleeping mats laid out. They had also erected a bathroom tent complete with portable toilet, a kitchen tent, their tents, and mess tent with a table, chairs, snacks and drinks. I could not believe how much these guys were carrying. Their outfits were also notable. In contrast to our high-tech expensive mountaineering clothes, these guys were wearing secondhand slacks and office shoes.

In the morning, Alpha, who worked in the kitchen, would knock on our tent, and say, "Good morning sir, good morning madame, would you like tea or coffee?"

We would make our selection, as he would open the vestibule and take a seat. It was freezing. We were still in our sleeping bags. He would meticulously pick out a tea bag, put it in the cup and add the boiling water.

Alpha would continue, "Sugar?"

"Yes, please," I would reply.

He would then slowly stir the sugar as if he was trying to dissolve every grain. Once we finished our tea and coffee ritual, it was straight into the mess tent where a full breakfast would be waiting for us.

Full and hydrated we hit the trail. The guides emphasize going slow. In fact, "polé polé" meaning "slowly slowly" in Swahili, has become a catch phrase on Kilimanjaro. While we were moving on, the porters would stay behind and pack up the camp, including our tents, sleeping bags, and personal effects. They would then proceed up the same path, pass us, make it to the next camp, and set up before we arrived. We were all blown away. This would happen day after day, camp after camp.

The second to last camp is called the Karanga Camp, 4,040 meters. The last stretch to this camp crosses the Karanga River then follows an incredibly steep uphill for another hour before reaching the plateau and camp location. However, there is no water at this camp, nor the one above it. Therefore, once you arrive at this camp, the porters are already making their way back down to the Karanga river to get water. They then spend the next several hours ferrying 5-gallon buckets of water on their heads from the Karanga river up to Karanga Camp and further to the last camp Barafu Hut (4,645 meters).

As if that wasn't enough, that night at dinner the porters pulled out two, unopened, one-liter, condiment bottles.

"Are you kidding me?" I exclaimed. One was a hot sauce the other was ketchup.

Why didn't they just ask us at the bottom of the hill if we needed that? I would have definitely declined. But, that's just the way it is on Kilimanjaro.

On our summit bid, the line of headlamps seemed to reach to the stars. Kilimanjaro is one of the top 10 most climbed mountains in the world averaging between 35,000 and 50,000 climbers per year. Sarah's feet were cold. Dimitri was quiet. I was doing decently until about 5,500 meters. That is when the nausea and headaches began. We crested the summit crater, the sun was rising, and I was so dizzy. My head was pounding so hard I could barely see. I was still 45 minutes from the true peak.

A stranger approached me and said, "You don't look too good, are you alright?"

I replied, "I think I'm gonna puke."

He responded, "Go for it, get it out."

Still standing, I bent at the waist. I puked so hard that for a second I passed out, only waking when my face smashed into my own puke that covered the black gravel trail. I slowly got to my knees picking out the gravel from my mouth and forehead. The nausea vanished but my head was pounding like the worst hangover I had ever had in my life. Sarah was also puking, and Dimitri could barely see, his head was pounding so hard. Forty-five minutes later I reached the summit, but the headache was relentless. On the way up, the guides kept us together as a group. On the descent our team disbanded. The air thickened as I dropped below Karanga Camp and I picked up the pace. I needed to do whatever I could to lessen my altitude sickness. My head throbbed for 8 hours. I walked into Mweka Camp (3,100 meters) and the pain began to fade. Somehow, there was a tent waiting for me.

As mentioned before, the Kili-worlborn Safaris company made me rethink my opinions on climbing with guides and porters. I did miss the team of great friends that I had on Denali, but it felt good to be supporting this local group of guys that worked incredibly hard and always with a smile. When it came to tipping, even though the suggested amount sounded ridiculous at the beginning of the trip, I gave all I could and well above the suggested amount. I hate tipping when tipping feels required but not deserved. The porters and guides on Kilimanjaro made that trip what it was. I wish I could have given more. They were continuously positive, helpful, and humble. I often go to YouTube and play the Kilimanjaro song that they sang to us before we said our goodbyes. It always brings a smile to my face.

"Kilimanjaro, Kilimanjaro
Kilimanjaro, mlima mrefu sana (Kilimanjaro, long mountain journey)
Na Mawenzi, na Mawenzi (And Mawenzi, and Mawenzi)
Na Mawenzi, mlima mrefu sana (And Mawenzi, long mountain journey)
Ewe nyoka, ewe nyoka (As a snake, as a snake)
Ewe nyoka, mbona waninzungukaa (As a snake, it winds all around)

Jambo, jambo Bwana (Hello, hello Sir)
Habari gani (How are you?)
Mzuri sana (Very fine)
Wageni, mwakaribishwa (Foreigners, you're welcome)
Kilimanjaro, hakuna matata (Kilimanjaro, there is no

problem)

Tembea pole pole, hakuna matata (Walk slowly, slowly, no problem)
Utafika salama, hakuna matata (You'll get there safe, no problem)
Kunywa maji mengi, hakuna matata (Drink plenty of water, no problem)"[5]

After the Kilimanjaro summit, I headed back to Japan. Mt. Elbrus was the next mountain on my list. Not as well-known as Denali and Kilimanjaro, Elbrus is located on the border between Russia and Georgia and is the highest mountain in Europe at 5,642 meters. Most people think the highest mountain in Europe is Mt. Blanc at 4,810 meters. However, geographically the continent Europe stretches from the Atlantic Ocean in the west to the Caspian Sea in the east.[6] This swath of land includes a significant portion of Russia and all of Georgia.

Dave Kellogg had told me that he never wants to climb another mountain again that he can't ski down. This was one of the reasons he turned down Kilimanjaro. On Elbrus not only can you ski down, but the majority of the mountain you can skin up (ski uphill). In 2013, after moving back to Tacoma, Dave Kellogg had married Karina Grishina, a Russian woman I introduced him to six years prior in Qingdao. The American wedding ceremony with Dave's family had been held. Now it was time for Dave to fly to Russia and have the Russian family wedding ceremony. With no convincing required, Dave and Karina started planning the wedding together. Dave and I started planning his honeymoon - just the two of us skiing up and down the highest mountain in Europe. How romantic!

After getting different forms of Acute Mountain Sickness (AMS) on both Denali and Kilimanjaro, I decided to take a look at

---

5        Kilimanjaro Song.

6        Society, National Geographic. "Europe: Physical Geography."

how I was training. While Tokyo, where I lived, was still at sea level. Mt. Fuji could get me up to 3,776 meters. I committed to climbing Mt. Fuji as much as possible to gain strength, altitude, and confidence skiing on steep ice. Between August 2013 and June 2014, I had climbed Mt. Fuji seven times, including twice with skis, skiing down from the top.

School was out in June again. I traveled to Ishigaki, a group of islands belonging to Japan that are actually further south than Taipei, Taiwan, then Armenia and Georgia for two weeks before meeting up with Dave and Karina 500km south of Moscow in Veronezh, Russia. The traditional Russian wedding was incredible. It was made even better by Karina requiring Dave to dress up as a good ole' American cowboy. Yee-haw! During the wedding week, we stayed in shape by running and swimming through the Veronezh Nature Reserve, an expansive park with rivers, backwaters, and trails. We would relax sipping vodka at Karina's parents' house, eating dried fish, getting naked in a sauna and being whipped with eucalyptus and oak branches, leaves and all, by a 300-pound Russian. This is "the good life" in Russia. The rest of the time was spent planning our climb.

Kilimanjaro did turn my aversion to guided climbs, however, Dave and I had been on so many adventures together we wanted to do this one on our own. He also needed to practice his incredibly poor Russian language skills.

One of the most difficult tasks on Elbrus was getting all our gear sorted. We did not want to haul our own alpine trekking skis with us, not to mention our personal skis are made for powder skiing, not ice. Therefore, we needed to track down alpine trekking skis that fit our boots, skins to put on the bottom of the skis to help us climb, and stove fuel. We figured this was a mountaineering town, it would be easy. Granted, it wouldn't be as easy as it would be in Seattle where we could buy all that gear and a Starbucks on every corner, but we did not expect the amount of running around that it actually involved.

Upon finding the ski shop, we began scrutinizing the gear. My ski setup seemed to work well. For Dave's setup, we had to jerry-rig the skins to the skis, which seemed to work great in the store. For white gas camping stove fuel, the town was dry. Luckily, we foresaw this problem and brought the MSR Whisperlite International stove which is known for being able to burn just about anything. No, we did not use vodka. However, we did track down some helicopter fuel, crossed our fingers, and explored the rest of Terskol. We stopped for lunch at the Kurbol Cafe. There we ran into a runner and mountain climber named Dave Williams.

Like Paco, Dave Williams was also trying to complete the seven summits. However, he was trying to climb each mountain from sea level! This New Zealander had already summited Kilimanjaro from sea level. For Kili, he started at the Indian Ocean in Dar es Salaam. He then ran over nine marathons in nine days just to get to the base camp. He had also completed a sea to summit of Mt. Kosciuszko in Australia.

Kellogg and I were amazed. For Elbrus, Dave started at the Black Sea in Anaklia, Georgia. He was quickly arrested by the Gerogian Border patrol. After seeing Dave's website, sea2summit7.com, Dave was granted special access to approach the border through the closed Nakra Valley. Once he got to the border, he had to run back out of the valley, have his friend Rich Henry pick him up, and they drove across a proper border. Then Dave had to make his way back to the border that he reached from the Georgia side, and run to Terskol from there. I was inspired.

"This guy is incredible," I thought.

We got his contact information, told him we would look for him on Elbrus, and wished him well.

Most of the hotels in the area are at the base of the gondola. The gondola whisks climbers and tourists up to the snow line near the Barrel Huts 3847m. Ours was no exception. At our hotel, we attached our boots to our skis and our skis to our overstuffed backpacks. This made for an easy walk to the gondola. When we entered the gondola area to buy tickets, we realized this wasn't the best plan. Our skis were catching on everything within a one-meter radius of us. As we got to the gondola, the line of Russian tourists going up to the Barrel Huts was much bigger than expected. It was awkward. Joining in our awkwardness was Dave William's buddy Rich Henry. Rich was bringing up Dave William's equipment for him. As the packed gondola departed the station, we looked out of the window and saw Dave Williams running up the mountain.

We exited the gondola carrying our unwieldy backpacks with skis still attached, smacking innocent bystanders along the way. Looking around, it seemed that we were in the midst of a photoshoot. Russians were everywhere taking photos of each other in the snow. Men with shirts off were taking pictures on snowmobiles and women in high heels, jeans, and bras were laying in the snow. My initial thought was this is a fantastic base camp. However, we needed to get higher on the mountain.

We set our high camp about halfway between the Barrel Huts and the Pastukov Rocks. It was a spot known as Prijut-11 or the Shelter Maria (4,100 meters). Dave and I were having a fantastic time catching up, cracking stupid jokes, and moving slowly up the mountain. During the days we would skin up the mountain for a couple of hours and then ski back to our tent. At the tent, we were having some issues. We had set up our camp on the side of a snow drift that appeared that it would block the wind. This was not the case.

The wind in this spot was testing the durability of our tent, thrashing it from side to side. To make matters worse, for the life of us, we could not get the stove lit with the helicopter fuel. The MSR Whisperlite International is called "international" because you can take it anywhere and light it up. It was not cooperating. We would prime the stove, then light it. It would stay lit but all we were getting out of it was huge flames, nasty black fumes, and carbon monoxide. This smoke was filling the tent. We could not keep the doors of the tent open because the wind was blowing hard outside. Without proper ventilation, our situation was serious. On an Everest expedition, as recently as 2017, climbers have died in their tents due to carbon monoxide poisoning.[7] Dave and I were actually starting to feel nauseous and lightheaded, but we had to melt snow for water. Frustrated, we took the stove apart, put it back together, and even changed the jet (the nozzle that the fuel comes out of). It was not working. We could not continue cooking and melting water with the stove in the condition it was in. Dave kept messing with it. It still wasn't working. As a last resort, he pulled out the soot-covered instruction leaflet, wiped it off as best he could, and read the fine print. For different fuels there are different jets. Although we had switched the jets out, we must have had one of the jets in backwards. It was a dumb mistake that we should have caught way earlier. We took the stove apart again, changed the jet again and got a solid blue flame.

The night of our summit push, we awoke at 2:00am. We were on our skis and skinning up the mountain around 3:00am. After about 2 hours of solid skinning, freezing on the outside but sweat soaking our inner layers of clothes, we turned around to see a snow cat driving past us delivering tourists and climbers to a higher section of the mountain. It was annoying.

The wind howled. We put our heads down and traversed back and forth up the mountain. Through the Pastukov Rocks Dave was having problems with his skins detaching from the bottom of his skis. Every time he put weight on his right ski it would slip. This was also annoying but more so, a colossal waste of energy. Regardless, we had made it to the beginning of the section of the climb called the traverse.

---

7     "Everest 2017: 4 Found Dead in Tent at South Col – Updated."

From lower on the mountain, we would always notice people climbing the traverse which was looking more like a walk across the mountain than a climb. The trail goes from the top of the Pastukov Rocks to the saddle located between the West and East Summits of Elbrus. They seemed to take an eternity on this perceptively flat section. Once we arrived at the traverse however, it was a different story. The trail, marked by fluorescent orange flags every 50 meters, was steep, long, and at an awkward angle; this, in addition to some clouds that rolled in making our visibility approximately 5 meters, slowed our progress. We now intimately understood why the traverse took so long. We trudged on blindly.

The fog was thick as we approached the saddle. We saw three figures from 5 meters away. As we approached, it turned out to be two Polish guys and Dave Williams. We sat down next to Williams on a snow berm. Williams was wasted. He was having a really difficult time as he had been climbing straight from the Barrel Huts. After a quick chat he shoved off. Dave Kellogg and I were a little worried about him as he disappeared into the fog. Soon, we caught up to him. He was in even rougher shape. He mentioned heading back down but would probably carry on. Dave and I respected his decision and continued on.

We reached the last steep face and finally the fog cleared. We saw Dave Williams behind us and decided that we would wait for him and climb the rest of the mountain together.

A couple hours later, in high winds as clouds flew by just above our heads, the three of us reached the summit hill. There was no one on it. Dave Williams was doing better, and we told him to take the summit first. Dave Kellogg and I waited below and got our skis ready for the descent. Dave Williams came down from the summit. We made a date to meet back at the Kurbol Cafe for a beer in two days' time. We high-fived and Dave Williams descended into the clouds. Dave Kellogg and I crawled on our hands and knees up the last steep pitch to the summit of Mt. Elbrus. We had a solid bro hug, took some pictures, then decided it was time to descend. We removed our crampons, stepped into our skis, and passing Williams on the way down, skied all the way back to our tent. It was one of my longest and most memorable ski descents. We were exhausted but felt great.

Just as planned, we met Williams at the Kurbol Cafe. The beers were fantastic. He thanked us for giving him the summit alone and then told us about his upcoming adventure. Williams' next sea to summit was going to be Aconcagua. He would be leaving from the coast of Chile and running up the Andes into Argentina before getting to the basecamp. I was excited to follow his monumental effort.

Looking back on Elbrus, I felt that I did it really well. I didn't vomit, I never got a headache, and never got dizzy. This meant that I could indeed climb high, I just needed to be in great shape and acclimatize as much as possible. I also didn't realize how this chance encounter with Dave Williams would impact my life.

Similar to Dave Williams, I was also looking at Aconcagua for my next adventure. The acclimatization for Aconcagua is serious. At 6,960 meters, it is the highest mountain in South America and 766 meters higher than I had ever been before.

While I was focusing on Aconcagua, in April 2014 Patrick McKnight, the climber I met on Denali, had signed up for a Mt. Everest expedition. I was following his Everest preparations on his blog: Climbing on Purpose.[8] Patrick had employed the use of the Hypoxico Altitude Training System and created a Google Spreadsheet which recorded his training progress in excruciating detail. He is a statistician after all.

The Hypoxico Altitude Training System is composed of an Altitude Generator, a sleep mask, a training mask, and a tent. The Altitude Generator, a 26kg box the size of a small washing machine, is where all the magic happens. It extracts

---

8     Climbing, Swimming, and Sailing on Purpose.

nitrogen from the air and pumps it into your mask or tent that encapsulates your mattress, effectively decreasing the amount of oxygen available to you. The generator changes the composition of the air you breathe from 21% oxygen (what is available at sea level) to about 8.8% oxygen (equivalent to around 6,700 meters). Scientific research has shown that this system enhances athletic performance, prepares your body for high altitude, and can also be used in physical wellness therapy.[9]

Patrick put in a year of heavy, documented training, paid his money and made it to Everest Base Camp on the south side. Then disaster struck. On April 18, part of the overhanging ice cliffs above the notorious Khumbu Icefall crumbled, killing 18 Sherpa. The tragedy ended the climbing season. Patrick's first attempt on Everest went only as far as touching the ground above Base Camp.

Patrick was not done with Everest. He signed up for another expedition in 2015. We kept in contact. Over a Skype conversation, I asked if he would be interested in climbing Aconcagua in December 2014. He thought it would be a perfect training climb and acclimatization check before his second Everest attempt. I also inquired about his Hypoxico and physical training.

Being gun shy from my numbed mind on Denali and my AMS on Kilimanjaro, I discussed the advantages of the Hypoxico Altitude Training System with him. He could not recommend it enough. There was only one disadvantage, the price. I was also living in Tokyo at the time and the shipping alone was $500 USD. However, I thought if I am planning on completing the seven summits and doing it right, then this is an advantage that I want. I put in my Hypoxico order.

In September 2013, with help from a spreadsheet that Patrick had set up called Aconcagua Workout Progress Madden[10], I

9      "Hypoxico.Com - Altitude Training Systems - Altitude Tents - Altitude Masks."
10    "Aconcagua Workout Progress Madden Sharelink."

started using the Hypoxico system. Sleeping in the tent and getting used to the buzz of the generator was easy. However, the one to four-hour bike workouts with the training mask were brutal. During the bike rides I was simulating the altitude between 1,524 meters and 6,483 meters which was only 477 meters short of Aconcagua's summit.

One way to measure progress is data logging your Saturated Blood Oxygen Levels (SPO2). At sea level most healthy people have an SPO2 of 97-99%. Climbers at altitudes above 8,000 meters have SPO2s between 55-65%. As you train using the Hypoxico system, a positive trend would be to see your SPO2 increase at higher altitudes over time.

Another way to measure your progress is how you are feeling. One of the first times I finished a workout at a simulated 6,000 meters I got off my stationary bike and went to the kitchen to make a protein shake. In the blender I put milk and protein powder. I peeled a banana, threw the banana in the trash and put the peel in the blender. I caught my mistake before hitting blend. I chuckled. I was glad I was learning the effects of extreme altitude on my brain in the relative safety of my own kitchen.

Finally, to see how the training was working on a real mountain, I would head over to Mt. Fuji and do a climb. After one of the climbs Patrick and I exchanged messages:

> Hangout with pem725@gmail.com
> October 28, 2014 Brendan Madden - 7:43 AM
> Holy crap the climb was great
> pem725@gmail.com - 7:43 AM
> yeah, the tent and training works, eh?
>
> Brendan Madden - 7:44 AM
> i've never felt so good at 12,000+ feet this weekend was a big test
> I wanted to see if I could push it
> pem725@gmail.com - 7:44 AM
> I tell you....this training method just works.

Brendan Madden - 7:44 AM
the trail that usually takes 5 hours i did in 3.5! and felt great
at the top

Patrick and I were stoked. The training was working.

Since it was the holiday season, Patrick decided to invite his
wife and son, 16 years old at the time on the Aconcagua climb
with us. If they felt good, they could move up higher on the
mountain with us and if they were feeling the altitude, they
could stay at the main basecamp called Plaza de Mulas (4,350
meters).

Patrick and his family arrived before I did. They made the final
arrangements in Mendoza, Argentina. The final arrangements
turned out to be a huge run around that I'm happy I missed.
Patrick had to get permits, hire a mule, and establish basecamp
services, mainly a dining tent that we could make our meals and
eat in.  Some places would only take US dollars, some places
would only take Argentinian Pesos. "That is no possible," was
the most common phrase Patrick heard. The bureaucracy was
wearing on him and he eventually relinquished our self-service
trip to a company called Lanko Atlas Montañas. They solved
all our problems in a day and Patrick and his family made it
to Plaza de Mulas (PDM) the same day I arrived in Mendoza
with missing luggage. I didn't want to inconvenience Patrick
or his family in any way and felt bad about arriving late without
baggage. Patrick made it clear that there was no rush and I
should relax.

Penitentes, the closest a road can get you to Aconcagua and
PDM, where Patrick and his family were waiting, took me the
prescribed two days. I arrived late in the afternoon to Penitentes
and was a bit worried about making it to Confluenza, the first
camp, before dark. The evening was gorgeous and starting
out on the trail I had a full view of Aconcagua including the
summit. The trail winds through the official park parking lot,
then up to Laguna de Horcones, 2,950 meters, and across the
Horcones River. There you will reward yourself with great views

of the mountain at Mirador Del Cerro Aconcagua. Further up the trail you go through the Horcones Valley to the Quebrada del Durazno Ravine to the first camp. I arrived at Confluenza Camp, 3,400 meters, just as the sun was going down. Patrick had told me to look for the Lanko tent; they would sort me out with a place to sleep and they did.

The next morning, I woke at sunrise and wanted to get going. This day was going to be a long one through desert to reach PDM. Just as I hit my stride at the beginning of the trail, Kilian Jornet, a Spanish professional mountain runner, came running by me at an incredible pace. I cheered him on. He was going for a speed record of climbing Aconcagua, which he ended up achieving in 12 hours and 49 minutes. Incredible. However, less than two months later his record was beaten by the Ecuadoran-Swiss mountain runner Karl Egloff in a time of 11 hours and 52 minutes. To put this in perspective, my time from Confluenza Camp to the next camp Plaza de Mulas was eight hours. Not that I could come close to Kilian's pace, however, I was in no rush. I took many pictures and videos, stopped several times for multiple lunches and admired the vastness of this high desert and surrounding peaks. I frequently pulled off to the side when the mule heards carrying gear to and from Plaza de Mulas would come through. I also spent the majority of the time talking to myself. On a very steep ascent that dropped even more steeply down climber's left, bones of mules, even full mule skeletons, were scattered. I knew I must be close to PDM.

I arrived at Plaza de Mulas (4,389 meters) out of breath and tired of talking to myself. One requirement of the Aconcagua climb is that you stop by the Park Ranger Station at PDM for a medical check. I was tired but not feeling the altitude at all. I was also excited to meet up with Patrick and his family. The Park Ranger cleared me with an SPO2 of 89%.

PDM is a valley of commercial guide company tents located before the next steep section of the climb. It took me about 20 minutes to locate the huge red Lanko dome tent. Adjacent to it was Patrick's yellow North Face tent. Now the fun began for Patrick and me. His wife and son were not doing too well with the acclimatization, although they were mostly in good spirits.

After a day resting at PDM, Patrick and I made a push to stash equipment up at Nido de Cóndores (5,550m. We decided to skip Plaza Canada (5,050m) altogether as we heard that people were getting sick from the water at that camp.

I knew Patrick was an athlete: swimming for Notre Dame in college and doing his long-distance cold-water swims. I also got a glimpse of how fit he was on Denali. However, this was the first time we were hiking together.

We left PDM with heavy packs headed for Nido de Cóndores. Patrick asked if I wanted to set the pace. I confirmed.

"Nice and steady, polé polé," I was thinking as we zig-zagged on the trails back and forth pushing hard up past Camp Canada.

After an hour or so of leading I asked, "You want to lead for a while?"

"Yeah," Patrick said, "Nice and easy."

Patrick continued at the same pace that we had established, then he started cutting corners of the meandering pathway, slowly picking up the pace. Before I knew it, I felt like we were running straight up the scree slope. Exhausted, we made it to Nido and camped for the night. I was having some slight headaches but did not feel nauseous at all. We headed down for a recharge before making our summit push.

Three days later we were back at Nido an hour before sunset. It was cold, desolate, and my headaches had returned. Patrick was feeling great, so he took a hike to fetch some water. I stayed in the tent with my pounding head. Patrick returned and we discussed our plans for a summit that next day. Patrick gave me some aspirin for my headache, and we went to sleep.

At 4am we woke up, ate some soup, and hit the trail. My headache was lingering but the forecast called for beautiful weather that continued for the next week. This was it. The mountain seemed relatively dry and we had not encountered much snow. Taking that into account, we both decided that we would start our summit push in our approach shoes, packing our mountaineering boots and crampons in our packs. I swallowed a couple more aspirin and we left for the summit.

The trail wound around the back side of the mountain and meandered up more scree fields. By the time we reached Plaza Berlin (5,930m), a common camp to start a summit push from, we were just going through the motions. My mantra of family names, following Patrick, and enjoying the desolate scenery kept me moving. Not long after, we encountered a snowfield. This snowfield was approximately 35 meters across. It bisected the path like a long finger pointing downwards. It was too icy and long to attempt a cross with our running shoes. Just on the other side of the snow finger the dirt trail started up again and continued for several hundred meters before a large cliff. In addition, we were bolstered by each other's laziness and decided we didn't want to put on our mountaineering boots and crampons which would allow us to cross the snowfield directly. Instead we decided to descend about 40 meters to where the snowfield was only about 5 meters wide. There, we crossed without incident.  There, we also realized we made a huge mistake.

The entire side of the mountain was scree. Scree saps energy. Every step we took to get back up to the main path required considerable effort with minimal gain in elevation. The mountain was sinking in and we were sliding backwards. Our frustration with our decision was clear to both of us but there was nothing we could do except flounder our way upwards, whispering profanities under our breath. It was 45 minutes before we got back onto the main trail. We shook our heads at each other.

"Idiots," we both murmured.

We knew better but were shockingly poor at learning lessons. Later in the day than we wanted, we arrived at a huge overhanging slab of conglomerate rock called La Cueva, the Cave which sits at 6,650 meters. From the cave we could see the summit. We could also see what we thought was the entire route to the summit. It seemed to be a rock path that held very little snow and ice. We carried our boots and crampons all this way and hadn't used them yet, so we decided to stash them at La Cueva and continue to the summit in our trail shoes.

Almost immediately, there was a snowfield to cross. We again floundered slipping and sliding digging into the icy snow with our ice axes to give us some climbing purchase. Several times we also went to the side of the snow path and struggled through scree, sending shards off the mountain down towards other climbers. I often picture us on this section of the mountain from an experienced climber's point of view.

"Who are these idiots? They are endangering themselves, and others. These guys need to go."

Fortunately, we made it to the summit ridge path where we passed groups of climbers and their guides. Several climbers were taking one step, then laying down on the ground. The guides were encouraging them to get up and take another step. Patrick and I skirted around them the best we could, clamored up a couple of boulders and made it to the top of Aconcagua. My headache had dissipated and, on that crystal, clear day we could see the majority of the majestic Andes.

# CHAPTER 3

# KIWI CRUSH

Back in Mendoza, Argentina we celebrated. Delicious Argentinian steaks and Malbec wines filled our afternoons and evenings. Patrick and I were reminiscing on our recent success. We were a great team of two and we swore that we had learned from our asinine mistakes. Future adventures were thrown down on the table.

Within four years of my Denali summit and first hearing about the seven summits objective, I was staring down the last three of the Seven Summits. The most remote: Carstensz Pyramid, Indonesia. The most expensive: Mount Vinson, Antarctica. And the highest, also not cheap, and most deadly: Mount Everest. From here, my plan was to save and save for Antarctica, eventually bag that peak, find enough time to get out to Carstensz and cross that one off too. Then, and only, if Patrick was successful on his Everest attempt, would I consider the feasibility of an Everest climb. We laughed, planned, drank more wine and ate more steak.

Dave William's who, due to exhaustion 300 meters from the top, failed a sea to summit attempt of Aconcagua in 2013 was back for his second attempt. We met up with him in Mendoza, just before he would head to Aconcagua for another summit attempt. Dave was in great shape, especially for someone who just ran up the Andes. I was enthralled.

We chatted about life, his Sea2Summit7 project, my Seven Summits dream, and Patrick's upcoming Everest climb. Chatting with Dave Williams, an inspiring human being, it all seemed possible. Dave also needed to start planning his Carstensz, Vinson, and Everest attempts. He also needed to climb Denali. I offered to help him with logistics. I felt that this meeting was no coincidence. I had met him in Russia and now in Argentina. It was fate. My next adventures seemed like they were writing themselves.

Dave had to get back on the mountain. He thanked me for my willingness to help with his Denali logistics and we would start looking at Antarctica.  It was settled. I was excited to start seeing what it would take to complete a "sea to summit" of Antarctica. That sounded like an epic adventure. Patrick and I were committed before we finished our next bottle of red wine.

After Aconcagua, Patrick was psyched. He felt fantastic and was more ready than ever for Everest. I was carefully following his blog. More than anything, I wanted to see how he did on Everest to get a feel for how I may fare. Patrick made his second payment to Summit Climb, a mountain guiding company, for his second Everest expedition, and in April 2015, Patrick was back at Everest Base Camp on the Nepal side, in the exact spot he was a year ago. He and his teammates from Summit Climb made it through the Khumbu icefall safely. Upon reaching Camp 1 at 6,250 meters disaster struck again. At 11:56 AM on April 25th, a 7.8 magnitude earthquake rocked Nepal, and Everest.

Patrick recalled the disaster.

> "We got up there, on the 25th we felt the Earthquake and the avalanche hit our campsite. This was a catastrophe of epic proportions and here is a helicopter helping us evacuate from camp 1. After our evacuation, we came back to this…...other than seeing a campsite with a large array of fully erected tents, we saw nothing but debris spread out, mattress pads, tent shreds all over the place, sleeping bags down, there was just about everything spread throughout camp. It was a nightmare."[11]

11      "Comfort Zone Exit: Exit 17: Patrick McKnight - 2018 Mt Everest Recap"

The climbing season was over. Patrick's second attempt on Everest didn't even get him to test his preparations past Camp 1. Patrick decided to hold off on any more Everest attempts and instead, in 2016, completed the Triple Crown of swimming. This endeavor consists of three historically significant swims: around Manhattan, Los Angeles to Catalina Island, and crossing the English Channel. Patrick completed all three swims in a world record timespan of 34 days.

Also, in 2016, Dave Williams made it back to Aconcagua. It was his third attempt. On a crystal-clear day, Dave along with two of his New Zealand friends, finally reached the summit. Dave recounted this moment on his blog:

> "This was finally the moment I had dreamed of for so many years, as this was the summit that had eluded me and caused so much self-doubt and anxiety but was now providing me with the greatest sense of pride and fulfilment of my life. Sometimes we build something up in our head so much that it actually transforms into something we perceive as intangible and even mystical. When you manage to finally rise above that perception and take control of your destiny the feeling is actually indescribable with my very limited diction. I was now standing on the roof of South America and this bastard was officially knocked off! Third times a charm! Now lace up your shoes, take the path less traveled and take control of your life with no excuses or justifications. The harder the challenge the greater the reward."[12]

I couldn't imagine climbing Aconcagua from sea level much less doing it three times. I was honored to be in his company and was excited to get planning Antarctica. It was going to be Dave Williams, Patrick McKnight, Dave Kellogg, and I. This was my dream team.

When I got back to Tokyo, I immersed myself in Antarctica. I

---

12      Sea2Summit7 "Summit Day- Part 3 of 3."

constantly read articles and books on modern exploration. Some of my favorites were, Alone in Antarctica by Felicity Aston and Antarctic Tears: Determination, adversity, and the pursuit of a dream at the bottom of the world by Aaron Linsdau. The grit and drive to continue over extremely tenuous terrain was engrossing. Their descriptions of how their body reacted to the inhospitable climate was eye-opening and exciting. The cold bit at their core, the arid landscape sucked them dry, and the headwinds blew doubt into their minds.

Along my Antarctica journey I also uncovered a couple of Australian YouTube characters: Cas and Jonesy. They are a traveling duo like Dave Kellogg and I that really pushed the edges of adventure. They had sea kayaked the incredibly dangerous Tasman sea from Australia to New Zealand and in 2012 walked from the edge of Antarctica to the South Pole, unsupported. Both of these adventures were near-death experiences. We were next, I could feel it.

My research was slow but necessary. Planning a route from some coast in Antarctica to the highest peak, an attempted feat, was surprisingly difficult and rewarding. I took detailed notes on routes, terrain, food rationing, equipment, training regimens, mental afflictions on Antarctica, and other logistics.

Modern Antarctic expeditions start and end with Antarctica Logistics and Expeditions (ALE). For any non-government expedition, they oversee every portion of your expedition: planning; flying into their main air strip at Union Glacier Camp; flying anywhere around Antarctica; activities at the camps; safety; fuel; environmental concerns; and climbing Mt. Vinson. I first contacted them in March 2016. They sent a massive amount of paperwork for us to fill out. I sent the paperwork to Dave Williams, Dave Kellogg, and Patrick and we got to work.

I had narrowed our expedition down to two possible routes. The first, and less sexy of the two, started at Hercules Inlet. There was no visible liquid sea at the inlet. The sea was approximately

600m below the ice. The plan would be to get a plane to drop us off there, a popular starting spot for a coast to South Pole expedition, but instead of heading south, we would head west back to Union Glacier. We would stop at Union Glacier camp, resupply, and then ski the remaining 180km to Mt. Vinson base camp. From there we would climb, summit, and then get flown back to Union Glacier and off of Antarctica. This option would take an estimated 33 days from once the plane took off from South America.

The second option, Gould Bay, was a world class expedition in the making. Gould Bay is where ALE takes clients to go see those loveable, adorable, penguins. Gould Bay has sea ice access and would be the ideal place to start a "sea to summit" of Antarctica. From Gould Bay it would be 50 days of cross-country skiing just to make it back to Union Glacier Camp. Then another 12 days to get to Vinson Base Camp. This option, about 650km of skiing, most of which across the Ronne Ice Shelf, had never been attempted. From my reading, I knew the terrain would be soul-crushingly difficult, but this was my preferred option.

I was in constant communication with Patrick, Dave Williams, and Dave Kellogg. Everyone filled out their paperwork and submitted it in August 2016.

I edited together a video pitch for our Sea2Summit7 Antarctica[13] adventure. I narrated the sizzle reel and it went as follows:

> Thank you for your interest in the Sea to Summit Antarctica Expedition. I think the best way to introduce you to this grand feat, is through to my friend, pioneer of the sea to summit expeditions, and fellow teacher, Dave Williams:
>
> Dave Williams: "Basically, I run, crawl, or walk my way from the nearest coastline or beach to the mountain and then climb it. The first one, I've done it. Kilimanjaro was 440km

---

13      YouTube. Sea2Summit7 "Antarctica."

*that I ran from the coast of Tanzania. Mt. Kosiosko 240km. Mt. Elbrus, in Russia, 210km that I ran from the Black Sea, Aconcagua 240km, Mt. McKinley, and Mt. Vinson Antarctica."*

This is where the team and I come in. Antarctica. The goal of this expedition is to support Dave in completing the first ever "Sea to Summit" of Antarctica. This will entail starting from sea level on the coast of Antarctica near Gould Bay Camp, and cross-country skiing approximately 650km (15 marathons by Dave's count) to the base of Vinson Massif, Antarctica's highest prominence. Once there, the team will climb 4,892m to the summit. From the summit, there is no way we are walking down, we are gonna ski it.

In addition to Dave Williams, we have Dave Kellogg: mountaineer, travel writer and videographer; he currently resides in Tacoma, Washington USA where he teaches underprivileged youth videography and photojournalism.

Patrick McKnight, a statistics professor at George Mason University, who has survived both Everest disasters of 2014 and 2015. He also just completed a swim of the English Channel.

And finally, me, Brendan Madden, a Physics and Biology teacher at the American School in Japan. I've run into Dave Williams, or rather he has run into me, on the 7-summit quest.

A team of four educators, pursuing their passions, paired with state-of-the-art technology sets the perfect stage for bringing this expedition into classrooms around the world.

We are currently looking for schools and institutions that want to follow the expedition, and institutions and companies that can provide technology, logistics, equipment, and financial support. Finally, we welcome any input-on ways to make this expedition immersive and global, sparking students' interest in STEM, storytelling and adventure.

I thought we hit it out of the park. Now it was time to make some contacts and find some sponsors. Hercules Inlet would probably cost around $60,000 USD per person, while the Gould Bay would probably cost around $100,000 USD per person. With a minimum of four people, this was not a cheap trip.

I started in Tokyo. I had talked up the trip to several friends who had connections with people who raised funds for a living. I was doing ski videos for GoPro Japan and was friends with a guy who ran an adventure TV syndicate. I was sending out our press packs to all my friends and asking all their friends. I was also in touch with Google Explorations, Shindig, UNESCO, Ice Cube Neutrino Observatory, Antarctic Search for Meteorites, and PolarTrec Education Outreach. Nothing was coming back yet, but I thought that was fine. We were planning to go in December of 2017. We had over a year to raise money.

Patrick had contacted his friends who worked for the Nestlé Global Food Corporation and from what he said: "The Amazon. com of Africa." To me those were two huge leads that I was sure would throw down some big money for our project. Patrick was also incredible at writing for grant money. That was a great asset.

Finally, Dave Williams had been digging up sponsors for all his adventures. He had connections at North Face and several companies and businesses in New Zealand. We knew it was a big budget, but we also knew the money was out there.

I also had to sell this idea to my school. In addition, to our normal three-week winter vacation, I was going to need another three to six weeks off on either side of our given vacation depending on the route. I had to show the value that this adventure would bring to the school.

The proposal I put together for the school was incredible. The objectives of the adventure met the strategic objectives of the school and the core values outlined in their handbook. I aligned the trip with lessons for every grade and fit it into their current curriculum. Also, every day after school I was training in the gym and dragging a tire with a 45lb. weight strapped to the top of it. Everyone knew I was training for a ski trip across Antarctica, I just had to make it official.

Nervous, I went into the interim Head of School's office and turned in the proposal. She said it was interesting but thought the time away that I was asking for was too long. However, she said it was not her decision and she would bring it before the school leadership board.

During that time, I was still contacting ALE often without any response. It was difficult to plan this trip with no on-the-ground beta of which routes were possible. I had not heard anything from ALE that would give us direction on our trip. There was no news, no information about the routes I had planned, or information about the final costs, until I received an email from them on October 28, 2016.

Hi Brendan,

Our Mountain Manager and Expeditions Manager reviewed your Expedition plan as well as everyone's climbing experience. From the information that was provided on everyone's questionnaire and we think that in order for the group to get the most out of this expedition and the best chance for success with the most enjoyment, it would be better for each of you to gain more experience in cold conditions at altitude before attempting an unguided Sea 2 Summit Expedition.
I am happy to put you in touch with the Mountain Manager,

Nick Lewis if you would like to chat to him.

With kind regards,
Melanie

"Are you kidding me?" I thought. I have skied in Iraq. I have ridden a bike to Mt. Everest. I have spent three weeks dragging a heavy-ass sled and pack up Denali, I've climbed Aconcagua in approach shoes, I have worked at ski areas for decades. "What do you mean I don't have experience in cold conditions at altitude?"

I was hurt, offended, and angry. I chatted with the team. We all agreed that we needed to get Nick Lewis on the phone.

On November 1, 2016 I was pulled into the high school principal's office. That is never a good sign. He said that ASIJ decided that they could not allow me to take that much time off. It was now my decision whether to keep this amazing job that I loved or follow my dreams of being an explorer. I had until December 1st to make my final decision. In my unsettled stomach, I knew my decision already. I was the one leading this charge to Antarctica. I did not want to let any of my friends down. I knew we could do it.

As I was in Tokyo and Dave Williams was in New Zealand, we asked Patrick to call ALE Mountain Manager Nick Lewis up until he answered. It took 25 days for us to get a hold of Nick from ALE.

Patrick took notes while he was talking with Nick and sent us an email summing everything up. According to what we had submitted in the paperwork, ALE had some concerns:

1. ALE is ultimately responsible for our expedition so they want to ensure that we are well-prepared and can enjoy a safe adventure. Thus, they vet these unique expeditions more thoroughly than with other more standard ones.

2. We didn't present ourselves well to ALE through our paperwork. It lacked information about our abilities to independently plan for the expedition.

3. We did not have enough evidence that our previous adventures were self-managed and self-monitored.

4. We did not have enough off the beaten path experience.

5. We did not show that we had the ability to make decisions in adverse conditions/extreme environments.

6. We did not provide enough evidence to convince ALE that we are fit and ready for this adventure.

7. Our planning was incomplete.

8. We needed to take this feedback seriously and not defensively.

9. We needed to train accordingly with adventures that would better prepare us for Antarctica.

I tried as hard as I could to not take the advice defensively but that was a huge blow to my planning, my ego, and the entire momentum of our trip. I didn't understand how they couldn't see that we were self-reliant, we had been way off the beaten path, we had been in adverse environments and had to make tough decisions.

I did agree with ALE that our planning was incomplete. However, I had been contacting them for nine months asking for information on the routes with no response. I needed to refocus. We had 13 months. All we needed was a 2-week trip pulling a sled across some frozen tundra. We could do that.

Patrick was a great voice of reason. He put together a list of places that we could meet.

- Norway - long stretches of open, mountainous terrain

- Alaska - huge mountains with tons of crevassed areas for route finding. Dave also plans to be there in May, right Dave W?

- North America (Cascade Range, Colorado Rockies) - tons of open areas where we can make it convenient for some with easy access in/out with flights

- Iceland - plenty of long stretches with route finding challenges

He followed up with some caveats,

"I have little if any restrictions since I can break away from work. Some of you, however, do not have that luxury. Money is also an issue for sure, but I think we need to be focused on the purpose here. If we are going to pull off this Antarctica expedition, we need to vet the details thoroughly and the best way is to make sure we are all prepared equally and are ready for the challenge."

Patrick was right. The only way this was possible was if we took the ALE recommendations and completed everything they wanted. They didn't say our proposed trip was out of the question. We just needed more extended cold weather experience.

Patrick also hinted at the other problems we were facing with ALEs recommendations. This trip would cost even more money and would require a lot more time.

That was two rejections, one from ASIJ and one from ALE. I was not going to let it hamper my drive. I had been planning this expedition for nine months. Perhaps I was blinded by my own stoke, but I had to fight on. This was a major setback but that's it, another step getting us closer to our goal. I had ample time off during school vacations, I was making great money, and spending very little on day-to-day activities. I could get in a two-week sled pull somewhere, anywhere in the world. I continued, full speed ahead.

December 1, 2016 came quickly. I had my 2017-2018, $86,000 USD contract in hand. It came down to Antarctica or one of the best jobs in the world. It was a tough decision, but I had a vision of Antarctica.

Dave Williams would be roped in, hanging over a 50-meter ice cliff that ended in the Weddell Sea. He would dip his crampons in and then ice climb up the translucent cliff. I would be flying a drone getting incredible footage. Dave Kellogg and Patrick McKnight would be at the top of the cliff with the sleds all packed up. Pods of whales would be surfacing near the icy coast and curious penguins would be gathered around wishing us well. Then a camera shot of all four of us departing across the Ronne-Filchner ice shelf on cross-country skis. The first ever sea to summit of Antarctica was on its way.

That was my dream. I walked into the Head of School's office. I said thank you for everything. I loved my job, the relationships I had with my coworkers, students, and the administration, however, I needed a grand adventure and would not be returning for the next school year. She asked me if I was sure. I said absolutely.

I was bummed that I had to give up my job, but it was all worth it for this Antarctica first. I continued to work out with a huge focus on dragging tires. I continued contacting funding agencies. Patrick had a couple of friends that might have been able to track down some big bucks, but they also wanted to be on the trip. If they were bringing money to the table, then I was all for it.

We were getting great feedback from schools and businesses.

The schools were interested in participating, but the timing was tough as the expedition would span semesters and Christmas break. Businesses were willing to support us with video distribution and logistics, but they kept coming back without any cash offers. I knew this wouldn't be easy so I continued on doing what I could to make connections to sponsors.

Patrick and Dave Williams were also reaching out to all the contacts they could muster. Guy Cotter, a famous New Zealand mountaineer and CEO of Adventure Consultants, Eric Larsen, a famous polar explorer, and Tom Sjogren another famous polar explorer and mountaineer. All of them said that our trip looked amazing, they had no solid way to help us with funding, and that we need to do everything through ALE. Patrick even reached out to Aaron Linsdau of Antarctic Tears, and I got a hold of Felicity Aston of Alone in Antarctica. They both responded quickly and favorably. However, again, they had no good connections for sponsors and directed us to ALE for logistics.

ALE was busy. They were still not responding to my emails about information regarding the possibility of the Gould Bay approach. However, through my research, the Hercules Inlet seemed extremely feasible. Dave Williams, although busy planning for his Denali sea to summit attempt in the spring of 2017, chimed in and said,

> "Well from what I can see it is 100m above sea level? Is that cheating? I want to do it right but if it is deemed by adventure folk that it counts then I am totally open to it, especially if that means we get the green light."

There was no green light in sight. The same obstacles kept coming up and it seemed like we were in this vicious circle of Catch-22. We needed to confirm the trip in order to get sponsors, but we needed sponsors in order to confirm the trip. It started to sink in that I didn't know the first thing about getting sponsors, business, and selling our expedition.

Dave Williams was doing a good job getting funding for himself. He was from New Zealand, a land of adventurers. They were a close-knit community that supported each other. Small businesses were supporting Dave because they believed in a Kiwi that could be the first person ever to tackle the 7 summits from sea level.

Dave was supported by Bivouac Outdoors, Radix Nutrition, Zealand's Family Wines, Physio mechanics, and the Mental Health Foundation of New Zealand. These are all wonderful companies and could support Dave, but not a team of four looking at a total price tag of close to $400,000 USD.

The big "why" of Dave's sea to summit objective was noble but hard to sell on a worldwide sponsorship scale. As it says on his sea2summit7.com website:

> A few years ago, my life came to a crossroads… I was in search of a new adventure, one that would test my limits both physically and mentally. At the time a good friend of mine, Ryan, invited me on a sea to summit of Mt Taranaki from the West Coast and it was here where the idea of sea2summit7 was born. The overall goal being to become the first person to climb the highest mountain on each continent from the nearest feasible coastline. I soon realized that this adventure was about more than just challenging myself, I wanted it to be about something bigger and better than that too. I had recently lost two friends, both with adventurous spirits, to depression and as a school health teacher I have witnessed daily the importance of the issue that is male mental health in New Zealand. Too often we try to tackle all our mountains in life alone, brought up with the "she'll be right" attitude and thus prevented from asking for help.
>
> And so, the inspiration to complete this adventure truly began, with the aim of raising $100,000 and awareness for the Male Mental Health Foundation, and to write about

every great, hard, brilliant, petrifying moment of it, no "she'll be rights" in sight. My hope was that these mountains would be a team effort, my steps but your support.

It probably was never a deciding factor for sponsors in the first place but saying that we are going to Antarctica to raise money and awareness for men with mental health issues in New Zealand did not seem like a "catch-all" charity that the world could rally around.

I had friends and acquaintances that urged me to start a www. gofundme.com page. However, I didn't want to take people's money so that I could have a great experience. I'm sure all the money that would have come in would have just been from relatives. I definitely didn't want that. Other people suggested that I choose my own noble charity and raise money under their banner. However, I have always questioned people spending tens of thousands of dollars on expeditions to raise thousands of dollars for charity. To me, if you really want to raise money for a charity then all that money for the expedition should go to the charity and the expedition shouldn't happen at all. With me not willing to go down those avenues and the corporate avenues not working out, it seemed that the expedition might not happen at all.

The expedition might not happen at all? More like, the expedition, as it stood now, was not happening at all. It hit me like a Mike Tyson jab to the ribs. We have no money, no sponsors, no solid plan, not enough experience, and we were already on the bad side of the only company that can help us navigate an expedition in Antarctica. I just quit my job. Dammit.

The email communications and skype calls between the team, Dave Williams, Dave Kellogg, Patrick, and I slowed down during the new year: 2017. Dave Williams was focused on his upcoming sea to summit of Denali. Dave Kellogg had foreseen many of the issues and was staying rather quiet. Patrick was still reaching out to polar explorers who were responding with positivity, but nothing that would save our sinking ship. I was at the helm watching it all go down.

In February, Dave Williams and I had a Skype call. I think we had come to the realization a while ago, but we had to say it to each other. Antarctica, for now, is over. I needed to find a job.

I continued to help Dave Williams plan for Denali. It was going to be incredibly difficult. Running over terrain that starts as melted permafrost tundra and evolves into glacier runoff sounded like a nightmare. I sent him an HD video of what the flight over the terrain looked like. The dense forests, raging rivers, and glacial ponds that led to the Kahiltna Glacier on Denali were fierce.

I also started looking for jobs. Could I be a substitute next year? Could I find a school that would give me the time off just in case the trip miraculously got the green light? I shot out emails to all my friends that were teaching at schools around the world. It was difficult to get an interview when I was still asking for an extra month off around the Christmas vacation.

My girlfriend at the time, Tatiana, was also living with me. Any decision I made would affect us both. Maybe she could continue working for the British School of Tokyo and I could just take the year off? Maybe I should be a ski instructor in Hokkaido? Maybe I should just get a cabin in Hakuba and ski bum again? I was clueless.

My coworkers and students were still stopping by my classroom, checking out the map on the wall. They were all excited for me and so interested in the Sea2Summit7 Antarctica. I acted like nothing was wrong. Questions flooded in about the expedition. The students were really looking up to me on how bold and adventurous I was. I did not want to let them down or let myself down in their eyes. I would answer as if the trip was full steam ahead.

Every day after school, I would put on my climbing harness, attach it to the tire with the 45lb plate on it, and wave to students as they were heading home. Then I would drag the tire around the adjacent park for an hour. The burden of Antarctica was much heavier now. Stupidity, anger, and loss consumed my thoughts as I continued to smile and wave.

I was embarrassed. Despite the red flags, despite the early warnings that this was an enormous undertaking that would take much longer than we understood, I had put all my eggs in one basket. I had smashed that basket over my own head. I couldn't believe I was leaving ASIJ, the best paying and most rewarding job I ever had, for nothing.

# CHAPTER 4

# COMMITTED

My time felt meaningless. I had no direction, no goals, no job. It was April 2017; Dave Williams was heading off to Denali. Dave Kellogg was in Tacoma getting ready for his daughter to be born. Patrick and I were still in contact with each other often, even though it had been three years since our adventure on Aconcagua. Patrick said that he wanted one more shot at Everest. He was signing up for a 2018 expedition to the north side of Everest and said that I should come with him.

Once Patrick invited me to climb Everest with him, the spark came back. I decided it was time. I refocused on my new adventure and new goal: Mt. Everest.

The first thing I needed to do was secure the logistics. I did not want this to fall through like Antarctica did.

Both of Patrick's first two Everest attempts had been with the Seattle-based company Summit Climb. The company's founder is the renowned mountaineer Dan Mazur. Dan has numerous accolades for climbing, conservation, and charity work in the Himalayas but is most well-known for discovering and assisting in the life-saving rescue of climber Lincoln Hall around 8,700 meters on a 2006 Everest climb. Most recently, he received the "Sir Edmund Hillary Mountain Legacy Medal for remarkable service in the conservation of culture and nature in mountainous regions."[14] Summit Climb is a no-frills company that operates on very little profit margin, passing the savings onto the climber. At the time, the cost of my full-service Everest climb was $28,450.00. I got a 5% discount for being part of

14      The next Hillary Medalist: Mountaineer and Philanthropist Daniel Mazur.

Patrick's group which knocked it down to $27,027.50. Patrick's cost, $25,605, was an additional 5% off since he had climbed with Summit Climb twice before.

According to Summitclimb.com,[15] the Full-Service Price Includes:
1. Leader David O'Brien
2. Expert Sherpas
3. Climb permits
4. Oxygen
5. Hotels in KTM
6. Transport from Kathmandu (KTM) to Chinese basecamp (CBC)
7. Comfortable but modest CBC accommodations
8. Comfortable but modest advanced basecamp (ABC)
9. Tents at each camp, (individual tents at CBC tent per member, because of our numbers we also each had an individual tent at ABC)
10. Expedition costs (on the Tibet side the permit cost paid to the Chinese Tibet Mountaineering Association (CTMA) is $8,000 USD)
11. Meals & food
12. Climbing equipment
13. Fixed ropes and fees
14. Radios
15. Internet
16. International phone

Also, on the Summit Climb website it says, "New Flexible Date Option: arrive anytime at your convenience during April or May."[16] This brought a smile to my face because as I was living in China with a "Z" working visa, Chinese government restrictions did not allow me to enter Tibet from Kathmandu, Nepal. As with any foreigners entering Tibet, the Chinese government wants to stop contraband items, ideas against the Communist Party, and notions that support the Dalai Lama. If

---

15      Mt. Everest Climbing Expedition in Tibet via Northside Route.
16      Mt. Everest Climbing Expedition in Tibet via Northside Route Lhasa Itinerary.

I were to fly to Kathmandu, they would cancel my visa. I then would have to apply for a new tourist visa to enter Tibet for the climb, exit after the climb, and reapply for my "Z" work visa to get back to my job. To avoid that pain in the ass, I would just fly into Lhasa, catch a ride across Tibet and meet up with the team when I could.

Once I told Summit Climb my predicament, that I would prefer the "Flexible Date Option," Sue Crisp, Summit Climb's office manager replied to me:

> "Dear Brendan. If you want to enter from Lhasa, we can organize it and the cost is $3,624.00 for the two-way trip and we now need a good scan of your China work and residence permit. Tibet is huge and you would be driving across it twice in a car, so that is the reason for the expense. It takes three days to drive across Tibet. Thanks for letting us know."

"Are you serious? Another $3,624.00?" I yelled at my computer.

I had already dug deep into my accounts to pay the $27,027.50. This new "Flexible Date Option" just raised the most expensive thing I've ever paid for to $30,651.50. What was I to do? I could not just back out now. I was in.

Dan called me on the phone the next day and we talked at length about what was happening in Tibet, the cost of the trip, the CTMA requirements, and the climb. He was not aggravated like I was, but I could definitely tell that he really did not want to ask me for that money either. I also informed them that I could return with the team to Kathmandu after the climb.

After some phone wrangling, Dan got back to me and informed me that since I was not returning to Lhasa that the extra fee I was quoted earlier would be cut in half: $1,812. This covered my permit to get into Tibet, my driver, my liaison, registration paperwork and one-night accommodation in Shigatse and Tingri and finally the drive from Lhasa to Mt. Everest Base Camp.

My new total expense, minus flights and equipment I bought for the climb, was $28,839.50. For an Everest expedition, this is about the cheapest out there.

Spending money for an Everest climb doesn't stop there. On Patrick's second attempt on Everest, when the Earthquake struck, he was stuck. There was no going up or down. However, Patrick had purchased the 90-day individual medical and security membership from Global Rescue LLC. As everyone was scrambling to get off the mountain, a helicopter landed. An associate from Global Rescue came out and asked,

> "Patrick McKnight?" "Yup," Patrick replied. "We are getting you out of here," the man responded, motioning to the helicopter.

Global Rescue flew him back to Kathmandu, which was in ruins due to the earthquake and put him and other clients up in one of Kathmandu's premiere hotels, the Yak and Yeti. Water was a scarcity, so they were encouraged to drink at the hotel bar. The tab was covered by Global Rescue. While sitting at the hotel reflecting on the events that shook the nation Patrick wrote in his blog:

> "Global Rescue earns top honors... an organization that not only deserves praise but also deserves more subscribers. Go ahead and ask anyone who has climbing insurance from Global Rescue or from one of their competitors. The folks at Global Rescue organized our evacuation from start to finish. Once we realized that our climb was over and our situation at Camp 1 remained precarious, I placed a sat-phone call to my wife to initiate our evacuation. That call started a cascade of events that required little on my part. The Global Rescue folks knew me, my mates, and our situation. My wife called several times and felt complete confidence in their handling of the situation. My two climbing pals - Sam Chappatte and Alex Schneider - used British Mountaineering Council insurance and found the experience with them to be less-than-satisfactory.

How unsatisfactory? Well, Sam essentially told the BMC representatives to contact Global Rescue to coordinate their evacuation. Yep, no faith in BMC. Meanwhile, my mate Jim Grieve, and I simply sat back and watched the great service unfold before our eyes. Global Rescue also evacuated our entire Summit Climb team from Camp 1. I am and will remain a die-hard supporter of Global Rescue."

With the stakes as high as they are on Everest, Patrick's enthusiastic recommendation, and pressure from my girlfriend, I also purchased the $855 USD, 90-day policy.

An Everest expedition takes at least a month and a half. I would still have a hard time finding a job that would give me that time off. I had settled on Tatiana working and I would just take the year off for training, tutoring, and whatever else I could do. I would be poor, but prepared. Tatiana was fully supportive.

One of the people I had reached out to during this time was the director of the school that Dave Kellogg and I had helped start in 2006: Qingdao American International School. It was now called the Qingdao Amerasia International School but was still QAIS. The director asked me what I needed to come back to the school.

"Give me a job, give my girlfriend a job and I need a month and a half off in April and May to go climb Everest," I said.

He replied: "Done."

Things were looking up. I would be able to work, Tatiana would get to live in Qingdao, a city that I love, and I would get to climb Everest with the support of a school. We immediately signed contracts.

The school year came to an end. I was chosen by the students at ASIJ to be the speaker at their graduation. It was during the commencement speech that I told everybody and was the first time I heard myself say it out loud, to anyone, that Antarctica fell through and that I was leaving the school to go climb Mt. Everest.

I concluded, "Thank you Japan, thank you ASIJ and thank you and congratulations class of 2017."

The Japan chapter of my life was closing. A new one in China, with a girlfriend, and Mt. Everest as my goal, was about to start in high gear.

Via the United States and Central America, Tatiana and I moved to Qingdao, China. It ended up being a great move for training. The city is sandwiched between a couple of small mountain ranges, Fushan and Laoshan and is bordered to the south by the Pacific Ocean. Not long ago it was a sleepy fishing village known for its imperialist German architecture and beer: Tsingtao. Now, it is known as one of the most elite cities in China and its beer. Between 2006 and 2012 when I lived in Qingdao, I was also known as someone who loved to drink that beer. This time around, in preparation for Everest, I had to distance my "new" self from my former self.

I made a decision to give up alcohol. During my Aconcagua training I continued to party. Several times I had drank too much to sleep at high altitude in the tent. Furthermore, the planned workouts the next day would be brutal. I would put in minimal effort, or the workouts wouldn't happen at all. While I did fine on Aconcagua, the stakes for Everest and this life changing move, were much higher. I wanted to avoid missing any days of training because of partying.

The school, although not the educational caliber of ASIJ, had come a long way since I had left it five years previously. The campus was a 10km, beautifully paved, oceanside bike ride from our apartment. We rode our bikes to school every day which was a great warm up for a day of teaching and training. It felt strange to be back "home" in Qingdao, but I loved it.

# CHAPTER 5

# TRAINING

Starting in August 2018, Everest was the focus of everything I did. I believe it was the intensity of this focus that was the largest contributor to my success and enjoyment of my Everest climb.

To keep track of my training, I used a Google Spreadsheet similar to the one that I used on Aconcagua. However, the new spreadsheet, "Madden 230 Days of Training for Everest"[17], had been fine-tuned by Patrick through his two previous Everest attempts.

The training list was daunting. I could see there was absolutely no time for anything but work, training, and sleep. Previous to signing up for this adventure, gym time to me was lifting weights. I wanted the big pecs, the big biceps, and shoulders. Through the years I had even gotten into squats and Olympic lifting. Patrick's new training list felt like every exercise except the ones I loved. It ran the gamut from Wim Hof breathing, to movement prep, to biking and elliptical workouts.

The spreadsheet was detailed. It had the expected time per exercise on one half of the spreadsheet and the other half I would input my actual minutes doing each of the exercises. The most intimidating days were the ones that required 459 minutes of training. That is over 7 hours. There was an area to record qualitative comments, successes and shortcomings. Many days I wanted to pad my numbers but realized that by doing so, I wouldn't be the only one being cheated. If there was any trouble on the mountain, I didn't want to put myself

---

17    "Madden 230 Days of Training for Everest 2018."

or others at risk because I wasn't physically prepared. So, I prepared my body and, in many ways, my mind along with it.

Overall, I focused on hypoxic training, breathing and cold exposure, as well as physical and technical training.

## Hypoxic Training

Every morning I would wake up in the hypoxic tent that was situated on our bed. The temperature in the tent was always a little hotter than I wanted it to be. Often there would be a layer of dew that would also drip on my face as I was waking up. Before leaving the tent, I would use an ambient oxygen meter and record on my phone the percentage of oxygen in the tent and what elevation this simulated.

The next step was to scrounge around for my small pulse oximeter. This allowed me to check my SPO2 levels and heart rate. At first, the standard issue Hypoxico 2-person Deluxe Altitude Tent was sufficient. It allowed me to get the oxygen levels down to about 12% simulating 4,500 meters. However, I needed to get higher. The volume of Deluxe Altitude Tent was approximately 5 square meters which was taking too long to fill with nitrogen and the tent was not sealed tight enough to keep it in and the oxygen out. I decided to make a new tent with dimensions of 0.8 meters long, 0.7 meters deep, and 0.5 meters high for a new volume of 0.34 meters. I termed it the fish tank. It could get the oxygen level down to 8.8%, simulating 6,700 meters. That is what I was looking for. There were many sleepless nights, but I was so extremely focused. It didn't matter.

All of this data I inserted on a separate tab within the spreadsheet (see Madden 230 Days of Training for Everest).

Analyzing the data shows exactly what I hoped to accomplish. In order to get a good night's sleep, I had to keep my SPO2 rather high, in my case above 80% all the while nudging up the altitude. At the end of February, with 46 training days remaining, I employed my small tent. I was then able to increase the altitude gradually to 6400 meters, even reaching 6,705 meters on my last night. As shown on the graph below, My SPO2 dropped. These nights were the hardest, but I knew they were necessary to give me the edge on Everest.

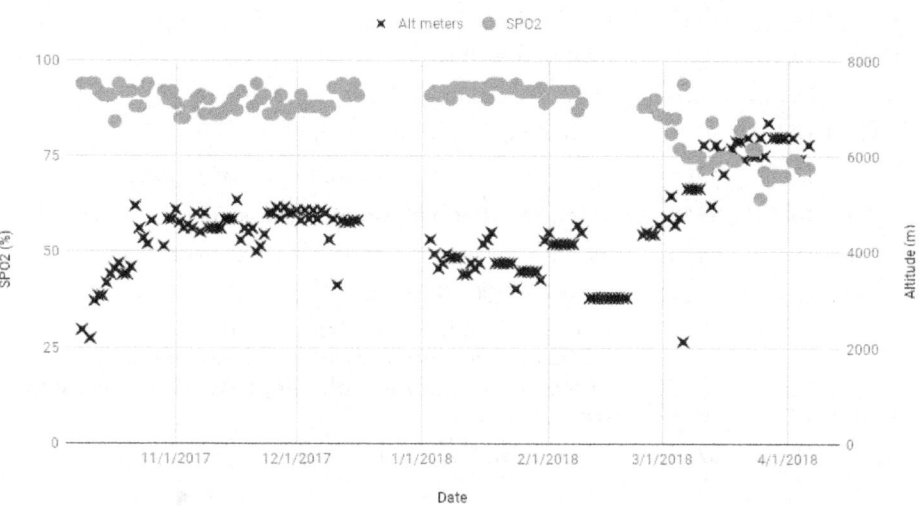

The Effect of Sleep Altitude on Saturated Blood Oxygen Levels

My qualitative comments for when I was sleeping above 5,000 meters can also be found on the Madden 230 Days of Training for Everest spreadsheet and below. It paints a realistic picture of what the day to day grind of pre-Everest acclimatization feels like.

| Date | Altitude (m) | Comment |
|---|---|---|
| 2/27/2018 | 4373 | woke up with headache |
| 2/28/2018 | 4572 | small tent |
| 3/1/2018 | 243 | hose was unplugged |
| 3/2/2018 | 4724 | up at 1:00, 2:45-3:00, 430, $O_2$ fluctuated between 14 and 11.2 |
| 3/3/2018 | 5181 | woke up twice but $O_2$ was at 11.3 and 10.8 need to keep blanket between chain and legs |
| 3/6/2018 | 2133 | need to fix the fish tank to make it more consistent if not going to do mask |
| 3/7/2018 | 5334 | slept with a mask. i woke up so many times. |

| 3/8/2018 | 5334 | mask brutal |
|---|---|---|
| 3/9/2018 | 5334 | mask brutal |
| 3/10/2018 | 5334 | mask brutal |
| 3/11/2018 | 6248 | NEW SMALL TENT |
| 3/12/2018 | 5724 | peed in a bottle twice, it was awesome. |
| 3/13/2018 | 4968 | woke up every 2 hours but not for a long time. |
| 3/14/2018 | 6248 | had a big headache this morning at 3:30 and was up since then |
| 3/15/2018 | 6096 | little headache |
| 3/16/2018 | 5638 | keep waking up at 4:00 |
| 3/17/2018 | 6019 | up at 4:00 feel good though |
| 3/19/2018 | 6324 | woke up at 3:00. felt great but couldn't sleep |
| 3/21/2018 | 5943 | when I'm asleep it's great but woke up at 4 again |
| 3/22/2018 | 6400 | when I'm asleep it's great but woke up at 4 again |
| 3/23/2018 | 6019 | up from 1:00 - 2:30 then up at 5:30 |
| 3/24/2018 | 6019 | not sure what happened but I'm guessing around 12:00 or 1:00 I jumped out of the tent and stayed out for the rest of the night. slept like a baby angel in oxygen bliss. |
| 3/27/2018 | 6705 | woke up with a little headache |

In addition to sleeping at altitude, I was exercising with the training mask as well. Unfortunately, my stationary bike had stopped working as a bike. It did however work great as a coat rack. I had to figure out a different way to exercise using the training mask. I decided to settle on a simple step up and squats. The training would start by velcroing the often-wet training mask on my face, putting on the backpack I would be using on Everest filled with 20 kg of water bottles, then stepping up on a chair, stepping down, doing a squat, and repeating that sequence for hours. It was tougher than I expected and had to stop several times and get my eyes to focus so I wouldn't fall off the chair.

Straight after recording my sleeping data in the Google Spreadsheet, still under the darkness of night, I would turn on meditation music "528Hz Release Inner Conflict & Struggle | Anti Anxiety Cleanse - Stop Overthinking, Worry & Stress"[18]

18    YouTube. ZenLifeRelax. 528Hz Release Inner Conflict & Struggle

I would lay down on an exercise mat and start my Wim Hof breathing.

Wim Hof is a Dutch man who tried to climb Mount Everest in shorts. I first heard of him from a student of mine. I thought, well, Wim has to be doing something right to even try that and I started researching and practicing his simple method. Through breathing, meditation, and cold immersion, the Wim Hof method has shown to increase your blood oxygen levels, tolerance to cold exposure, and increase your focus. For an Everest expedition, this is exactly what I was looking for.

The Wim Hof Method's breathing involves taking deep breaths through your mouth or nose or both filling the bottom of your lungs first, and then filling the rest of your lungs up to your head. To release the breath you just let go, not forcing anything out on the exhale. This is repeated 30-40 times. At the end of those breaths, you exhale everything out and just lay there, not breathing in. When you really need to breathe again, you take a deep breath and hold it for 10 seconds squeezing the muscles throughout your body. You then exhale, relax and take a minute or so before your next round. It is recommended to repeat these 3 or 4 times. I would complete 3 rounds. As I became more adept at the breathing process, I would sometimes do 4 rounds followed by exhaling all my air and doing knuckle push-ups without breathing.

The first week of breathing blew me away. My entire body was buzzing with oxygen overload. Before starting the breathing techniques, I could only hold my breath for approximately 45 seconds. As I progressed, I was able to hold my breath for up to two minutes.

Also, while holding my breath hold, I would envision myself framed in Tibetan prayer flags, walking along the top of the North Col.

## Cold Exposure

Right after breathing in the morning, my cold exposure routine would start. I would take three quick deep breaths, turn the shower on fullblast cold, and go under the stinging stream without hesitation. I kept track of my progress using Wim Hof's "20-DAY COLD SHOWER CHALLENGE,"[19] .

Like electrocution, the cold showers were difficult at first but became routine. After a week of minute-long cold showers, I pushed even further into Wim Hof's 10-week Video Course.[20] During week four of this course, one 10-minute shower is required. Week five requires a 10-minute cold shower every day. These were the hardest. I broke them down into three phases. The first phase, the electrocution phase I liked to call it, lasted for the first two minutes. The second, relaxed phase was great as my body was used to the cold and from two minutes to eight minutes I was completely at ease. Around eight minutes to 10 minutes I reached the 'I'm over-it phase.' I was getting cold headaches and was ready to get out. These showers were much easier in the fall and spring than they were in the winter. With that routine, I was absolutely energized, focused and ready to take on the day before 6:30 am.

After a quick bite to eat, every working day, regardless of the temperature or weather, I would ride my bike 20 kilometers to my school in shorts and a t-shirt. Before I left the house, I would check the outside temperature. I intimately felt the changes in weather from the cooling of the fall, the bloody cold winter, and the warming of the spring. When the temperature was above -3° Celsius, I would walk outside, the doorman laughing at me, and be refreshed. It felt wonderful. Any time the temperature dipped below -4° Celsius, I knew it was going to be a tough ride. The coldest day was -13° Celsius. My eyes would start watering, my knees would feel like rusty hinges, and my fingers would turn bright red before going tingly, then numb. Upon reaching school, I was glad to step into warmth. I would repeat

---

19    "Wim Hof Method - Cold Shower Challenge."

20    Learn the Wim Hof Method | Classic 10-Week Video Course.

this on the way home from school as well. By riding in any weather, with minimal clothing, I trained my body to know what it was like for my extremities to go completely numb, and warm them just before frostbite crept in. This would come in handy on the climb.

My cold training didn't stop there. During the winter, with the outside temperature around -10° Celsius, I would stroll down to the Shilaoren beach in Qingdao, China, in a Speedo. There, I would sit on the sand, do a round of deep breathing, then head into the 4° Celsius water for a 10-minute swim. I would do these swims once a week. On the days that I had planned these polar plunges, my nerves would be counting down the minutes until I was face to face with the ocean. I spent the entire day psyching myself up.

The feeling in the salty ocean water was similar, but more intense than the showers and bike riding. Immediately upon entry into the water my body would want to start hyperventilating but I would force it into taking deep breaths. My extremities would start pulsating and around 2 minutes after my submersion they would start to tingle. Then all feelings would disappear. I ducked my head underwater to get a dose of instant brain freeze. Looking down into the water it was crystal clear like swimming in a mountain lake. The Shilaoren waterfront would sparkle with its apartments and office buildings. Behind it, the Fushan and Laoshan mountains, white and brown from a dusting of snow and the cold of the winter, would shimmer. It really was beautiful to be in that moment. I would then check my stopwatch and agonizingly wait out the last two minutes.

Walking out of the water, my feet and hands felt like blocks, my entire body was bright red, and with a smile, I would nod to onlookers. My girlfriend was usually waiting for me with a towel and a sweatshirt. My thought was to put these on quickly, but with the limited use of my hands, it took longer than it needed to. Standing out in the cold, slowly putting my clothes on, did not bother me at all. I was proud of what I had done and completed. I was achieving mind over body, at least for six of those minutes.

Many of the ideas and cold training techniques came from the book, "Becoming the Iceman; Pushing Past Perceived Limits" by Wim Hof and Justin Rosales.

## Physical Training

The majority of my physical training (11,567 minutes or 8, 24-hour days) was spent on an elliptical machine. The elliptical machine provided ample resistance, was easier on the knees than running, and could allow for other activities. To help me get through the hours on the elliptical machine, I watched and re-watched YouTube videos on Everest. They ranged from great to mediocre to terrible, but I always felt hungry for more information no matter the quality.

One excellent video in particular documented the actual climb more than any other: "Mt. Everest Climb from North Side 2016"[21] by a Chinese man named Li-Lan Cheng. I watched this video several times, trying to understand exactly what I was getting into and it helped me kill time and give focus in the thick of my long workouts. In addition to the Everest videos, I listened to all the audio books of Game of Thrones, and several other audiobooks that Patrick recommended. In many ways, the long elliptical workouts were training my mind to deal with the repetitive movements for hours on end. The training was mental as much as it was physical.

Other activities I did in the gym included spin classes, leg workouts including squats and lunges (very little upper body workouts), yoga and core exercises. One of the best core exercises I found that always felt like it went by fast was through the Fitness Blender YouTube channel. In particular, their "60 Minute HIIT Cardio and Abs Workout - Fitness Blender Tabata HIIT, Abs and Obliques Workout"[22] was fun, difficult, and made the core exercises a brainless activity. Just hit play and go.

21      YouTube. Li-Lan Cheng. Mt. Everest Climb from North Side 2016. YouTube.

22      YouTube. Fitness Blender. 60 Minute HIIT Cardio and Abs Workout

Outside, in addition to biking to and from work, about twice a week I would run 5km along the beach, in shorts and a t-shirt of course, no matter the weather. Whenever possible, I would use the local mountain, Fushan (360m) to train.

International Mountain Guides (IMG) web page provides excellent information on how to train for Everest. I incorporated their yo-yo method of climbing mountains and applied it to Fushan several times:

> "Near the end of your training do a "mental hike." You should be in good shape to take a climb like this: Mt. Baldy... start in the parking lot, and go all the way to the summit... four miles and 4,000' and then all the way back to the car... tag it and then do the climb again... called a "yo-yo!" (don't complain... just suck it up... a nice 10 hours of getting your buns kicked.) Not pleasant but will get you ready to handle the mental part of being tough. Remember it and how prepared you really are when the going gets tough on your summit day."[23]

I yo-yoed Fushan in the sun, in the snow with crampons, with students, and met tons of Chinese people along the way. They would see my Olympus Mons boots (I wore them on all my climbs) and hear them say "Ah ta shi zhuanye de," he is a professional. I would politely respond,

"No, I'm not, I'm just trying to break these boots in."

The challenge of Fushan was waning. To up the physical output, I went down to the beach and did a sea to summit push of Fushan with a full 19-liter water bottle in my backpack.

I started rock climbing in 1995 but was never that good at it. I loved going to rock climbing gyms. The outdoor clubs that I ran always had an aspect of rock climbing in them. But, I was

---

23      How to Summit Everest -- Advice from IMG Climbers.

out of practice. It had been at least two years since I had been on a real rock wall. I needed to brush up on my skills.

Luckily, Fushan also has several steep cliffs up to about 40 meters high. It was on the cliffs, that I would rehone my rock climbing and rappelling skills. It had been several years since I was looking down a 40-meter rock face for rappelling and, admittedly, I was very nervous. However, with the help of a coworker and excellent rock climber Chris Boredenko, we would take down and set up the rigging a couple of times a week so that it became second nature again. We even re-established the school's outdoor club so students could learn how to tie knots, camp, climb and rappel.

I continued climbing and rappelling outdoors. Our school, serendipitously, also just installed a 10-meter rock wall in the gym. Chris' wife Lauren, Tatiana, and I would hangout on the wall after school to climb, joke around, and teach students how to climb.

All aspects of training were going smooth until Novermber 6th. On that day, 64 days into my training, I started having knee pain, enough to where I noted it in my training spreadsheet. I tried to ignore it. Most of my training pains seemed to dissipate after one to two weeks. On November 7th and 8th the pain got worse. I had too much at stake to not get my knee checked out. This was crushing. I had been following the training regimen extremely well and now I was facing a serious setback. If I couldn't complete the training, I wouldn't belong on the mountain. I would be putting Patrick's and possibly numerous lives at risk. At the time it felt like a game ender.

I went to the best medical clinic in Qingdao. The temperature outside was 15° Celsius and I showed up in shorts and a t-shirt. The doctor sat me down, stared deep into my eyes and said,

"You need to wear pants. The cold and wind are getting into your knee joints, that is the main problem."

I nodded. I knew he was serious and without him asking, I explained the amount of physical training I was doing. He sat there staring at the ceiling for a couple of minutes not saying a word. Finally, he looked directly into my eyes again. It felt like he was staring into my soul. This was one intense Chinese medicine man. He said I needed to stop all exercise for 3 weeks and start physiological therapy. He laid me down on his massage table and started digging the knuckles of his thumb into all sorts of places I did not know you could get into with fingers. He even got his thumb under my patella. After 20 minutes on each knee he put warm towels on them and walked away. He came back five minutes later with needles.

It started with a prick. Then the needle was slowly forced into deeper tissues. The first needle was inserted directly above my patella. This was followed by 5 other needles. One on each side of the first. Then one on the outside of my knee and one on the inside of my knee. The last one was stuck in below the patella. It was a strange sensation. The tiny pinch when the needles entered was fine. However, when he pushed the needles in further it felt like my ligaments and muscles were turning into stone. Once all the needles were in, my knee was stiff as a board. I was also trying as hard as possible not to move my leg to avoid any unnecessary jabbing's. On its own rolling stand, he brought over a bright orange heat lamp. Translucent waves of water vapor could be seen rising above the lamp. This thing was hot. He positioned it directly above the needles. They cooked for 15 minutes. The heat conducted through the needles into my deep tissues. It was a numbing sensation but far from pain relief. This was repeated with my other knee. The treatment was finished and surprisingly, there was minor immediate pain relief. Perhaps I was just glad to get the needles out. I was instructed to return to his office three times a week for the next three weeks.

This knee pain was a serious setback. I could not fulfill the times that were outlined in our training spreadsheet. I was concerned.

This led to a minor case of depression. It was imperative that I match Patrick's training numbers in order to arrive at Everest completely prepared. I wanted to train but I had to recover. If my knee did not get better fast, would I even be able to get my fitness to a point where climbing Everest was an option? Is this over? Did I make another huge mistake? I thought deeply about my options.

To take pressure off of my knee, I dropped the spin classes. I also cut back on my elliptical training and running. Unfortunately, these exercises made up the bulk of my training. In the graph below, Scheduled and Actual Training Time Leading Up to Mt. Everest Climb, after November 6, my actual numbers (Xs) were nowhere close to where they needed to be (circles).

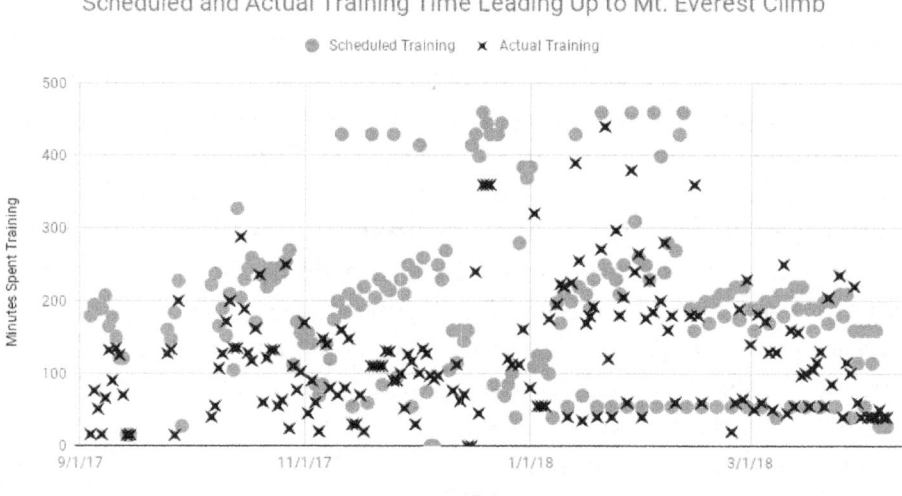

Scheduled and Actual Training Time Leading Up to Mt. Everest Climb

It was difficult to squeeze the extensive hours of exercise into my day. I would exercise before work, on the way to work, at work, coming home from work, and late into the evening. The hours just weren't available. My girlfriend was even preparing all my meals and bringing snacks to the gym for me to help give me the training time I needed. With my knee injury, I was now consistently 1 to 5 hours below my training goals every day. Initially, I held this information back from Patrick.

I came to the realization that If we were to rely on each other on the mountain, I needed to come clean. I called up Patrick and told him the bad news. I was in a slump. My training numbers were low and were not going to improve until my knee did. Patrick, as easy going as they come, reassured me. He told me that there were days that he had knee problems, shoulder problems and/or back problems that caused him to dial down or skip a workout. He said it was all part of the training: overcoming obstacles and setbacks but continuing forward. He emphasized that as long as we were doing everything we could, especially the long workouts and hypoxic training, we would be fitter than most non-Sherpa climbers on Everest. Patrick motivated me to not give up and to find a way to cope with this setback.

I needed to replace the lost exercise time. I decided on a positive step that addressed what I thought the problem with my knee was. I self-diagnosed that my big issue is my horrid inflexibility, so I developed a routine that I called Core Stretch Roll (CSR). It looks like this:

| Core | Stretch (1 min. each leg) | Roll (10x) |
|---|---|---|
| V-Ups 30 | Standing Quad | Quad Flat spread 2 sides |
| Plank 1 min | Back outside hip | Hips outside |
| Reverse Crunch 30 | L sit at wall | IT Band |
| Elastic band twist 20 | External Hip rotation - Layovers | Glutes |
| Supermans 20 | Wall push calf stretch | Calves Flat Outside Inside |
| Sit ups 50 | Butterfly | Inside Ham |

I would start in the top left corner and move to the right from top to bottom: a core exercise, stretch, and roll. The roll means I would massage out the muscles on a big blue foam roller. It wasn't as rewarding as a spin class or a long slog on an elliptical machine, but I had no choice.

My knee was feeling better, but not 100%, by December 2017.

I was nearing the halfway point in my training and felt I needed to measure up, face to face, with Patrick's training. We decided to meet in the Pacific Northwest at Dave Kellogg's house. I had not had any alcohol since I started training for Everest, however, Dave had a hot tub at his new house. On the first night we all got in. He brought out a couple Rainier Beers for each of us. I knew saying anything but "thank you" would have brought on a barrage of insults and I would have folded eventually. So, I gave my thanks, we cracked the tops, and relaxed in the hot tub under some Pacific Northwest drizzle.

We spent just under two weeks in the Pacific Northwest staying in shape. We did several runs through a forest by Dave's house. We took two trips for backcountry ski touring: one on Mt. Rainier and the other near Crystal Mountain. We skied a couple of days at Alpental and Snoqualmie Pass. We even ran into Garrett Madison, one of American's most renowned Himalayan climbers at Dru Bru, a microbrewery. Even with the beers, Patrick felt great. I felt great. The training was working.

Back in China, I kept going. I would ease off if my knees were acting up and tried to spend more and more time outside. I knew my gear well. Patrick put together his equipment list and left room for me to add my gear. This way we were checking that between the two of us we had everything covered and were not doubling up on any equipment unnecessarily. The entire sheet can be viewed at: Everest 2018 Planning Sheet Shared[24] and in the appendix.

March arrived quickly. It was time for one of my last equipment tests. As best I could, I wanted to simulate what I would encounter during the summit night of Everest. On the Tibetan north face of Everest there are three steps -- cliffs -- that you must surmount. The summit push begins at 10:00pm for most climbers so you have to scale the cliffs with just a headlamp. On a weekday night, I made my way up to a cliff on Fushan that was similar to the second of the three steps. This cliff is about

---

24      "Everest 2018 Planning Sheet Shared."

300 meters above sea level. There was no wind and it was 15° Celsius. These were not the same conditions that I would face on Everest, but it was the best simulation I had. It turned out to be an important test.

Tying off to two boulders and using a cam as a backup, I fixed a rope to the top of the cliff and rappelled down the 20-meter cliff. Then I put on my Olympus Mons Boots complete with my Grivel crampons, my Mountain Hardware summit suit, my Mountain Hardware gloves, my harness with cow's tail, my Petzl ascender, my Black Diamond figure 8 descender, my Black Diamond headlamp, and my Oakley goggles. Before I could even try fixing my ascender (jumar) on to the rope, I was soaked with sweat.

I practiced going up and down the cliff. On the bare granite, the crampons were spraying orange sparks until they bit the rock, and when they did, they stuck much better than I thought they would. That fact made me feel good. However, it was immediately evident that the big puffy summit gloves were going to pose a problem. Putting my gloved hand in the ascender was tough. Trying to manipulate the levers that cause the ascender to lock on the rope was nearly impossible. Adjustments to any equipment with these gloves on was an energy-draining struggle. Once I was moving up the cliff, I was great, but any extraneous movements like taking the jumar off the rope, or a simple task like opening a carabiner, was a struggle. I had to rethink my glove options for summit night.

That was it. The time for training and preparations had come to an end. The recorded physical training that I put in prior to leaving for Mt. Everest totaled 21,842 minutes, or just over 15, 24-hour days. Also, on the IMG site, there are some words of wisdom that I took very seriously:

> "Train hard. Be in the best shape of your life and believe that you are."[25]

---

25      How to Summit Everest -- Advice from IMG Climbers.

Virtually training alongside Patrick, my own focus, and the support of those closest to me had allowed me to be in the best shape of my life. And I believed it. Patrick and I had done everything we possibly could do to control every aspect of the climb that was controllable. This included our ability to adapt to altitude, knowing our gear and the route, and our physical and mental fitness. I knew from my previous mountain experiences that Everest was going to test my preparations to their limit. I felt ready. However, I had a nagging concern of the uncontrollables during summit night. Most disasters, tragedies, and mistakes happen then.

That was a problem I would face in a month. It was April 6, 2017 and my current problem was trying to fit all my equipment for that next month into three bags: I only had my new Mammut duffle, relatively new South Col OutDry 70L backpack and my ole' reliable 1995 navy blue Kelty internal frame pack. My gear was spread out over an entire room. I did not see how all of this equipment was going to fit in three packs. I carefully placed gear in my bags as if it were a 3D jigsaw puzzle. It took two hours. Everything fit in perfectly.

I did a final check of my statistics:

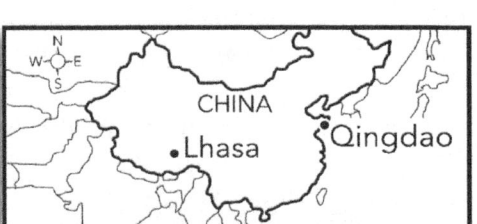

**April 12, 2018**
Day 0: Qingdao, China (22m)
Ambient Oxygen: 21%
SPO2: 99%
Heart Rate: 68 BPM

The next day I departed Qingdao, China on a Sichuan Airlines flight headed for Lhasa, Tibet.

# CHAPTER 6

# THE TIBETAN PLATEAU

Sichuan Airlines' main hub is in the city of Chengdu. My flight landed there at 11:00pm and my connection was leaving at 6:00am the next morning. I had one night of sleep in the Chengdu airport. In those 7 hours I managed to lose a pair of brand-new red Beats bluetooth headphones, all my back-up batteries, one headlamp, and my solar power charging battery packs. It was the first day and already I was making mistakes. I was angry with myself. I had left them behind while boarding the plane from Chengdu to Lhasa. I sat there in my cramped airplane seat staring out over the foothills of the Himalayas and had a little chuckle at my avoidable mistake. This could have been a bad omen, but I thought about how it was a good one. I find that on every adventure something goes wrong. I'm glad I got that out of the way within 10 hours of leaving my house.

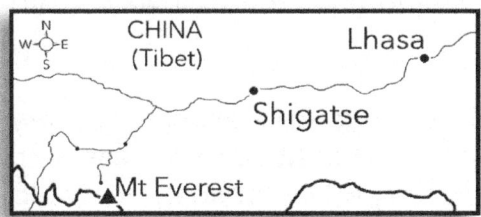

**April 13, 2018**
Day 1: Lhasa, Tibet (3,655m)
Ambient Oxygen: 13.3%
SPO2: 98%
Heart Rate 71 BPM

Lhasa overwhelmed me with nostalgia. Eleven years earlier I was here with Dave Kellogg. Then, the Internet did not contain any information about biking across Tibet. The research that we did beforehand was through books and calls with Tibet permit agencies. We were here as true explorers, only a guidebook to show us the way. We had no Google Maps, no Air BnBs booked, no 3G connection nor did we have a backup plan if things went wrong. The Tibetans we ran into on our mountain bike ride did not speak English and most didn't speak Chinese. It was just us and the open, usually gravel, road. I was back but here under different terms. Tibet had also been changed.

The stakes of my adventure were just as high or higher, but the unknowns were much less. Summit Climb arranged a jeep, a driver, and a government appointed liaison that met me at the airport. The liaison's name was Linlin. He was not a native Tibetan but a college student from outside of Beijing. He spoke great English. The China Tibet Mountaineering Association (CTMA) hired him to help foreigners like myself navigate the paperwork required at every city and checkpoint across the Tibetan Plateau. He was also hired to make sure I wasn't bringing any trouble to Tibet. Once he realized I could speak Chinese and most likely didn't have a Free Tibet flag with me, he relaxed, and we were on our way.

The highways had all been freshly paved. I had the entire back seat of the jeep to myself. The plan was to head west across the Tibetan plateau to meet the rest of the Summit Climb team who had been making their way up from Nepal. This road that stretches from Lhasa to the Nepali border, over some of the highest passes in the world, is named the Friendship Highway. Although, with the amount of security on the highway, it did not seem to be friendly.

The road was noticeably being watched. Approximately, every 5 km there was a slow zone with flood lights and no less than 12 cameras pointed at the road. Every 80 km or so there would be a roadside checkpoint. In addition, as we drove from Lhasa to our first stop, Shigatse, there were several new housing developments. The Tibetan architecture and colors were present, but the dwellings seemed prefabricated. Each flat-roofed homestead carried two new Chinese flags. This was a Tibet I had not seen in 2007.

The 273-kilometer drive to Shigatse took six hours. It is the second largest city in Tibet, with a population of 117,000.

Linlin headed to the government office to register my arrival. He suggested that I stay in the hotel. I told him I needed to walk after being in the car for so long. I also told him that I had been here before and there wasn't much to do anyway. I didn't have favorable memories of Shigatse. On our bikes, the city was just another stop between huge mountain passes with a decent restaurant. Dave nor I were impressed. I stepped out of the hotel and immediately felt different.

The weather was gorgeous. Large fluffy clouds floated beneath the bluest skies, characteristic of Tibet. Prayer flags rippled in the wind off of every surrounding peak. The markets were bustling with Tibetan tourists buying hand-held prayer wheels, prayer flags, and incense. I quickly toured the Tashi Lhunpo monastery's alleys and earth-toned buildings. Exiting the monastery, large prayer wheels lined the entire outside perimeter. Buddhist devotees were prostrating, circumambulating the monastery clockwise. I decided to walk their path. The path led me up the hills in back of the monastery. It brought me to a high point that overlooked the city, its markets, and the Xigatse Fortress.

I fell in love with the city. Tibet had reinvigorated me. I was talking to the locals, eating local street food, and enjoying being so familiar with a city that so few people in the world visit, much less understand. I was traveling again. I was on an epic adventure. I was living life to its fullest. It was an incredible feeling.

On my way back to the hotel, I strolled through the city center which is packed with hardware stores. I easily tracked down a USB charging solar panel. They were bulkier than my sleek REI solar chargers but were a fourth of the price. I picked one up for 120 RMB, about $20 USD. I wouldn't carry it from camp to camp, but it would be nice to have it at Chinese Base Camp.

That night, I took Linlin out and showed him around the city. We had a delicious yak steak with fries. It was enjoyable but I was eager to reunite with Patrick and get this climb started.

Finally, we were heading to Chinese Base Camp, or so I thought. We climbed and descended several passes including Gyatso la. At 5,220 meters, I stepped out of the car for some fresh, low-oxygen air. I distinctly remembered Dave and I biking up this pass. By that time, we were both in great shape and had adapted well to the altitude. My body was again adapting well to the low oxygen.

Back in the car, we descended the pass, drove through a little town named Selkar which also carries the names of Shegar and New Tingri. Just beyond this truckstop town was the largest checkpoint on the Friendship Highway, outside of the China-Tibet border crossing. Here, they thoroughly checked my paperwork. After an hour, we were on our way without incident. Just after the checkpoint is the entrance to the Qomolangma (Mount Everest) National Park, but we drove right by it. I asked the Linlin why. He said we were headed to Tingri, another outpost that Dave and I biked through after Mt. Everest on our way to Kathmandu. I was confused but didn't feel like pressing further as Linlin was just following the directions of his superiors. I sat back and enjoyed staring out the window at the desolate landscape.

Driving into Tingri, population 523, is like entering a wild west town. The city is located in the middle of a large glacial flood delta. It's a kilometer of storefronts that line both sides of the road. Just behind the stores was an empty, high desert. Horses, tractors, and semi-trucks parked wherever they decided to stop or breakdown along the Friendship Highway. Other semi-trucks plowed through the town at high speeds not breaking for anyone or anything. Grease monkeys, cowboys, herders, and ranchers meandered into the automotive, hardware, and feed stores. At the far end of town there was a new housing development complete with numerous Chinese flags. Atop a hill in the direction of Everest, renovations to the Gelung monastery were underway.

We stopped at the only restaurant in town, the Base Camp Restaurant. It is used as one of the last tastes of civilization and comfort on the way to Himalayan climbs from the Tibetan side. It was the beginning of the climbing season and the restaurant was hopping. Guides, Sherpas, drivers, and climbers overflowed the restaurant and were loitering in the gravel parking lot. Linlin, our driver, and I entered the restaurant. We passed several tables of Sherpas eating noodles and climbers eating french fries. I sat down and looked through the menu. From across the restaurant there was a loud boisterous, excited voice that I recognized. I looked up. It was Patrick! I wish I had done something more clever as neither of us knew the other was there, but the team had been together for a week already, and I wanted to meet everyone.

I got up from my table and when I did Patrick spotted me. We were excited. It took months of planning, training, and sacrifice to get here. Finally, we were reunited. Patrick got up and asked what the hell I was doing there, we embraced, and then he introduced me to the rest of the team.

The majority of the team was sunken into the sorted couches assorted around a large square knee-high wooden table in the back of the restaurant: Franz Rassi, Dominic Renshaw (Dom), Heikki Koskinen, Jon Lawrie, Jon's wife Lucy, and co-guide Martin Szwed. Two climbers from the Summit Climb team were sick: Grant Maughan and Magnus Nerve. They were given a stern suggestion to stay in their rooms to avoid passing on their germs. Two other climbers, a Singaporean man named Sanjay and a Swedish woman, Violett, were just climbing to Advanced Base Camp.

David O'Brien, at almost 200cm and looking like a skinny Santa, ducked into the restaurant. Patrick introduced him as our head guide. He said he was looking for me. Linlin had informed him that I was leaving today for Chinese Base Camp. David and the rest of the Summit Climb team were staying in Tingri for another night. Dave explained that the camp they were taking me to, Chinese Base Camp (CBC) was nothing but pebbles and rocks. He didn't know what the CTMA planned to do with me once they ferried me to CBC. There were no tents, people, Sherpas, food, yaks, nothing. I had been in China long enough and I knew what needed to happen. I needed to talk to Linlin, get his boss on the phone and reason with them.

In Chinese, I tried to reason with Linlin's boss, "If I stay here tonight, you guys save money by not having to take me to Chinese Base Camp. You can also skip all the permit hassles. I am so troublesome; you don't want to deal with that. And what if I'm a spy, then you are really gonna be in trouble."

They chuckled but still weren't budging. Linlin, got on the phone. My permit said I was going to be at CBC that night. It seemed the entire CTMA could not understand how I could possibly stay in Tingri if my permit said I needed to be at CBC.

"Also, if we were supposed to be at CBC tonight, why did we drive 8 hours out of the way?" I continued to reason.

"No why," he responded. Welcome to Tibetan China.

A black Toyota Land Rover veered off the side of the road and four large Chinese men stepped out. Linlin walked over to them. They took out their clipboards and lit up their Zhongnanhai cigarettes in front of the restaurant. This was the CTMA. I was out of earshot, but I could tell Linlin was fighting for me. I waved. A couple of cigarettes later, Linlin came back over to me. The CTMA guys got on their cell phones. Apparently, none of them could make the final decision either. They said they were relaying the request through the proper channels to see what could be done. There was nothing Linlin, or the guys from

CTMA, or I could do. It was all up to the decisions made on the other side of the phone calls. David was by my side, the entire time urging them to let me stay in Tingri with the team.

David said he would continue to push his connections and see what he could do. Patrick and I decided to wander around the city with our goal being to hike up to the Gelug Monastery. A dirt road between two auto repair shops led to a small one-road village. School had just been dismissed and the children ran out after us as we walked by.

"Hello?" they would say and laugh.

"Tashi delek!" we answered back in Tibetan

They laughed out loud. We found a community park consisting of a pull up bar, a metal leg swinging device, and a what appeared to be a back-massaging medieval torture tool. With the entire elementary school cheering us on, we each did 10 pullups, high-fived the onlookers, and walked on breathing normally. Not bad for 4,399 meters.

At the back of the village a trail wound up the side of the hill. Two children, around six-years old were still following us. They had tattered clothes and incredibly dark skin that looked as if it had seen many winters at this elevation. We stopped to talk to them, and they asked in perfect English, "Money?"

We moved on. As we approached the monastery the trail steepened, Patrick wore his normal footwear, flip flops, and was slipping and sliding on the loose rock. We looked south over our shoulders. Between scattered dark clouds we saw Everest and Cho Oyu. At 8,201 meters, Cho Oyu is the fifth highest mountain in the world.

This quickly turned into a disagreement of which mountain was Everest and which was Cho Oyu. I had been at that exact spot before on a clearer day. Everest was on the left and Cho

Oyu was on the right. Sorry Patrick, you were wrong.

We got back to the Base Camp Restaurant and my predicament had been settled. I was now under the full control and responsibility of the Summit Climb team. David was going to have his work cut out for him.

I thanked Linlin for his understanding and persistence with the CTMA. He said he was going to be back and forth between Tingri and Everest. We exchanged WeChat contact information and then he got back in the truck that picked me up at the airport and drove away.

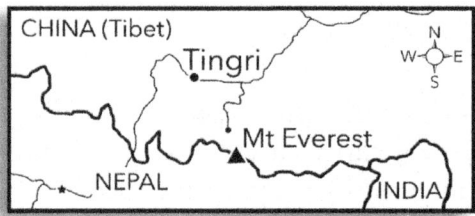

**April 15, 2018**
Day 3: Tingri (4,399m)
Ambient Oxygen: 12.1%
SPO2: 98%
Heart Rate: 66 BPM

For the Summit Climb team, this was another acclimatization day in Tingri. As the team moved up from Kathmandu, they were staying two days at each stop to help the acclimatization process. Today, we were all encouraged to go for a hike.

The rolling foothills start at the edge of the glacial flood plain on which Tingri sits, one-kilometer east of the Base Camp Restaurant. Jangbu, our Sirdar, head sherpa, took the lead. Pushing 160 cm tall, he is a very unassuming Sherpa from Eastern Nepal. Soon, I would learn the superhuman feats he had accomplished. Patrick, in flip flops, was right on Jangbu's tail, followed by me and the rest of the team. We encountered false peak after false peak. The hill continued south where it turned into mountains, which turned into the ridges leading to Everest. After 3 hours of hiking we reached another false peak shrouded in Tibetan prayer flags. As a team we took pictures, enjoyed the views, and headed back to Tingri for dinner.

We dined at the best restaurant in town, the Base Camp Restaurant.

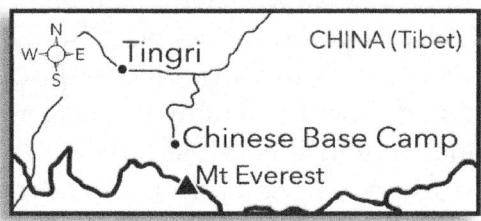

**April 16, 2018**
Day 4: Tingri (4,399m)
Ambient Oxygen: 12.1%
SPO2: 98%
Heart Rate: 64 BPM

After breakfast at the Base Camp Restaurant, our team took to the streets for last-minute shopping. Tingri is the spot where you can pick up very thick, cheap, and well-worth-it mattresses that can be kept in your tent at CBC, IBC, and ABC. Patrick and I, as well as the majority of the team, each bought two. This purchase is highly recommended.

You can also acquire USB solar chargers here. Our team bought the store out of Coca-Cola. We bought juices, teas, and snacks that we probably could have done without. In Kathmandu, Patrick had loaded up one full-size duffle bag with snacks. The bag was now difficult to close.

Our mattresses, and all the other equipment, food, and fuel required for six to eight weeks on Everest was loaded up into one of the four colorful Nepali dump trucks that, with the team, had driven up from Nepal. It felt excessive.

The drive from Tingri heads back towards Shigatse but then takes a turn south at the entrance to Mt. Everest National Park. At the entrance of the park, we took a team picture. During the picture line up, I couldn't help but contemplate who would make it and who wouldn't. There was even a possibility that one or more of these people might not return with us. Could it be me?

Back in the vans, we continued through the town of Qiecun. Here, 11 years ago on mountain bikes, Dave Kellogg and I went around house to house looking for a place to sleep and a meal.

Back then, a gracious host let us into her house. She fed us as much popped barley and yak butter tea we could handle. Yak butter tea tastes like yak manure mixed well with used french fry oil. We could hardly drink it. The dry popped barley was barely edible. The next morning, grateful and starving, we headed up the seemingly never-ending switchbacks of Gawula pass at 5,198 meters. This time, in a cramped van, it was less strenuous but much more nauseating. In addition, since I had been here last, the road was completely paved, not a gravel trail.

The top of the Gawula pass offers one of the best views of the Himalayas. Unfortunately, in 2007, when Dave and I got to the top of the pass on our bikes it was raining, and the visibility was 20 meters. This day, with the Summit Climb team, there wasn't a cloud in the sky. We had unprecedented views of Makalu (8,485m), Lhotse (8,516m), Cho Oyu (8,188m), and Everest (8,848m). Coming down from Gawula pass you reach Zhaxizong Cun in Chinese or Tashizong in Tibetan. This town is a true outpost. The vans stopped. We spread out like kids in a toy store. Some climbers went to track down fresh fruit. Some went to find a bathroom. Others went to eat noodles and stock up on more Coca-Cola. Patrick and I picked up a couple more packs of Oreos just in case. The road continues along the Rongbuk River until making a left turn south up the Rongbuk (Dzakar Chu) Valley. The river continues to rush on the right. The road steepens substantially while continuing to zigzag up the valley. About halfway up the valley, Everest shows itself. It is a view that I could never get sick of. Everest was playing hide and seek in the clouds.

A couple of kilometers later the vans stopped short of a thick rope that bisected the road. The new Rongbuk Monastery was on the left and on the right, six modified army-green shipping containers with stenciled characters: 中国边防 (Zhōngguó biānfáng) China Border Defence. This was our final permit check on the way to CBC. After a relatively minimal amount of grief, we were let through. We drove past the tourist Chinese Base Camp, called 珠穆朗玛峰大本营 (Zhūmùlǎngmǎ fēng dàběnyíng) and crested a steep hill. The road continued in the direction of Everest. We reached a flat outwash plane covered in stones. Here we saw the first of the huge dome tents and knew that we finally arrived at the climber's Chinese Base Camp (CBC): 5,200 meters.

# CHAPTER 7

# SETTLING IN

We stepped out of the van. The Sherpas had beat us to CBC. I suspected they would be beating us to every camp on this mountain. I didn't know they drove faster as well. We started unloading the vans. The Sherpas were hard at work cinching down the final swaths of black canvass on our dining tent. They also fixed guy lines extending 3 meters out from the tent that we would all be sure to trip over. This tent would be used for our meals, meetings, hanging out, and the location of Mr. Heater, a butane blasting tent warmer. Twelve yellow and orange two-person Kailas tents were scattered haphazardly around the black dining tent. The Kailas tents had a very recognizable sun logo reminiscent of an ancient cave etching. David instructed us to each pick a tent. Patrick and I got tents next to each other and began ferrying loads from the van. The Sherpas stopped what they were doing and immediately helped us. We told them we had it taken care of, but they wouldn't have it.

A short, stocky looking Nepali man in a green hat and blue North Face jacket grabbed our case of Coke and brought it to our tent. Patrick hugged him like they were best friends. He then introduced me to Geljie Sherpa. Geljie was one of the Sherpas that was with Patrick during his 2014 and 2015 Everest Summit attempts. Patrick was excited to see him again. Geljie had impressed Patrick in those previous years with his ability to carry enormous loads at high altitudes. Patrick, emphasizing this ability, jokingly called him "man-beast."

Mountaineering in the Himalayas starts and ends with the Sherpas. During the 1924 British Expedition, famous for the disappearance of George Malory and Sandy Irvine, Sherpas were the backbone of the expedition. In fact, that expedition brought along 150 porters. Many of those porters were Sherpas and helped the foreign climbers get above what is now Camp 3. In 1953, the British Expedition that put Edmond Hillary and Tenzig Norgay on the summit of Everest had 350 porters and 20 Sherpas.[26] Sherpas were and are the muscles on the mountain. There is no doubt us yahoos would not be here without them.

Most of the Sherpas along for our expedition were for the group as a whole. They set up camps, help cook food, stash oxygen bottles, and most importantly carry a tremendous amount of equipment from Advanced Base Camp (ABC) to higher camps on the mountain. However, it is possible for you to hire a personal Sherpa. As the Summit Climb website explains:

"For those who do not wish to carry their own rucksack, or prepare their own meals and drinks above basecamp, we offer full personal-private Sherpas (or, you may wish to share one with another member). A personal Sherpa climbs and camps with you at all times and carries approximately ten kilos/22 pounds of your personal belongings. He also helps with boiling water and making your meals on the mountain. The cost of hiring a personal-private Sherpa is $10,850 USD, which includes full oxygen and equipment for your Sherpa."[27]

Neither Patrick nor I opted for the personal Sherpa.

Magnus decided to go all in and got himself a personal Sherpa. His name was Ang Pasang. He was strong and looked out for Magnus' activities on the mountain as well as teaching him the ways of the Sherpa.

The majority of us took our time putting our camp together.

---

26      "Sir Edmund Hillary and Tenzing Norgay - 1953 Everest."

27      Mount Everest Tibet Expedition Climb Cost | Summit Climb.

Martin Szwed, David's assistant leader, was as tall as David, half his age, and took care of the smaller important tasks that the camp required. He took it upon himself to make our spot at CBC more holy, friendly, and Tibetan. He strung prayer flags between all of our tents. This way we were all connected in a common mission. When he wasn't helping out, he was on Skype calls with his girlfriend back in his home country of Germany.

Several of the Sherpas were also taking their time and chatting. It was apparent that we were now on mountain time. Jangbu, however, was in full hustle mode. As the head Sherpa, he was responsible for communication between David and the entire staff, including four drivers, one head chef, three kitchen boys, as they are called, and eight climbing Sherpas. Jangbu was calling the shots for what needed to be done at base camp and leading by example. He carried clients' huge base camp duffel bags to their tents, helped the kitchen staff unload the food, and when it was dinner, he served us soup and noodles. He came around to each of us with a giant smile making sure we had eaten enough.

Apparently, Jangbu was also on the Nepal side with Patrick during 2014 and 2015. During supper Patrick leaned over to me and whispered,

"Yeah, that guy serving us soup, Jangbu, he has summited Everest 17 times."

Soup sprayed from my mouth. "What?" I questioned.

"17 times," Patrick repeated.

I was floored. Here was this mountaineering legend treating us like kings.

"I should be serving him dinner," I whispered back to Patrick.

Due to the steepness of the Rongbuk Valley walls, the sun goes down early. When it does, the temperature drops substantially. The wind was picking up outside. We finished dinner, chatted, and checked the Internet. The connection speed was not fast but very acceptable for a 5,200-meter base camp. I was getting to know more about our teammates. I also was trying to drink as much water as possible. It helps with acclimatization. Filling up two Nalgene water bottles with just boiled water, I stuffed them in my jacket and exited the tent. The stars sparkled with a clarity I had not seen in years. Tents were lit like Chinese paper lanterns across the valley. Entering my tent, I tossed my water bottles into my sleeping bag, stripped down to boxers and a t-shirt, and pondered what lay ahead. I was still nervous but comforted knowing that Jangbu would be going to the summit with us.

**April 17, 2018**
Day 5: CBC (5,200m)
Ambient Oxygen: 10.9%
SPO2: 71%
Heart Rate: 68 BPM

I had wanted to wait for sunbeams to hit my tent before getting out of my sleeping bag, but I was anxious to see Mt. Everest in the morning light. In addition, like the ratatat of a machine gun, Martin's prayer flags were relentlessly smacking my tent, Patrick's tent, and everyone on our team's tent. Everyone was up. I unzipped my south-facing tent vestibule and said good morning to the mountain.

"Thanks for putting those prayer flags up Martin!" we all joked.

"Sorry, guys," he replied in his German accented English, "I'll take them down."

"No way. They are good luck, and we are gonna need all we can," I replied.

I would much rather have the thumping of prayer flags at base camp and a successful summit than the alternative.

The temperature was hovering above freezing and we got to the first order of business: emptying our pee bottles. Admittedly, peeing in a bottle, in your sleeping bag, in your tent, rather than getting up and going to use the designated bathroom may sound preposterous. However, when it is cold outside or you are camping on snow, it is more convenient and less disturbing (sleep wise, not morally) for you and your climbing partners if you can pee in a bottle. It is difficult to fall asleep at altitude. Once you are asleep, you try to avoid waking yourself up fully. Peeing in a bottle is a better alternative than putting on shoes, a jacket, hat, and trudging across camp to the toilet. It allows for the ultimate nighttime relaxation to rejuvenate your tired bones. That, and drinking upwards of 8-liters a day, means you save yourself from getting up several times.

Patrick and I both had the 96oz Nalgene Canteen, a must for any expedition. Too many climbers have used the regular Nalgene bottles as pee bottles and mixed them up in the middle of the night when reaching for a drink. We heard several stories even within our own team of this mistake. After that first night, I realized I was acclimatizing too well, drinking too much water. I was close to filling the 96 oz.

Patrick and I dumped and rinsed our pee bags in the designated pee spot. We then headed into our black Tibetan Tea-House themed tent. Martin was already inside apologizing to Dominic and Magnus for the whipping flags. They were all huddled around Mr. Heater.

Dominic was a self-employed digital marketing entrepreneur from Oxford, UK. Climbing Everest had been his goal for the past 15 years. This year, he finally had time in his life to give it a shot. Dominic had the stature of a Sherpa, made surprisingly more obvious when he stood next to Martin. Delightful in conversation, he gave his opinion but wasn't opinionated about any topics.

Magnus, who was feeling better but still had a bit of a cough, was a Swedish expat living in Hong Kong. He worked for Haglöfs, a Swedish outdoor apparel company. While he wasn't a sponsored Haglöfs climber, his gear would lead you to believe otherwise. Magnus had climbed with Summit Climb before. They had successfully guided him to the top of both Manaslu (8,163 m) and Cho Oyu (8,188 m). Magnus has also successfully summited Aconcagua, Elbrus, and Kilimanjaro. Magnus' wife is Japanese. I believe his numerous conversations with her over the phone in the dining tent would have been incredibly annoying if in English.

After an hour or so huddled next to Mr. Heater, the camp assistants, kitchen boys, as they are called, Nobu and Tashi came in. Nobu and Tashi are Tibetan. They had dark, weathered skin and thick braided hair that was ornamented with a doughnut-sized bead made from a yak horn. Their name brand puffy jackets were well worn. With ear to ear grins they brought in several two-liter Chinese thermoses filled with boiling water. We mixed the water together with our morning elixirs: tea, coffee, Horlicks (a malted milk powder), hot chocolate and/or some combination of those options.

The Summit Climb dining tent was simple. It followed an authentic Tibetan tea house motif on the inside and outside. The black canvas walls rose up 1.5 meters and peaked in an A-frame. The inside was adorned with a smooth, brightly colored Himalayan Mandala-inspired fabric. The room was lit by two hanging iridescent bulbs. Cushioned metal and spring couches lined the walls. Fake wood vinyl flooring covered the pebbled ground.

In front of each of the couches was a Tibetan Buddhist altar table: wooden boxes painted in colors matching the Mandala-inspired fabric. The entrance to the tent was a steel framed canvass door that required constant attention. To keep it shut, a latch on the inside of the door had to be fastened. However, minutes after someone put the latch down, someone else would want to come in. Or, if someone went out, then someone else would have to latch it on the inside. Even when it was closed it was never airtight. The cold Himalayan wind would blow through the cracks. Adjacent to the door was another Tibetan altar table with the Internet router and numerous extension cords. This was the charging hub for everyone on the expedition. In the center of the room was a single metal pole that provided support to the entire structure as well as a post for climbers to lean on while being warmed by Mr. Heater.

Nobu, Tashi, and Jangbu brought breakfast. This was the first and last time I had eggs and "sausage." The rest of my days on the mountain I would stick to porridge with Nepali granola, sometimes adding a sprinkling of Horlicks on top. Further investigation of the "sausage" patty origins would lead to its nickname "the worm."

Across from our black tent was the yellow kitchen tent. It was two meters high and square. Inside was where all the cooking was done for us at this camp. Hanging from a string in the far corner of the tent was a tube of some meat concoction about one meter long. It had one open cuttable end that faced the ground and harmonically swung back and forth in the mountain air. Once I saw that, I was glad I was not indulging in the worm any longer.

Our expedition leader David ducked below the entrance into the dining tent.
"Good morning campers!" he exclaimed.

This quickly became his morning tagline. He found his seat at the head of the tent next to a giant duffle bag filled with all the drugs that a Nepali pharmacy would let you buy, no prescription needed. He gave us our morning briefing,

"It's a take it easy day today. If you are feeling good there is a walk up the hill behind us to gain some altitude, but preferably it's a take it easy day or get your gear ready. The yaks are coming on the 19th. There will be a whole lot of bells and clanking going on, so that with the addition of Martin's prayer flags, you may have another sleepless night."

We all had a good laugh.

David had set a perfect tone for the trip: take your time, relax, enjoy, have fun, be safe, and give people a razz. He had approached Patrick on the way up from Nepal and revealed his worry that Patrick and I were going to be our own team. His desire for this climb was that we would all be part of the Summit Climb Everest 2018 team. Patrick reassured him. We were both here for the experience. We had no plans to defect.

Later in the climb, David confided in me that the most rewarding part of guiding on Everest was making a team. He said he loved taking a bunch of people with different backgrounds and getting them to act like a team under stressful circumstances. With David's knowledge, experience, mutual respect, and zingers, I was fully on board.

By 9:00am, direct sunlight made its way into the Rongbuk Valley and onto our Tibetan-themed dining tent. The temperature inside rose considerably. We all made our way outside for our first full day at the foot of Everest.

The Sherpas sorted gear. We sorted gear. The goal was to get everything ready for moving up the mountain. While the yaks would be constantly traveling between the camps, this first big movement of equipment is when you want to organize everything you will need higher up. The better you can plan for what you need at successive camps, the less shuffling of gear and carrying you will have to do later on. This was information that I did not have before I left for the mountain. If I was to do it again, I would have brought three sleeping bags and three sets of mattresses. Then I would have a complete sleeping set at CBC, IBC and ABC. This would save a ton of effort during the acclimatization rounds. My gear at ABC would be used higher up on the mountain.

Patrick and I took things slow. We continued to drink as much water as possible. It was hard to stay focused on a task as the great mountain, and all the possibilities that came with it, stood in front of us. The views were jaw-dropping. I would take a video of the peak, then Patrick would. Then I would take a picture, then Patrick would. Often, I would start something and then become distracted by the beauty and just gaze at it. I caught Patrick doing the same at times -- just looking at it. I could not stop taking pictures and filming Everest. It was enchanting.

From our vantage point, the peak lined up with the center of the valley. To the right of the snowy, cragged peak, the West Ridge dropped precipitously as its knife-edge arête creates the border between China and Nepal. To the left of the peak the mountain gradually sloped downwards before being concealed by Changtse, a neighboring peak at 7,583 meters. I squinted my eyes to find Everest's Camp 3, the Exit Cracks and the Three Steps: large cliffs that are known as the crux of the North Ridge Route. Even with the 20x zoom of my Sony FDR-AX53, it was difficult to determine which cliff was the second step or where I thought Camp 3 was located. For all the Everest climbing books and videos I had studied, the mountain remained mysterious.

I was nervous. This climb and the people here were world class. I wasn't sure I belonged here. To calm my nerves, I wandered around to find a peaceful spot to practice deep breathing. Towards the northwest, a mound rises up in the glacial rubble. Atop the mound is a two-meter-tall white stone monument placed in 2005 by the Chinese State Bureau of Surveying and Mapping[28]. The top was carved in the shape of Everest. Red inscriptions in Chinese, Tibetan, and English read, *"Monument to Mt. Qomolangma Elevation Measurement. Altitude 8844.43m."* Four strands of Tibetan prayer flags were wrapped and tied off around the base of the monument and

---

28      完. 北大登山队登顶珠峰 成2018年首支北坡登顶队伍

extended six meters to the top of a wooden pole. The flags blew in the breeze. The scripts on the flags are blessings and the constant Tibetan winds disperse them. Everest stood tall to the south. The jet stream was blowing from west to east on the summit and had created its own white prayer flag.

I sat down, closed my eyes and got comfortable. The whipping prayer flags were the only sound I could hear. I applied the same breathing routine that I had practiced at home leading up to the climb. I did three rounds of 30 breaths. On the 30th breath I exhaled completely and envisioned myself climbing higher up the mountain.

After breathing, I took more pictures of Everest and CBC. The survey monument looked over the entirety of the camp. From this perspective, it was clear who the big players were and hard to not be intimidated. A new breed of mountaineers has been attracting attention and high-paying clients. This year the bar was raised again, and it was impressive.

My climbing resume was not as extensive. I had puked, fell and hit my head on the summit of Kilimanjaro, 5,895m; I had hallucinated that I was in a movie on the summit of Denali 6,190m, and I had splitting headaches on Aconcagua 6,960m. I doubted my credentials.

In front of me were the new idols of high altitude climbing. Their enormous shiny dome tents were complete with pool tables, espresso machines and full bars that made CBC look like a classy outpost on Mars. These were the spring homes of world class, professional athletes: Lukas Furtenbach, professional high-altitude skier, Alex Abramov, professional mountaineer with over 100 high-altitude ascents, and Adrian Ballinger, a social-media savvy entrepreneur who at the time had summited Everest six times, once without oxygen.

The Furtenbach team's dome tent was located closest to the trail that led to the higher camps. This year they had two teams on the mountain: a regular climbing team who paid $63,375.73 USD/person and a rapid ascent team -- "Flash Expedition" -- that paid $106,770.00 USD/person.[29] The Flash Expedition required that clients have to be acclimatized prior to showing up at CBC. This would be done in a similar way to Patrick's and my training regimen. Once all the camps and ropes were set and a weather window opened, they would make their summit push. Each client is provided with two Sherpas to carry as much oxygen as needed. The Flash Expedition was looking to cut a minimum of three weeks off of an eight-week expedition. To add to their client's comfort, they had brought up a four-person ski gondola that had been repurposed as a sauna. In cooperation with the manufacturers, New Enerday, the Austria-based company set the world record of highest sauna.

Alex Abramov's business endeavor, 7 Summits Club, stood out as well. This Moscow-based company had the most elaborate set up of all the camps. An enormous white dome tent, with the company's logo in bright red, stood out no matter where you were at CBC. Upon entering the dome though a protruding entryway with double doors, you were met with a fully stocked bar on the right. On your left was a foosball table and couches. On the far side of the tent there was a full-size pool table. Past the pool table was a corridor that connected this dome tent with another smaller dome tent. The smaller dome tent contained a gym and a massage area. Extending south from the dome, 40 tents, as large as our mess tent, were in three perfect rows as if Putin was present for an inspection. These two-room tents, one per client, were the ultimate in base camp luxury. They provided full size beds off the ground. They had installed lighting and a separate room with a desk and chair. The 7 Summits Club also set up streetlights in the main corridor between the tents so that climbers could make their way back from the bar.

Next to them was Alpenglow Expeditions. This company is the brainchild of Adrian Ballinger, a professional mountaineer

29      Furtenbach. Everest Flash.

who, like Furtenbach, has started to cash in on speed ascents. Alpenglow was also using nearby mountains like Cho Oyu for acclimatization. This made for great publicity. The company could boast that they were completing two speed ascents in the time it takes most companies to do one Everest expedition. The Alpenglow speed ascent also carries a hefty price tag of $85,000 USD[30]. Their dome tent was also large, new, and the interior made you feel like you were in a private ski lodge. They only had nine clients, but they were notable.

One was Neal Beidleman, a former Everest guide for Mountain Madness who in 1996 was one of the few climbers from Scott Fischer's team to survive a storm high on the mountain. Eight climbers ended up dying. The tragic tale was made famous in the book "Into Thin Air," by Jon Krakauer.[31] Other clients included Jim Morrison, a professional athlete for The North Face, and Greg Penner, grandson of Sam Walton, the founder of Walmart. This team was stacked and set to boost Alpenglow Expeditions' already reputable name.

There were the elite teams, there were others just living large, and there were those that were just large. The Transcend Adventures Team based in Hyderabad, India had the biggest team with 36 clients reported, and the biggest camp. It consisted of 60 two-man tents, four large mess tents, two large kitchen tents, eight-bathroom tents, two giant dome tents, four supply tents, and one medical tent.

Another large one was the Chinese team. Granted, it was their home turf. After I visited with them it seemed that they had two main teams with about 16 people per team. Their camp was expansive and orderly. The Chinese also had a team of rope doctors that were in charge of fixing all the safety ropes on the north side of the mountain.

---

30      "Mount Everest North Side Rapid Ascent Expedition." Alpenglow.

31      Mutrie, Tim. "Finally, Ready to Confront Everest After Fatal Climb of '96." The New York Times.

Several other teams, including Altitude Junkies, Adventure Peaks, 7 Summits Treks, Climbalaya, Kobler & Partner, Satori Adventures, had camps of different magnitudes spread through the valley[32]. I went to bed that night questioning if I was ready to be with so many incredible athletes. The last thing I wanted was to be put in a position where I was slowing others down on the climb, or worse... Did I mention I was intimidated?

**April 18, 2018**
Day 6: CBC (5,200m)
Ambient Oxygen: 10.9%
SPO2: 80 - 91%
Heart Rate: 68 BPM

In the middle of the night, I had to pee. My Nalgene Canteen was again on the verge of overflowing. I decided to just get up instead of pushing my luck. I left my tent and saw one of the most intriguing scenes of my life. It was dark. There was no moon light. However, there was a lightning storm in Nepal. The lightning was shooting up behind Everest and lighting up the outline of the mountain. It left a silhouette of Everest with each strike. It was otherworldly. I stood and watched as long as I could.

A couple hours later, Martin's prayer flags rattled me awake again. I didn't mind. It was a clear, crisp, and quiet morning. Yet it was cold enough to wear gloves. It seemed as if I was the only one at CBC. Everest was lit up like a sepia lantern from the early morning sun. The surrounding peaks and our camp were still in the shadows. At the south end of the camp, a 20-meter berm of sand and rock, one of the recessional moraines, towered above the dome tents. To the looker's right, west, the Rongbuk River's rushing meltwater carved shallow paths through the glacial debris. To the looker's left, east, was the trailhead for all Everest expeditions that were utilizing the northwest ridge route.

---

32     "Everest 2018: May 25 Team Locations and Headlines." Alanarnette.Com.

Those first steps past the trailhead towards the peak I took alone. CBC was still asleep. This was my first hike on the flanks of Everest. The beginning of perhaps the greatest test of my life. For the same reason I surf at dawn, I headed up the trail, testing the waters with no one around to see me fall, flail, or fail. I kept my breathing deep, my pace slow, and the placement of my feet purposeful.

Remnants of the receding Rongbuk Glacier were all around me. To the left, several massive boulders were precariously perched on debris spires. To the right, a 10-meter berm was marked with several wandering yak paths leading up to the main moraine. I followed a path, sandy grey silt filling my shoes. Atop the moraine, several glassy kettle lakes reflected the image of Everest. My mind was clear, confident, and concentrated on being in the moment.

I made it back to camp, which was now buzzing like a hive. Shaggy yaks and shaggier yak herders were making their way from their winter homes at lower elevations. They careened through and around CBC. The brown beasts were hairy, strong, weighed close to 900kg (2,000 lbs), and drooled like babies. For the most part, it seemed like the herdsman had them under control, but every now and then one would go rogue, plowing through a tent, knocking over supplies, or just not moving where they were supposed to.

In Tibetan culture, the yaks are a cornerstone animal. They plow the fields. Their milk is the essential ingredient in the greasy, putrid, unpalatable (in my opinion) yak butter tea. Their skin and fur is used for clothing and blankets. Even their dried feces, often seen plastered to the walls of a domicile, a fence, and all around Tibetan farms, is used as heating fuel. In the summer, all across the Tibetan plateau the yaks are celebrated during the Yak Festival.[33] In the winter they can survive at high altitudes where the temperature can get down to -40° Celsius. Lucky for us, they can carry heavy loads at high altitudes. Included in the

---

33      "The Significance of Yaks for Tibetan People." Tibet Travel and Tours

expedition cost is the yak hiring. Each yak costs $350 USD to carry gear from CBC to Advanced Base Camp (ABC). This was the time of year for them to earn hard cash.

A group of herdsmen and yaks started congregating around our kitchen tent. Everything going higher up on the mountain was in duffle bags or reusable blue barrels. The pile of gear included extra mattresses, glacier travel equipment, summit suits, oxygen bottles, food for all of us, extra cases of Coke, snacks, Mr. Heater Jr., and anything else we did not want to personally carry up to ABC. It was all lined up.

David and Jangbu started the intense negotiations with the lead herdsman. The rest of the Sherpas met with the other herdsman and, using a shoulder-pole scale, started weighing the packaged gear. The gear was then brought over to a yak and fastened to its harness. The yaks waited patiently as each load was balanced and secured.

David suggested that we, as a team, take a hike down to the Rongbuk Monastery. Even though I had been to the north side of Everest before, I did not know that there are two Rongbuk Monasteries. The Rongbuk Monastery that we passed at the shipping container border patrol was the original Rongbuk Monastery. It was destroyed during China's Cultural Revolution between 1966 and 1974. While this destruction was occuring, the Buddhist monks took many of their relics and moved them up the Rongbuk Valley towards Everest. There, caves dot the cliff walls and another Rongbuk monastery was established. The Rongbuk Monastery hidden in the cliff walls was our goal for the day.

Throughout the Tibetan Everest valley, the names Rongbuk, Rongpu, and Rongbu are used interchangeably for the monastery as well as the two glaciers, the river, and valley itself. The temple's original name in Tibetan is རྫ་རོང་ཕུ་དགོན་, pronounced, rdza rong phu dgon. The Chinese transliterated this to 绒布寺, pronounced Róngbù Sì. In the 1920s, the British explorer G.H. Bullock, looking for a route to Everest wrote,

"There are a number of monks living in separate houses or huts scattered throughout the valley or district, which is called Rongbuk."[34]

This is considered the earliest written account of the valley by a western explorer and most likely the reason in English it is written Rongbuk.

The hike from CBC down to the hidden Rongbuk Monastery took an hour. A small set of rock slab stairs led up to a pile of enormous boulders that provided the structure of the complex. The Sherpas had come with us. We followed them into a musty smelling, candle-lit room. There, we were instructed to light a candle and be blessed by the resident monk. At the back of the room, the Sherpas were signaling us over to a square open hole in the floor. The hole had a ladder that led down 1.5 meters into a cave.

The cave was tiny. It was filled with candles, thangkas, bracelets, buddhas, demons and divinities. Our whole team could not fit in the ceremonial cellar. Jon, Patrick, Franz, Jangbu, and Gelje made an offering, took a couple of pictures and ascended the ladder so other members of the team could do the same.

Some members of the team headed quickly back to camp. Patrick and I stuck around to admire the view of Everest through the colorful Tibetan Prayer flags that adorned the monastery. The monastery also offered several hidden caves behind the central buildings. We explored these, took photos, and started the climb back to CBC.

The rest of the day was spent reading, playing cards, and getting to know the others. While the unknowns of what lay ahead were daunting, I kept my mind busy. I washed clothes,

---

34      Bullock, G. H. (1962). "Everest Expedition, 1921. Diaries of G. H. Bullock (Part I)" (pdf). Alpine Journal.

admired the spectacular views, and practiced my Wim Hof breathing. One of the afflictions that Everest climbers face is called the Khumbu cough. It is a result of inhaling extremely cold, dry air, and dust from the moraine. This combination irritates the lungs and results in a chronic cough. High up on the mountain the cough can halt a climber in their tracks. I have heard stories of climbers breaking their ribs from coughing so hard. In order to reduce my chances of getting the Khumbu cough, I always did my breathing with my air pollution mask on. This would warm, filter, and moisten the air I was breathing.

I climbed into my tent to test my SPO2. It measured 95%. At 5,364 meters, having an SPO2 of 95% is very high. However, what surprised me was my breath hold at the end. During the breath hold my SPO2 and heart rate both decreased, however, my heart rate continued to drop. It decreased from 110 beats per minute to 50 beats per minute. That was something I wasn't expecting. My body must have been learning to relax and use as little oxygen as possible.

Sitting in my tent after the breathing I gazed at the summit. I was feeling nervous about every step after this camp. Tomorrow, we would leave for Intermediate Base Camp. The day after we would head higher to Advanced Base Camp. Advanced Base Camp was high: 6,492m. I just hoped that my training would allow me to adjust quickly and perform well at these altitudes.

I peeked out of my tent often to watch the coming of the night. Jupiter rose over the broad valley and I fell asleep watching shooting stars and the Milky Way.

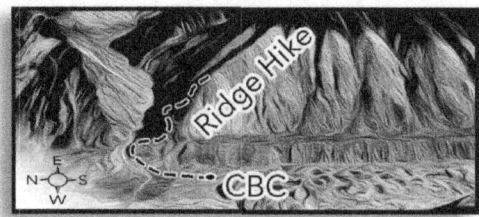

**April 19, 2018**
Day 7: CBC (5,182m)
Ambient Oxygen: 10.9%
SPO2: 95%
Heart Rate: 68 BPM

This was our fourth morning at CBC. The yak brigades were

still loading up. Other climbing teams were setting up. We had just learned that our team was not going up. Summit Climb was staying another day at CBC. Supposedly, the ropes up to Camp 1 on top of the North Col were not in place yet. David thought it would be better if we stayed down here at CBC an extra day.

The first team on the north side of Everest every year is the Chinese Tibet Mountaineering Association. They choose the route and fix safety ropes to the mountain. The safety ropes allow climbers to be connected to the trail at almost all points above Advanced Base Camp. If you should slip on one of the steeps faces the safety ropes would keep you from falling to your death. Your jumar, a device that grips the rope with the ability to slide forward but not back, can also be clipped into the rope. This allows climbers to stay mostly upright while climbing the steeper sections. If climbers use their equipment and the safety ropes correctly, the risk of injury or death due to falling or tripping is greatly reduced. Sherpas, with their extensive experience and heavy loads, often skip using the fixed ropes.

While the ropes were being set by some serious mountaineers, David suggested that we climb up a ridge on the east side of the valley. It didn't seem that bad of a climb until I saw people the size of little ants making their way up. It reminded me that these mountains are enormous. Everything is much bigger than it looks.

After a relaxed breakfast, the whole Summit Climb team decided to hike the ridge at the same time. We all left camp together except for David who said he would catch up to us later. Apparently, he was still making deals with the yak herders.

The trail was steep out of the gate. It passed by a valley of prayer flags and came to a cliff band where other teams were practicing their technical skills. We decided to take a quick break to allow David to catch up and tell us why the yak negotiations had taken so long that morning.

David explained that they drove a hard bargain. Basically, additional yaks cost about $250 USD per yak. This is expensive considering buying a yak would be about $1000 USD. There is also a yak waiting fee: $100 for a bag of straw. As much as David tried to negotiate, the yak herders knew that there was nowhere else we could take our business.

We wanted to climb higher but as we did the rocks became less and less stable. This hill was not worth risking a rolled ankle. We took in an almost aerial view of CBC. The tents were tiny specs of yellow huddled around larger mess tents. It was cool seeing the variety of setups from this elevation. I was surprised at how many tents there were. This year the CTMA issued 300 summit permits. This count did not include Sherpas or support staff. Looking down on the entire spread, just based on tent real estate alone, it was easy to see how the Chinese, Indian, and Russian teams took the majority of those permits.

On the way down, we stopped by some of those camps. I introduced Patrick and myself to the Chinese teams. I was wearing a shirt with Chinese characters that I had made. On the front it said, "The foreigner is coming," and on the back, "The foreigner is leaving." They thought it was great and we took pictures with most of the team.

We also stopped by an international team that was preparing to break a world record for highest formal dinner. They were doing a practice run at CBC in their tuxedos and dresses. Their goal was to have that same dinner atop the North Col. There, they would also be in their tuxedos and dresses uncorking champagne bottles. They would be dining on miso soup, lamb tagine and chocolate pudding.

Back at our not so luxurious dinner tent, the whole team was in good spirits after the hike. Jangbu lit Mr. Heater while we were sipping tea. He then reentered with a huge smile and surprised us with maybe the highest apple pie in the world. I would take that over chocolate pudding any day.

As a team, we thoroughly enjoyed the pie and swapped life stories. Looking back at the day's hike, everyone seemed to be relatively at the same fitness level. There were some climbers that were huffing harder and moving slower than others, but nobody quit. Some of our teammates were feeling the altitude as well, but nothing that a day or two at this altitude wouldn't fix. It also seemed that everyone I met at the other camps were extremely welcoming. People were just focused on their goals. I knew that there were people up here with much more experience than me, but at the same time, there were probably just as many with less experience. I belonged here as well. I smiled at my teammates and finished off my apple pie.

We were all enjoying the comforts of base camp. We knew they wouldn't last. Tomorrow we had to move up the mountain.

# PINNACLES AND PUJA

**April 20, 2018**
Day 8: CBC (5,182m)
Ambient Oxygen: 10.9%
SPO2: 95%
Heart Rate: 68 BPM

It was our fifth day at Chinese Base Camp. The wind was noticeable. The sun shined brightly but the cold was biting. The morning required gloves and a hat. Patrick and I were psyched to get moving up the mountain. Our team left Chinese Base Camp in a couple small clumps. Everybody matched up with someone that they felt they could enjoy the next 4-7 hours with.

The Northeast Ridge Route is the most popular route for those wanting to climb Everest from the Tibetan side. The trail starts at Chinese Base Camp and meanders at a slight grade along the north side of the Rongbuk Glacier for approximately 5km. Upon reaching the confluence of the Rongbuk East Glacier you take a long left. There, the trail gets much steeper as it follows the west side of the Rongbuk East Glacier and its tributaries another 5km to Intermediate Base Camp. Most teams spend a night here. The next day, you have some very steep ups and downs as the trail, the Miracle Highway, provides you safe passage through an otherwise impassable glacier. After approximately 10 km, you reach Advanced Base Camp.

We were just starting. My goal was to go as slow as possible to conserve as much energy as I could. The problem was Patrick likes going fast. I decided to go a little faster than I was comfortable with in order to keep up with Patrick. I didn't want him to think I was any less prepared then he was. So, we cruised.

Patrick brought along his pink Olivia sailing flag and had it hanging from the back of his backpack. He led and the flag was always part of my view. It was his token of remembrance for his good friend's daughter who died at age 13 in a sailing accident. He has carried it with him on all his big adventures. It has given him strength when he needed it most. This was the beginning of the journey and he intended to take Olivia's flag to the top.

As we walked, I thought about a picture I had seen of this section from 1921, when the entire valley was a glacier[35]. The glaciers had receded and left behind massive piles of debris. I couldn't imagine how difficult this must have been back in the 1920s. Those were some true adventurers.

A highlight, and one of the main reasons to climb Everest from the north side, are the stunning views. You can't help but rejoice in where you are and what you are doing. The peak was just showing off the entire time. Another hour up a steep grade and we all took a break at what became known fondly by our team as lunchtime corner.

Lunch had been packed by Nobu and Tashi. We had no idea what was in the brown paper bags we were carrying until then. We unwrapped the aluminum foil to find a boiled egg, some fried bread, a chunky slice of the worm, and a Kit-Kat. It wasn't lamb tagine, but it would do the job.

After lunch, as we headed up the East Rongbuk Glacier, the mountainside came to life. We were joined on the trail by Tibetan Blue Sheep - not as blue as I imagined, but friendlier than I could have ever expected. We all chugged along and before we knew it we caught up to the yaks. The yaks were

---

35      1921 British Mount Everest Reconnaissance Expedition.

very shy the entire way up. We learned that unless you wanted a staring contest, it's best to move off the trail to let them pass. After five and a half hours of hiking, I arrived at Intermediate Base Camp (IBC). My heart rate was 103 bpm. My goal was to take it easy, which according to my heart rate, I accomplished. I was still tired and looked forward to sitting down. That was more difficult a task than I thought. It wasn't snowing but everything looked wet. It was also clear that the yaks ran this spot. They ran through tents when they wanted, they ate where they wanted, and they defecated everywhere. Jon and Lucy found a pile of yak dung inside their vestibule. I surveyed the scene in sincere disbelief at the sheer quantity of yak manure at 5,742m.

Patrick signaled me over to a tent that he had picked out. We couldn't even put our bags down without contaminating them. We repositioned some rocks into the vestibule where we could put down our bags with some dignity. The rocks gave us a couple of clean square centimeters to work with. Like bank robbers dodging the red lasers in the vault, we took off our shoes, tiptoed over the backpacks in the tent vestibule, and sunk into the tent. Once we got inside, we realized our mistake. The tent was on a 15-degree slope. It was going to be a rough night. Nonetheless, it sounded better than tramping around Yak Poop Camp looking for another tent.

We relaxed with some tea that another Tibetan, Dough-Che, brought us. Apparently, he is the keeper of Yak Poop Camp for the entire climbing season. We joked that this was yak poop tea. The laughter stopped as we realized it probably was. I had my head outside of the tent when Magnus and Dom arrived. It was fun to watch them come to the realization that they too would be sleeping around in, and on yak crap.

IBC is also in a valley between two high ridges. The sun disappears well before the day is done. Once the sunlight left us, we ate a quick dinner also provided by Dough-Che. We thanked him and started an early night of slipping centimeter by centimeter towards the vestibule.

**April 21, 2018**
Day 9: IBC (5,742m)
Ambient Oxygen: 10.1%
SPO2: 76%
Heart Rate: 91 BPM

In the frozen morning air, I awoke. I could hear the deep breaths of yaks as they slept outside of our tent. The wind was blowing hard. Patrick and I got up, had a quick bite, a tea outside, and got moving. It was 10:00 am.

IBC is split by an enormous ravine. Our camp was at the top of the first section before dropping into it. Across the ravine, you could see several other teams' tents. It took us 20 minutes just to get to the bottom. From there, we crossed a glacial stream and worked our way back up the other side of the ravine. It was incredibly steep and took 45 minutes to get to where we were back at 5,742 meters. It was hard to swallow that it took more than an hour just to hike from one end of IBC to the other.

We finally passed a couple of other teams' tents at the end of IBC. We were now on the miracle highway. I was astounded by the size of the pinnacles, or penitentes as they are called in Argentina. Pyramids of ice, four stories tall, lined both sides of the trail. They are remnants of the receding glaciers.

The trail from IBC to ABC is known as the Miracle Highway. Since its discovery in 1921, expeditions from Tibet have been using this route to access Everest. The miracle of this trail is a result of the Rongbuk Glacier and the Changtse Glacier pushing massive amounts of earth together as they collide. The glaciers move downhill and the scraped earth has moved with them, creating a large undulating berm between them. This moraine provides a hilly, safe, and relatively quick passage up to Advanced Base Camp. Without this miracle moraine, advancing on Everest from this valley may never have been an option as crossing through the maze of ice pyramids would be treacherous and time consuming.

The undulations on the miracle moraine were tiring but the views were not. Magnus, Franz, and Martin had caught up to Patrick, Jon, Lucy, and I. We all stopped and admired a remarkable vantage point looking straight up the East Rongbuk Glacier at the base of Changtse.

"Hey, can you take a picture of me naked?" Martin asked.

"What?" I replied bemusedly.

He repeated the same question and justified it with, "I take pictures of myself naked in crazy spots around the world. I even have one of me on top of the Pyramids in Giza."[36]

He whipped out his phone and showed me the picture. I was impressed. It was an incredible shot. His girlfriend had taken it. Martin was atop one of the pyramids, hands raised, butt cheeks out. Another pyramid was in the background followed by the lights of Cairo.

"Then there is the one I have of me in Antarctica. I am known as the Antarctica Terrorist as I managed to get there without the permission of ALE."

I was intrigued. Everyone else walked on.

"Sure," I said. "Give me your camera and I'll take a couple of shots.[37]"

Martin stripped down quickly. Before I knew it, I was photographing a naked dude at 6,000 meters. Once he got his clothes back on, I asked him about the Antarctica Terrorist. According to Martin, he went down to Antarctica to climb Mt. Vinson. Martin wanted to do something else while he was in Antarctica as it was a relatively easy climb. While he was on the continent, he decided to ski from Hercules Inlet to the

---

36    Martin Szwed Facebook: Naked Pyramids of Giza
37    Martin Szwed Facebook: Naked Everest

South Pole. He did it. But there was a problem. He undertook the challenge without anyone's permission. He also broke the standing record by 10 days. News of his accomplishments quickly hit the Internet and with it a wave of problems. The German Federal Environmental Agency, responsible for Antarctica permits for German nationals, raided Martin's house and he was forced to dump all his pictures and GPS data or face prosecution. Without GPS data and pictures of his trip, the tight-knit polar explorers community questioned his claim[38]. Many dismissed him as a fake. He lost sponsorships over it. Now, Martin was on Everest to climb the last mountain of his seven summits.

I walked in silence listening to his story. I was jealous that he had made it down there and found a way around the paperwork. However, whether it was true or not, it definitely damaged his reputation.

The others of our team had slowed down as there is a section that leads off the moraine and into the large ice pinnacles. Here, at the base of Changtse Mountain, we had lunch. The Sherpas had packed us fried bread and a hard-boiled egg. It hit the spot just like yesterday's fried bread and boiled egg. Thankfully, this day, there was no slice of worm. We kept moving. The undulations of Changtse's skirt did not have the downhills that the miracle moraine had, but many steeper uphills.

The final corner to reach ABC is the steepest part. Your legs ache and breathing becomes more difficult. Now, you are at the doorstep of Everest. I was extremely excited to be here; I ran around our camp taking pictures; I ducked in and out of our new yellow dining tent; I enjoyed the moment with our team. After about an hour, the adrenaline wore off. I ate dinner and I crashed hard in my tent by 6:30pm.

---

38      Larsen, Eric. "Is the Greatest Record in Exploration a Hoax?" Outside Online.

# CHAPTER 9

# FAILURE ON THE NORTH COL

Summit Climb location at ABC

**April 22, 2018**
Day 10: ABC (6,492m)
Ambient Oxygen: 9.1%
SPO2: 72%
Heart Rate: 92 BPM

First thing after breakfast, Patrick and I explored ABC. Advanced Base Camp is a sprawl of tents approximately a kilometer long. It is scrunched up between the northeast face of Chigatse and the East Rongbuk Glacier. This is the last camp that the yaks reach with supplies. Therefore, the majority of Everest expeditions on the Tibet side funnel through here. This is another camp where you realize that, depending on your tent location, your climb may be an hour longer or hour shorter than expected. For us, our tents were located near the bottom of ABC. This gave us a welcome sense of relief when we arrived from IBC. But the convenience became an inconvenience. It added another hour to our climb, when we would move up to the next camp.

Patrick and I walked for about an hour towards Crampon Point. There, the magnitude of the North Col climb hit us. We could see dots of people on the enormous ice wall. Squinting, I could make out tents the size of yellow pinpricks at the top of the North Col. That was Camp 1. It was going to be an exhausting day to get up there. The risks would also increase exponentially. We stared in awe. It was gorgeous and intimidating. We headed back down to ABC shaking our heads at the thought of climbing that colossal col.

Back at the Summit Climb ABC camp our guide David was shooing away yaks. I was starting to feel the altitude. My head was hurting every time I moved too fast. I decided to lie down. After several hours in my tent sleeping, reading, and eating junk food, I physically felt better. However, I was feeling the external pressures of undertaking this challenge. My family, friends, students... they were all rooting for me. I had to do this. I had to feel better. I left my tent and headed to the mess tent. It was freezing outside, and I had to double back for my blue puffy jacket.

The cold shadow of Changtse quieted the camp. In the mess tent, Jangbu was lighting Mr. Heater Junior. This was enough to let your worries slip away. He would almost get it lit and we would all cheer. Then it would go out and we would all boo. He gave us a very kind and sarcastic laugh. Dinner started with soup. Then a main course. By the time it was dark, the temperature had plummeted. We had peaches for dessert, and it was time for bed.

**April 23, 2018**
Day 11: ABC (6,492m)
Ambient Oxygen: 9.1%
SPO2: 64%
Heart Rate: 88 BPM

This was our second full day at ABC. My headache had lightened, and I slept well. I did take 11 Aspirin interspersed throughout the night. I think that helped.

Instead of sitting around and playing cards, David wanted to make sure everyone was familiar with their equipment. A little late if you ask me, but I was going with the flow. In the mess tent, we checked our gear. David passed on his tricks of the trade and emphasized maximizing safety and efficiency. He said we must clip in every time we see a rope. One small slip on the northeast ridge could send you to a grave at the headwaters of the Rongbuk Glacier, 3000 meters below. Franz was happy because he had just learned how to use a figure 8 rappelling device.

"Franz is an expert now!" Patrick sarcastically pointed out.

It actually did not take too long to go through the gear checks. We were back to sitting around playing cards and BS-ing for the rest of the day and evening.

Puja Ceremony

**April 24, 2018**
Day 12: ABC (6,492m)
Ambient Oxygen: 9.1%
SPO2: 64%
Heart Rate: 87 BPM

The next morning, I awoke to a surprise. Our first snow day! Today was also the day of our Puja ceremony. In Buddhism, Puja can be used as expressions of honor, worship and devotional attention. David said the purpose of our Puja was to ask for safe passage on our expedition. Ever since I had heard of expeditions in the Himalayas, I was fascinated by the Puja ceremony. For me, it has always been a symbol of respect to the mountain.

The Sherpas spent most of the morning setting up the Puja. They had found a shaman who seemed to be a porter for another climbing team. I did not ask him for credentials. The set up consisted of making a 1.5-meter square chorten out of rocks. That got wrapped in tin foil. A blue yellow and red Buddhist fabric was then placed around the chorten. There was a pole in the middle that reached a height of three meters. Our entire team was asked to bring our boots, crampons, harnesses, and ice axes to be blessed. They were placed at the foot of the chorten along with puffed barley, yak butter tea, an apple, two cans of coke, some amulets, a hot water bottle, fried dough, paper cups, a giant bottle of dark rum, and two cases of Lhasa Beer.

Our Puja started out with some chanting. It then continued with more chanting. Tsampa, a roasted barley powder, was thrown and rubbed on our cheeks. Prayer flags were raised, and an offering was made. We were forced to chug a cup of the bad dark rum. I wasn't ecstatic about the rum, but it was for Buddha and our safe passage. I guess that's ok.

It was a fine ceremony. All of us clients went back to our tents while the shaman, the Sherpas and the kitchen boys stayed to finish off the rum and the beers.

Later that day, all warmed up from the ceremony, Jangbu had crossed the valley from our tents to where the ice pinnacles were. He set up ice screws and ropes that went 10 meters up one of the ice pinnacles, traversed 10 meters across the top, and came down. Our job was to make sure we were fluent with our crampons, jumar, carabiners, and figure 8s.

I was really excited. I love climbing steep faces and rappelling down. I waited in line filming some of the climbers. Everyone was going with the flow. Franz seemed to have a bit of a tough time, but he had just learned how to use a rappelling device the day before. Patrick front-pointed up the pinnacle and came flying down the rappel like a SWAT team expert. I followed with the same speed and style. We would be using these skills from here on up. The first test would be on the North Col. There, we would use everything but the figure 8. The figure 8 would only be needed once: to rappel down the 2nd step after a successful summit. I was definitely looking forward to that.

For my second round on the ice, I decided to retest my new Mountain Hardwear Absolute Zero mitts. I had tried them in Qingdao, and they were horrible for dexterity. However, they were the warmest mitts out there, so I gave them another test. They kept my hands warm, but I could not do anything with them on. I could barely grip my ice axe, I couldn't use my jumar, and clipping into the rope took way more energy and time than I wanted. I would have to go with my Black Diamond

Mercury Mitts on summit night. They weren't overly dexterous either, but they were better than the Absolute Zero mitts.

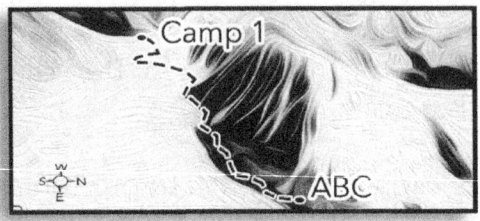

**April 25, 2018**
Day 13: ABC (6,492m)
Ambient Oxygen: 9.1%
SPO2: 64%
Heart Rate: 110 BPM

My head was not happy that night. It felt like there were sharks with lasers blasting my brain cells. I actually had to sit up and concentrate incredibly hard to make them go away. Then when I laid back down, the torture aquarium started up again. This time it took 12 aspirin throughout the night. It helped but I didn't get much sleep. Perhaps, I was nervous. Today was going to be a big one.

Looking at the North Col, it's hard to believe how long it takes to get there and how big it is. It took about an hour to reach the top part of ABC from the Summit Climb ABC camp. The Chinese team was camped here. From the last Chinese tent it was another hour to Crampon Point.

There are blue barrels at Crampon Point where climbers stash equipment that they don't want to carry up to the North Col. As an example, Patrick put his approach shoes in one of them. I had been wearing my mountaineering boots since we left ABC and they felt great. The blue barrels are also used to stash harnesses and crampons on your way down from Camp 1 to ABC. It didn't seem very orderly to me, so I decided to not put anything in the barrels.

Crampon Point is where you slap on your crampons and take a rest as the real climb begins. From here to the summit, there are additional dangers such as cravasses, overhanging seracs, avalanches and increasingly less oxygen. The walk from Crampon Point to the base of the North Col does not look far but it takes another hour before you even clip into the fixed ropes. Patrick and the faster guys on our team, Jon and Grant, were on the heels of Jangbu. I, on the other hand, was already feeling toasted as I labored across the field of ice.

Here we were on one of the most dangerous sections of the mountain. I was prepared for -40° snowstorms. Instead it was about 12° Celsius. I was roasting. The ice field is surrounded by vertical walls of ice on three sides. The solar radiation was bouncing off every shiny piece of ice and being reflected right at us.

The heat was slowing me down and I ended up at the back of the pack.  By the time I got to the bottom of the wall, Patrick, Jon, and Grant were already out of sight. I couldn't keep up. I was trying to save energy, but I had nothing to save. I was in trouble.

I clipped into the fixed line at the bottom of the North Col. It looked bigger than it did yesterday.

"Here we go" I thought. "Only 500 meters straight up an ice wall. I can do this."

The fixed lines on Everest are not endless. They span 20 to 70 meters depending on the terrain. At the end of every rope you must change over to the new rope. It seems like a simple task. You unclip your carabiner from the old rope and clip it to the new rope. Then you unclip your jumar from the old rope and clip it into the new rope. There are so many extraneous steps in this process that it begins to wear on you. It zaps your energy. You have to dig your crampons into the snow, position your ice axe, bend over, mess around with bulky gloves, and repeat this process. The entire time you are trying not to drop any equipment, or it is all tied to you, in which case the lines get tangled. It was a hassle but necessary.

The going was slow and became increasingly slower. I was so hot I thought I would pass out. The trail was  blue ice in sections and you really had to stomp your feet multiple times to gain purchase. The sun beat down on us and its reflection off the snow melted our energy away. Patrick, Jon, and Grant were still out of sight. I could imagine them on top of the North Col. Two hundred meters behind, I struggled.

We had been on the move for 4.5 hours from ABC and reached an altitude of 6,850 meters. However, we were still 250 meters short of our goal. Dom and I were beat. David sat down with us. He mentioned that it was difficult today. Hot and icy. David assured Dom, Magnus, Franz, and I, that today was a difficult day on the North Col. He continued saying that it would be easier the next time and that this was a great spot to turn around. A couple of Sherpas were with us slurping down some juice boxes next to me. They were laughing and said that they felt great. I got my butt kicked.

I was crushed and embarrassed that I couldn't reach Camp 1 and had to retreat to ABC. If I couldn't climb the North Col, there is no way I would be able to make the summit. My eyes were burning from sweat and suntan lotion, my legs were shaking, and my water bottle was empty. This may have been my worst day ever in the mountains. I was pissed off at myself. I tried to lessen this blow by telling myself I would have another shot, but at this moment my failure struck me hard. I sat in the dead center of the North Col looking out over the East Rongbuk Glacier. From my vantage point, my whole adventure was coming to a close.

There was no reason to sit in the sun, keep baking and sulking. The slower half of our team, Franz, Dom, Magnus, and I descended. I was at the back of the pack with the slow group. I couldn't believe I wasn't at Camp 1 with Patrick and the strong half.

Going down the face of the North Col we used a wrapped arm technique on some of the more mellow parts. Several sections we had to clip in our figure 8s and practically rappel down the slope. When we finally got off the wall we were still roasting from the sun.

Crossing the flats was tiring but the section from Crampon Point to ABC was absolutely painful. We couldn't believe how far it was. The trail just kept going and going. Even when we reached the top of the camp it took us another 30 minutes to descend to the Summit Climb camp.

I was the most trashed on a mountain than I had ever been. Arriving at our camp, I went straight into the mess tent and poured some water. I chugged half, filled it up again, and went to my tent. I flung open my tent and sat down on the ground. My feet were cooked in my 8000m boots. Quickly, I undid the laces and pushed them to the side of my vestibule. I could see Dom, Magnus, and Franz going through similar motions. I closed my tent fly, opened all the vents, undressed to my boxers and passed out.

My Nalgene bottle was frozen. I usually tuck it into my sleeping bag so that it stays liquid the entire night. However, in my haste to go to sleep I had left it out and it was a cylindrical block of ice. I was still thirsty from my failed attempt on the North Col and headed to the mess tent to see if there was any liquid water left in the thermoses.

It was a sublime morning and very quiet at the Summit Climb camp. I actually felt good which I was a bit upset about. I thought of Wayne Gretzky's biography and how his team, the Edmonton Oilers, lost the 1983 Stanley Cup Championship to the New York Islanders. He said that after the game he and his team were tired. However, he walked by the New York Islanders locker room and they weren't even celebrating. The entire team was hurt. They were dead tired, cut up. Their bruised bodies were covered in ice packs. That is when Gretzky realized what it would take to win. You had to give everything and get to the finish line with nothing left.

It was bothering me that I didn't give absolutely everything to make it to the top of the North Col. Granted, I would have had to leave enough in the tank to get down. Yesterday, I was tired, thirsty, and hot but that shouldn't have stopped me. If I really wanted to complete this goal, I had to reevaluate how I was climbing. I needed to make sure I was climbing at my pace. If I was tired, thirsty, hungry, or hot, I would stop and take care of those needs. If I was beat, it didn't matter, all I had to do was take one more step. One more step would get me closer to my goal. I would have to turn off my tired voice, go to my happy place, and continue on.

Frustrated, I headed into the mess tent. I hadn't heard from Patrick. Maybe he had stayed up at Camp 1.Magnus and Dom were already slamming down fluids in the mess tent. They were also talking about how big of a day it was on the North Col. I poured some hot water into a mug and made some tea.

An hour later, I went back to my tent. Patrick emerged from his tent. It looked like he had seen a ghost. He was shaking his head. He was sunburnt, his lips were peeling, and he was moving slower than normal. He was in good spirits but the first thing he said was, "Man, I am beat."

He recounted his day above the midpoint on the North Col, above where I turned around. He said that he, Jon, and Grant were just trying to keep step for step with Jangbu. They were all exhausted when they got to the top of the col. It was cold and windy with some flurries. Patrick said they watched the Sherpas set up tents and stash supplies. Patrick took a video of himself giving a shout out to the Olivia Foundation and then it was time to descend. He didn't get back to ABC until 7:30pm.

He could tell I was down on myself for not getting to the top of the North Col and tried to justify my turnaround.

"Yeah, it was hot on that wall," he explained. "I'm not surprised you turned around. I almost did several times. Also, we were only up there for a couple of seconds. You really didn't miss anything."

As he was saying this, I thought, 'but you didn't turn around and I did miss something, I missed meeting a milestone that I should have met.'

He was trying to make me feel better. I was definitely making myself feel worse.

Later that morning we headed back down the mountain. The air mercifully thickened and my head cleared. My aches were still with me, but they did not matter. I just kept stepping downhill. I was unsuccessful on the North Col but would have another chance. Next time, I will be better prepared. Patrick threw in his headphones and blasted down. I stopped often trying to enjoy where I was. Admittedly, I was also still tired and bummed because of my time on the North Col.

Without incident, I made it back to CBC in 7 hours. Round one was done. It felt great to be back at base camp. It was comparatively warm, the communal tent was comfy, and the amenities were plentiful. We could catch up on sleep, check the Internet, shower, shave, stare at the peak, and recover with movie night in our Tibetan-themed tent before going to bed.

The next day was a day to do nothing. I wandered around Chinese Base Camp in search of two grave sites. They were difficult to find as the majority of the gravestones used are rocks with small inscriptions.

On top of huddled boulders, inscribed plaques echoed those who had died on the north face of Everest. There was Irvine and Mallory, Auricht, Boardman, and David Sharp, the English mountaineer that died as people walked right over him on their way to the summit. There were also several graves in Ciryllic, Chinese characters, Hindi, and Korean. Every one of these mountaineers lived a story. I bet none of them thought it would end here.

The graveyard spooked me and reminded me that there were dead bodies scattered across the mountain. I had read about climbers who encountered the dead on their summit push. It seemed to affect most climbers the same. They would question mortality and the climb. I was hoping to get that part out of the way here. While there is always a chance of dying wherever you are, summit night on Everest was equivalent to jumping into the lion's den.

# A SECOND CHANCE

**May 1, 2018**
Day 19: CBC (5,182m)
Ambient Oxygen: 10.9%
SPO2: 87%
Heart Rate: 92 BPM

The snow continued from the evening into the early hours of the morning. Under the morning clouds, the lower sections of Rongbuk Valley were white from the storm. The snowline was much lower than the altitudes we would be crossing today. I didn't bring any hiking boots on this trip. I much prefer to wear approach shoes on any type of trail that is not snow. On snow, I prefer my 8000-meter boots. They are lighter, don't give me blisters, and provide more cushion. Unfortunately, there was snow and my 8000-meter mountaineering boots were safely stashed at ABC.

I was still in my tent when the sun hit Everest. The Rongbuk Valley remained shady and cold. I was not looking forward to today's hike up to IBC in just my approach shoes. They were going to be soaked and cold. The wind was blowing which was going to make the going even more miserable.

The view of Everest in the sunlight was stunning. I could no longer stay in bed. That, and Magnus' cough two tents down had woken me up. He wasn't sounding too good. I was a little worried that his cough was getting worse. I did not want to get infected. A sickness would be detrimental to my next acclimatization round. I made my way to the dining tent. Once again, I was one of the first climbers to rise and got Mr. Heater started. It was -4 degrees Celsius.

By 10:00am the weather improved. The sun had melted the majority of the snow, however there were many unavoidable drifts. Around 10:30 am we started on the trail. The team had split up their leaving times according to when and how was best for them to travel. Grant's backpack was packed and stacked taller than he was. I almost mistook him for a Sherpa. Dom, Franz, and Martin were taking it easy. Patrick had his headphones in and was playing air guitar on his trekking poles. He even threw in a few leg kicks and spinoramas. My feet were soaked but not cold. In fact, 1km into the hike I stripped down to just my softshell pants and a t-shirt.

The yaks brought up a second round of supplies for most teams. This was our second time on this trail, and we started naming landmarks. One of the larger boulders on the right had a pointed front end with a rounded top. He became "Angry Tortoise". We knew we were near the end of the flat section when we passed the skull and horns of a blue sheep - that became Ram's Head.

We took numerous pictures and videos. It was fun taking our time. I was much more relaxed than the first time up this trail. Patrick was still rocking out while keeping a solid pace. We passed another welcome landmark, a string of prayer flags that indicated the steep climb to the East Rongbuk Glacier.

We spotted more blue sheep as we neared the lunchtime corner - the halfway point between CBC and IBC. There is a steep cliff that looks down a ravine to the rushing waters of the East Rongbuk Glacier runout. Grant was getting dangerously close to the edge.

Everyone on the team stayed within eyesight of each other. Sherpas were passing us like we were standing still. It felt like there were fast people behind me and slow people in front of me. I ducked off to the side and took some film and pictures.

This impromptu stop allowed me to really go at my own pace. There was no pressure to go slow and no pressure to go fast.

By the time I rolled into IBC the snow had started covering all the yak poop, making shitty slushies everywhere. It took about 4.5 hours to get from CBC to IBC. I got to the tent; Patrick was already inside. My feet were soaked. I only had one extra pair of socks, so I dried my feet with a t-shirt and put gloves on them. It looked ridiculous, but it worked.

Tashi and Dough-Che brought us garlic soup as an appetizer. Then came the main course. They brought us pasta, rice, baked beans, fried potatoes, and chicken. This adventure was starting to feel like a vacation. We cracked ourselves up talking about it.

"We have been in bed in our tents since 4pm, we only hiked for 4.5 hours today, they just brought us dinner, I've eaten four KitKats, had tons of other junk food, and we sleep for 11 hours every night," I bellowed out.

Between laughs Patrick added, "We don't even get up to pee."

With that, it was time to listen to a podcast and fall asleep.

**May 2, 2018**
Day 20: IBC (5,724m)
Ambient Oxygen: 10.1%
SPO2: 87%
Heart Rate: 92 BPM

It was another spectacular morning at IBC. The sky was baby blue. We left down the steep ravine and up the other side. The start and end of this 9km hike were the most difficult. The middle section on the miracle moraine was pleasant. I focused on the fresh coat of snow on the majestic mountain. The summit appeared deceptively close. It felt like you could reach out and touch it.

The roller coaster-like ups and downs of the moraine led me into a hiking trance. It was peaceful and meditative. The penitentes reflected rainbows of light. The going was much easier than the first time we came up this route. Once off the central moraine, we stopped for lunch at the same spot we did during our first round of acclimatization. We named the lunch spot between IBC and ABC Martin's Rock, as he tried in vain to push an enormous boulder off of its icy perch.

While we were sitting there enjoying lunch Magnus kept coughing. It didn't seem like a Khumbu cough, but more like a phlegmy gurgle. It was concerning. It's hard to shun someone from the group as you are all a team, however, when your investments of several years come down to the next three weeks, you try to distance yourself from illness as much as possible. I offered to take pictures and film of the group. I climbed a berm several meters away. I set up my camera overlooking the lunch spot and enjoyed my lunch: one boiled egg and a piece of fried bread. The group finished their lunch. I told them I wanted to film them leaving the lunch spot and that I would follow up after. It was a way to courteously distance myself.

Three hours later, I arrived at ABC with a heart rate of 103 BPM. My SPO2 was surprisingly low at 84%. I was feeling great but that last hour of hiking was brutal on the legs. I heard the team chatting and drinking tea in the mess tent. I went directly there to say hi and grab some tea. David rolled in a couple minutes later in great spirits. We were all laughing at the fact that the Viagra and condoms made it up ABC in the medicine bag. Summit Climb was prepared for anything.

As it turns out Viagra has an active ingredient called sildenafil citrate. This causes vasodilation. Although not backed by scientific findings, there are stories that it helps with altitude sickness. I never got an answer to what the benefit was for the high altitude use of condoms.

Enough laughing for me, I headed to my tent to take care of a housekeeping issue. I needed to take off my shoes and tend to my feet. This is the best way that I have found to avoid blisters. My routine is to take off my shoes and socks. I then wipe down my bare feet with a wet wipe. I allow them to dry. Afterwards, I apply a large helping of foot powder or baby powder. The powder usually gets into my sleeping bag and tent but I figure a little freshness there doesn't hurt. I follow up by putting on a pair of dry socks and my camp booties. Since I started using this process my feet have always been in great shape.

For the rest of the day, I joked around with the boys in the mess tent and spent time in my own. I read, organized gear, and practiced breathing. With my activities at ABC, my SPO2 dropped to 68%. I was able to get it back up to a high of 91% through deep breathing exercises. During the breathing, my heart rate dropped from 108 to 57 beats per minute. I was relaxed.

**May 3, 2018**
Day 21: ABC (6,492m)
Ambient Oxygen: 9.1%
SPO2: 64%
Heart Rate: 84 BPM

The taste of spring was in the thin air. This brought its own problems. With the longer and warmer days our precious spot at ABC was melting into a land of lakes. Patrick found his tent in the middle of one. However, in the subzero temperatures at night, the lake refroze, sealing Patrick's tent floor in ice. This mishap required the attention of all Summit Climb climbers who were huddled around the tent like retired engineers at a new building project. Eventually, Tashi came by with an ice axe and chopped away at the ice until he freed the tent. That was enough excitement for one morning. Although today was a rest day at ABC, which meant that that was about as exciting as the day would get.

I went back to my tent and laid all my gear out on its floor so that it would dry. I examined the gear that would be going up to the North Col with me. Everything was in order. Alone, I hiked about halfway to Crampon Point. I wanted to size up the North Col again and mentally focus on my objective for the next day. I had to make a plan. I could see climbers slowly making their way up and the tents on the ridge at Camp 1. Several groups were also descending.

It was clear to see that several teams were having trouble on the wall just like I had had a week ago. This was an intimidating slab of ice. Technically, it was great. It was much more enjoyable than the hike from CBC to ABC. I would much rather travel on snow and ice with crampons than rock and scree in shoes. The amount of time climbing on the wall wasn't the problem either. The problem was the weather.

It was the heat that got me last time. When you leave ABC, you have to be prepared for some of the coldest temperatures in the world. Simultaneously, you must be prepared for blazing heat. I was not prepared for the latter. One of my biggest personal faults while hiking, climbing, and/or skiing is I hate stopping. A stop for water, or an equipment check, or putting on or taking off layers has always bothered me. That was one of the reasons I got so hot on that wall. I had to get over that idiosyncrasy if I was going to make it to the top. My plan would be to start out cold, warm up on the wall, and if I had to, I would stop and put a layer on.

With my camera, I zoomed in as much as I could to look at the route in detail. The bottom of the route started to the far left (i.e., climbers left or rather to the left as you look up at the mountain). The route travelled right across the bottom of the face before turning straight up the wall. After that turn, there was a shiny ice section that was slowing some climbers down. The trail then made a hard right across the heart of the North Col leading to a mellower slope, which was where I stopped and turned around the last time. Looking at it from this angle it was a horrible place to stop. Formidable overhanging seracs above the lunch spot looked like they would break off at any second. Past my highest point marker, the trail veered left up another steep section curving around the seracs. Once atop the seracs the trail finally gets completely flat. It loops far out to the right and back to the left around an exposed crevasse. This serpentine route leads you to a final long and steep section that ends on top of the North Col at Camp 1.

I went through the succession of this trail several times so I could repeat it in my mind, like memorizing rock holds on a difficult climbing route, or the way Olympic downhillers visualize sections of the run.

I scanned the North Col for answers in vain. Doubt clouded my ability to think it through. Was I going to make it tomorrow? And even if I did, from Camp 1 there would still be 1,828 grueling vertical meters to reach the summit? How can you make a summit if you can't even make a milestone ascent before the summit? I descended to ABC lost in these questions.

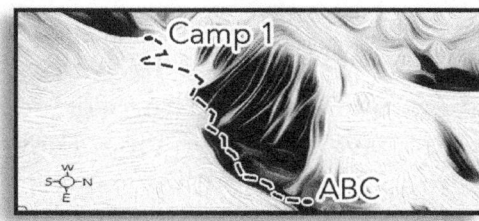

**May 4, 2018**
Day 22: ABC (6,492m)
Ambient Oxygen: 9.1%
SPO2: 74%
Heart Rate: 84 BPM

I awoke to a sparkling day. The sun rose like an ember out of the frozen pinnacles and the moon was setting into the grasp of the Changtse Mountain. The North Col was bleached white. The birds had been foraging for a while and the climbers were just starting to stir. Magnus was still coughing up a lung in the tent next to me.

This was it. Today was extremely important. I needed to get to the top of the North Col and spend the night at Camp 1. My earlier failed attempt was not sitting well with me. If I didn't make it up today, my chances of getting further on the mountain would be close to zero. Who would want to climb with someone to the top if they had failed on the North Col twice?

'Not me,' I thought.

Grant, Magnus, Patrick, and I were outside of our tents, stuffing our packs with anything we would need for the overnight excursion. David was by the yellow kitchen tent discussing something with the Sherpas. He shuffled over to us.

"The Sherpas have volunteered to take your sleeping bags up to Camp 1. If you want them to take your sleeping just put them in a pile outside of the kitchen tent," David said.

I was over the moon with the Sherpas' offer. A huge literal weight was off my back. These men were superhuman, supporting the vanity of people of a different culture. I was relieved and grateful. Now, I just had to relax, take it slow and put one foot in front of the other.

Time after time the Sherpas have come through. They are strong, kind, and humble. I wish we would have had more opportunities to interact with them one on one. However, so far on the trip, they definitely didn't have any down time. They were on the clock. In Nepal, the average monthly salary is approximately $270 USD. Our Sherpas would be making five to ten times that amount depending on tips. Their work was difficult and dangerous, but they seemed to enjoy it. They were elite mountaineers and I felt lucky to spend time with them.

Grant, Magnus, Patrick, David and I left the camp together. I knew David was going to take it slow. I tucked myself behind him on the trail and made sure I did not go faster than him. From the onset, his pace was agonizingly slow. I followed step by step. I wanted to make sure my energy was conserved for when I really needed it. Surprisingly, several members of our team were also feeling this way. We all matched David's pace.

David had been up this trail seven times before and he knew what it would take to be successful.

The path up to Crampon Point wound up along the side of Changtse. Again, the magnitude of this section was misleading. The stretches between a valley, or a rock you may recognize, to another point you remember, took twice as long as you thought they should. We passed through a winding section that has metallic looking rocks. I had named the section Goldie Rocks. I later changed it to Metallic Alley. I enjoyed geology in college and the different rocks at these varying elevations were fascinating. There was time to stop, but I decided to keep in step with the group. Further up, there are some small crevasses to cross marked with flags. We did not have crampons on yet, so we took it even slower.

Crampon Point was much quieter this time around. Everyone was focused on conserving their energy. That is, until we saw Ang Psang, Magnus's personal Sherpa. He was proving his worth in carrying capacity. He had a completely stuffed backpack. On the outside of the back there were three sleeping bags and three oxygen bottles. It made us all question why we were climbing this mountain in the first place. Maybe we didn't belong here. He dropped his load on the snow by sitting down with it attached to his back. It was heavier than it looked. We were all just staring in amazement. He made no huff, no groan, no annoyed noises at all. Once he was down on the snow, he didn't relax either. He stood up, walked over to the blue barrels, and started preparing himself and Magnus for the North Col.

The sun continued to shine brightly on the North Col. It was hot and the going was tough. The cold breeze helped to cool us off. We crossed the large, comparatively flat section of ice that leads to the first steep section of the North Col. We clipped into the fixed ropes and little by little moved up the face.

As with the trail up to Crampon Point, the route up the North Col continues to have sections that once you see, you remember, but they just keep coming. You crest a steep section and then you think you are arriving at a mellower section, but it turns out there are two more steep sections than you remembered. Even with my visualization techniques the day before, the trail seemed to have its surprises.

The Sherpas had been amazing throughout the trip so far, but from ABC upwards, they are the yaks. Their ability to carry heavy loads at these altitudes strikes you dumb from incredulity. I found myself questioning why I hadn't seen more of them in the Olympics. Our loaded-down Sherpas were passing us on the fixed lines. Several other Sherpa teams were on the way down, practically jogging.

I found the going hard. Careening over a berm, we arrived at the lunch spot. The spot we turned around last time. We had caught up to Patrick, Jon, and Grant; that is, the faster guys on the team. The day had cooled. It was not as hot this time around. I was tired but nothing like the first time. After our little rest, I was now higher than I had ever been in my life. The challenges continued. Before the final steep section up to Camp 1 on top of the North Col, we had to circle around a sizable crevasse. The last section, the final test of the North Col, consists of a vertical ice wall that requires front pointing, rope negotiating, and the rest of your energy.

It was all jumar with a touch of shaky legs that got me over the final berm. I laid atop the snowy plateau for a second to relish in the moment. I had done it. Making it to this camp at 7,020 meters was of huge importance. If I hadn't done it this time, I was going home. The next time I would climb the North Col wall it would be for the summit attempt. Dom, Magnus, Ang Pasang, and Jangbu were coming up the last steep face of the North Col. I stood up, positioned myself out over the edge and tried to give them encouraging words. The sherpas continued to blow me away. Ang Pasang and Jangbu were hot on the heels of those guys and looking eager to pass. They were carrying loads that would easily amount to the mass of another person. For the third time today I questioned, 'What the hell am I doing here?' I had a feeling they would continue to impress me the further we went up this mountain.

Once they got to the top, we took a quick break, high-fived and continued along the North Col. Our tents were supposedly the last set of tents on this ridge. Sure enough, after passing the other teams' tents, I arrived at the Summit Climb camp. David was directing people towards their living quarters for the night. I couldn't believe he was outside standing around. The wind up here was ferocious.

Camp 1 is located on the top of the North Col. The North Col is a spine shaped ridge, an arête, that creates a giant letter "U" between Everest's snow slope and Changtse. The bottom of that "U" is exactly where Camp 1 is set. The winds from Nepal hit this ridge between Everest and Changtse and accelerate over the top; as they do, the temperature drops. Clouds and ice form. They deposit drifts on the ridge. Luckily, that ridge has a giant ice wall and cornice that blocks the wind on the plateau. Unfortunately, by the time the Summit Climb sherpas arrived at Camp 1 with our tents, all of the good spots were taken. Our camp was in a wind tunnel.

Patrick was in the tent with his gear sorted and vestibule pit dug when I arrived. The pit makes it easier to take off and put on boots as well as allowing for additional storage space. He unzipped the tent with the enthusiasm and gusto of a decorated French restaurateur and gayfully said, "Welcome to Chez Louis!"

He caught me off guard and I started laughing. I coughed from humor, altitude, and extreme tiredness. I took a knee in front of the tent to see how he had set it up.

"Come on in! Take off your harness, I'll hang it for you," he said.

My exhaustion must have triggered my Neanderthal brain. I replied, "Take off harness?"

Patrick took advantage of it and replied in Neanderthal speak "Yes. Take. Off. Harness."

We were both giggling at the absurdity of it all. We were also super stoked to be at Camp 1. Once settled in the tent, I did a round of breathing to increase my SPO2 from 78% to 84%. It was cold in the tent, but my sleeping bag warmed up fast. Except for the occasional cough, it was quiet outside of the tent. All Summit Climb climbers and Sherpas were staying out of the elements.

Patrick and I used a Primus stove hung from the center of the tent to melt snow from the comfort of our sleeping bags. The hot metal wires hanging from a plastic hook with an open flame in a nylon tent was not a safe option. However, it was our preferred method. Watching snow melt was our evening entertainment. It took 2 hours to boil water for our water bottles, dinner, and replenishing our water bottles before bed.

At Camp 1, time for bed does not necessarily mean that you will get any rest. We had a rough, rough night. Snow was blowing into the tent from somewhere. In addition, a continuous cycle had developed. Our breath would freeze on the inside of the tent and the strong wind would throw the ice crystals off, showering our faces. It was not pleasant. I was awake for most of the night.

Camp 1 - N. Col

**May 5, 2018**
Day 23: Camp 1 (7,020m)
Ambient Oxygen: 8.4%
SPO2: 57%
Heart Rate: 89 BPM

I woke up groggy. My SPO2 was the lowest it had ever been. We realized we had made a complete rookie mistake. We left our boots in the dugout vestibule. The wind, which was still howling, had no problem filling the vestibule pit with snow. Our boots were under that snow. I was glad it happened on this rotation instead of the next one. We had just heard word that we were not going up the snow slope to touch Camp 2 but heading down to ABC due to the high winds.

In full blizzard gear, I stepped out of our tent vestibule. The wind was relentless. My boots were uncomfortably cold and wet. ABC was visible but miniscule below. I turned towards the snow slope. The path beyond stretched up in front of me. It led up to Camp 2, the traverse to Camp 3 and the Summit. It was calling me louder than ever. It felt dreadfully close.

For this rotation, this was the highest we were going. We started to head back down to ABC. It wasn't windy below the col; it was warm and beautiful. Our team spread out as we went down and everyone traveled at their own pace.

We made it back to Advanced Base Camp without issue. Snow was being blasted off the summit like an arctic smokestack. It was good to be back at ABC. We relaxed, drank tea, and played cards. Tomorrow, we return to Chinese Base Camp.

Tibetan Sand Grouse

**May 6, 2018**
Day 24: ABC (6,492m)
Ambient Oxygen: 9.1%
SPO2: 64%
Heart Rate: 84 BPM

It sounded like a freight train coming straight at my tent. That was how I woke up. I realized what it was. My tent would be still, but I would hear a katabatic gust of wind rampaging down from the North Col. It would hit the top of the ABC and shake the Chinese team's tents, then the Seven Summits Club's tents, then make their way down to my tent. The wind hit and shook my tent like a martini bartender to a tumbler. It was enthralling. I lay in my sleeping bag listening to these phenomena.

The sun had made it over the northeast ridge of Everest. I quickly slurped down porridge in the mess tent. A group of us were about to return to CBC. I closed up my tent and was waiting out front. Martin, Franz, Jon, Magnus, and Patrick hustled up and we headed down.

In high spirits, we passed the last of the tents marking the bottom of ABC. It felt like a fairytale alongside the East Rongbuk Glacier: the crisp air, the sunshine, the beautiful pinnacles. The walk was joyful.

We arrived at CBC and Dough-Che came out to greet us. Within minutes, he brought out tea and some of the best ramen I have ever eaten. I know it was just ramen, but I was a huge fan.

After the noodles it was time to get moving again. It wasn't a race, and everybody walked in their own headspace. The yak traffic was extremely light, contrary to their loads. The valley run out was more inviting than usual. I practiced what I preached: enjoying the present moment. Magnus caught up with me and I let him cruise by.

At the confluence of the East Rongbuk Valley and the Rongbuk Valley, I scrambled up a steep slope of scree to a large boulder so that I could get a view of CBC. It was far but didn't appear that far. It looked like it should be a 15-minute walk. Again, the mountains here are deceiving. It was at least another hour away.

Today was supposed to be a dreaded day. We were just walking for hours downhill over a path we have been on three times already. To me, it was awesome. During that last hour, I felt so fortunate to be where I was. I had time to sit and look for interesting rocks, stare at the summit, and think about my family and friends around the world that had made my life what it was. From the good influencers to the bad, I was thankful that they were all in my life. I felt like I did not have to wait until I reached the summit to feel appreciative. Perhaps it took getting away from society to appreciate my luck. I had one more big goal to complete. I felt strong, confident, and was as ready as I would ever be.

A couple of Tibetan sand grouses accompanied me on my descent. I got caught up in a tiny sand twister. I made it to CBC in time for dinner and bed. CBC felt like a 5-star hotel and it was about to get better. Tomorrow we were descending in a van to New Tingri. There we would spend three nights chowing down on local food, sleeping in beds, and getting legit showers.

# CHAPTER 11

# DOWN TIME

**May 7, 2018**
Day 25: New Tingri (4,300m)
Ambient Oxygen: 12.4%
SPO2: 97%
Heart Rate: 64 BPM

We arrived in New Tingri and went straight to the Qomolangma Hotel Tibet Tingri. Before we explored this government instituted bustling truck stop of a city, we had lunch at the hotel and a much-needed shower. The water was mostly warm.

I had lived in China for a total of seven years before this trip to Everest. In New Tingri, it was my time to shine. David told me the Summit Climb teams that have come down to New Tingri in the past haven't ventured into the city. They also ate all their meals in the hotel. After lunch at the hotel, I knew there would be tons of great Chinese food out in the streets. I rallied the troops and took them exploring.

For breakfast we would eat at 成谕友谊 Chéng Yù Yǒuyì, Chengyu's Friendship restaurant. They served great eggs with bread and some drinkable instant coffee. For lunch, we would eat instant noodles at the hotel and relax. The afternoons were spent on the Internet, playing cards, going for walks, and chatting in the lobby. For dinner, we went to a traditional Chinese food restaurant, a Sichuan restaurant, and a Xinjiang restaurant.

The Xinjiang restaurant was the most memorable. Xinjiang

is the northwestern portion of China. Their specialty is lamb, bread, and a chicken and potato stew called Dà Pán Jī (大盘鸡). This translates directly to Big Plate Chicken. The description was spot on. The 50cm wide plate was filled to the brim with a spicy cumin-based sauce. Like a volcano rising out of the sea, the middle of the plate was a pile of chicken, potatoes, green bell peppers, onions, and Sichuan mouth numbing peppers. The team was taken back by the chicken head at the top of the pile. We dug in. The thin slices of chicken had to be pulled off of bone shrapnel. The taste was spicy, exotic, and delicious. A couple of hours passed. We ate, chatted, laughed, and hydrated.

On one of our down days, David wanted to go visit a town called Shegar, now also renamed Tingri. However, David was told the town was closed to foreigners. "Let me see what I can do," I offered. I sent a WeChat message to Linlin, my CMTA liaison. I asked him if he could pull any strings. Linlin made some calls. The next thing we knew, he had arranged a 20-minute van ride to the Tibetan city of Shegar. The only stipulation was that pictures just in the town were forbidden.

The city was perfect. Where New Tingri is just restaurants and convenience stores, Shegar had Tibetans, in all manner of traditional clothes and headgear, walking around. There were Buddhist stores selling intricate religious items like prayer flags, singing bowls, and spinning prayer wheels. Of note, there was an ancient monastery that climbed up a nearby mountain. I also tracked down a great spot for lunch: a tiny, dilapidated restaurant with pork and cabbage dumplings. Most of the team turned down my recommendation and dined at the fake KFC that looked just a little less sketchy than my dumpling restaurant. I thought the dumplings were outstanding.

It felt so good to show the team how much China has to offer. I added a bit of culture to our short amount of downtime in Tingri. I am also positive that if David leads anymore Everest trips from Tibet, he will make Big Plate Chicken a tradition. Our time in New Tingri was up. I felt rejuvenated both physically and mentally. I was ready to rock this mountain.

# CHAPTER 12

# SUMMIT PUSH

**May 13, 2018**
Day 30: CBC (5,182m)
Ambient Oxygen: 10.9%
SPO2: 97%
Heart Rate: 68 BPM

We were all eagerly anticipating the final push. Over the last month, we completed two acclimatization rounds, reached 7,020 meters, and just spent four down days at New Tingri to rest up. Next, we spent the last two days at CBC doing last minute preparations. Now, we pushed off one last time from CBC to get to the top of Everest.

The sights were still breathtaking, the terrain familiar, the yak bells enchanting. Since we had arrived a month earlier, the lakes and rivers were melting, and we heard rock falls more often. We knew the pace we needed to conserve energy, keep our heart rates low, and SPO2 high. However, Patrick and I were excited. We hiked up the side of the Rongbuk moraine. I had to remind him often to slow down. After lunch Patrick bolted ahead. I felt confident hiking at my own pace. I would see him soon at IBC.

Arriving at IBC everything was as expected. Patrick relaxed outside of the tent and Dough-Che was serving noodles. Throughout the afternoon other members of our team arrived. Before we knew it, it was dinner time. I did a couple rounds of Wim Hof breathing before falling asleep.

**May 14, 2018**
Day 31: IBC (5,724m)
Ambient Oxygen: 10.1%
SPO2: 74%
Heart Rate: 103 BPM

With care, Dough-Che made us our morning tea - that got us up and moving. It wasn't as bright and sunny as it had been our last two times here, but the surroundings held their beauty. It started out as a pleasant hike. The trail was magnificent, the pinnacles bold, and Everest summit sat in the distance appearing to wait for us. Although the scenery was no longer novel, it is one of the most incredible places that I have ever been. I felt very fortunate to be there. Patrick was cruising and I cruised with him.

After a quick lunch at Martin's Rock, we made our way through the melting glacier. Grant caught up to us. Patrick soon sped off with him. I started to trail behind. I felt I was pushing myself a little too much that morning and I just needed to slow down. I finally felt that I had become my own mountaineer. I was no longer comparing myself to anyone. I was enjoying the trek and living in the moment. I was climbing the way that I knew would serve my goals best.

I had all day to make it to ABC. There was no rush. It was just the mountain, a bit of rolling fog, some snow flurries, a couple of yaks, and my slow stroll. An hour later, my legs were feeling heavy on the last steep hill to ABC. I had kept my heart rate under 110 BPM the entire day, but my muscles ached. I attributed it to trying to keep up with Patrick's brisk pace that morning. I stayed positive and kept going, step by step.

I arrived at ABC completely drained. I did not enjoy the last hour of the hike. I looked at my watch. It was 1:15pm. That did not make any sense. We left IBC a little after 10:00am. I thought the altitude was impairing my math skills. That meant it only took about 3 hours to get from IBC to ABC. That was a surprise.

No wonder I was tired. In comparison, the first time I hiked from IBC to ABC it took 6 hours!

Laying down in my tent, I did a round of breathing, increasing my SPO2 from 79% to 87%, and dropped my heartrate from 104 BMP to 65 BPM. Impressed with my accomplishments, I fell asleep until dinner.

Tashi and Nobu were serving. The dinner continued to please, and I left the dining tent stuffed. I hurried back to my tent and fell asleep while checking my SPO2.

Camp 1
View of N. Col from ABC

**May 15, 2018**
Day 32: ABC (6,492m)
Ambient Oxygen: 9.1%
SPO2: 64%
Heart Rate: 84 BPM

The splendor of Everest's brilliant North Face provided another spiritual awakening. If you want to see the Himalayas at their best, I highly recommend going during the month of May. The goal of the day was to rest, eat, drink, and get ready for the North Col climb tomorrow.

After my porridge breakfast, I strolled 20 minutes uphill to the Chinese camp at ABC. They were bustling with excitement as several of their climbers had gone for a summit the night before and could now be seen descending. They pulled me over to their telescope and told me to take a look. It was stunning. The climbers on the summit gave the mountain scale. It was huge. It almost seemed as if they were on the moon. I spotted two Chinese climbers coming down right from the summit and three climbers atop the third step. It was warm, sunny, and there appeared to be no wind. I imagined what a great feeling it must be coming down after a perfect summit day like that. My fingers were crossed for my own summit to be in similar conditions.

Later that day, the Summit Climb team gathered in the mess tent. David wanted to review how to use and troubleshoot the oxygen masks and regulator system. It turned into an oxygen mask lottery. In this lottery you either get a modern slightly used mask, or a 1980s heavily used Russian fighter plane mask. Dave put everyone's names in a hat and pulled them out one at a time. The modern slightly used masks went first. I lucked out. My name was drawn first, and I got one of the modern masks. I tested the oxygen. It was glorious.

The sun went down over ABC and I returned to my tent. Tomorrow, we head up the mountain. Here at ABC we were completely safe. The day-to-day schedule was predictable and there was very little risk of injury or death. However, the unknowns of the next four days could have severe consequences. These days would be exciting, difficult, and terrifying. The nights would be sleepless.

Then there was the low oxygen levels. I had been on the North Col, higher than I had ever been in my life, without any headaches or acute mountain sickness (AMS). However, I was gunshy from my experiences with AMS on Denali and Kilimanjaro. I knew I was susceptible. I had to put my faith in my hypoxic training and acclimatization. That, and I hoped the supplemental oxygen would help.

The mountain's obstacles did not stop there. Summit night it would throw everything at us. Climbing in the dark through the Exit Cracks, walking the narrow path of the Northeast Ridge, the three steps, the cold, and lack of oxygen presented real challenges. There were so many ways things could go wrong. I couldn't help but think back to the graveyard at CBC.

I knew I was as prepared. Patrick and I had controlled all the controllables. It was the uncontrollables and the unknowns that nagged at my nerves.

Before I left, my girlfriend had given me a stack of laminated post-it notes - each one with a different message. I had been reading them throughout the trip. They were a welcome distraction for my nerves. I had organized them into my favorites:

*"Before I do anything, I ask myself, "Would an idiot do that?" and if the answer is yes, I do not do that thing."* - **Dwight Schrute**

*"In the middle of difficulty lies opportunity."* - **Albert Einstein**

*"Drive fast, take chances."* - **Greg Spechalske**

*"Tough times don't last, but tough people do."* - **Robert H. Schuller**

*"If you're feeling cold, go stand in a corner. They are usually around 90 degrees!"* - **Unknown**

*"If I could, I'd give you the ability to see yourself through my eyes. Then you'd truly see how wonderful and amazing you really are."* - **Tatiana Gregorek**

With a big smile and a warm heart, I fell asleep.

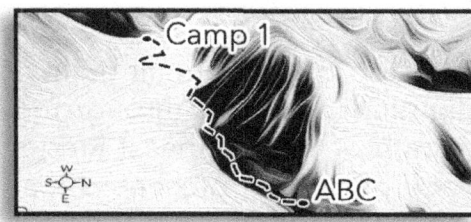

**May 16, 2018**
Day 33: ABC (6,492m)
Ambient Oxygen: 9.1%
SPO2: 74%
Heart Rate: 84 BPM

There was a new thin coat of snow on the ground. We said goodbye to Tashi and Nobu and started the familiar hike to Crampon Point. I asked David what the plan of attack was for the day.

"The plan of attack is to take it nice and slow and easy," he answered. "It is going to be hot, hot, and even hotter on the

slope going up to Camp 1. I'm going to take it easy, take this jacket off, look at the enjoyable scenery, and possibly the bum of anyone in front of me."

David was right. It was time, more than ever, to take it slow. We tramped through the rest of the tent settlement at ABC, and through Metallic Ally. I was breathing heavily but kept a comfortable pace. With a fresh coat of snow, there was more danger of falling in a crevasse. We approached Crampon Point. The larger crevasses were marked with flags. The small crevasses we had to watch out for ourselves.

Patrick, Dom, Grant, Jon, and I had been at Crampon Point for 20 minutes and were ready to push off. Grant blasted out of the starting gate and quickly became a dot with the North Col looming over him. David, Franz, and Martin were just pulling up. Martin got his gear on quickly and decided to go up with me.

"This is it," I kept hearing myself say. Every situation that "this is it" came up felt like a do or die moment. A moment where I had to cognitively understand that I was about to push myself out of my comfort zone and to the next level. "This is it" applied to when we arrived at CBC over a month ago and I saw the snow blowing off the top of the peak. "This is it" applied to my second test on the North Col. "This is it" applied when we left CBC for our summit push. "This is it" applied when I left ABC this last time. Now, I was at Crampon Point staring directly at the North Col's cragged ice face and yes, this was it.

"This is it," became the shortened version of "This is a point in my life that I have a purpose; that time is meaningful; that I need to prove something to myself in order to feel complete and give myself meaning."

If I didn't continually test myself on that never-ending refrain would it be like I had never left my cubicle more than a decade ago? Would the Everest summit "this is it", the granddaddy of them all, fulfill me in some way that would sustain a sense of purpose after the fact? What if I failed on the summit "this is it?" Would I feel meaningless? Would I be satisfied enough to screw down the cap, bottling up the adventures of my life and move on without having to push myself to these extreme physical and mental limits anymore? Would I be dead?

Was I soon to be ready to gladly return to the cubicle? Was I ready to settle down? Was this whole adventure a last effort to prove I could do something before my life ticked away? Or was I overthinking it? Was "it" a midlife crisis?

I wasn't doubting my abilities at this point. I was doubting if I still needed these adventures to give my time meaning. At this moment, I knew I could get up the North Col, and I was confident I could climb this mountain. I realized on the North Col that with the time, money, physical and mental effort that I put into this climb, this was not the moment to give up because I might be over "it."

This was it. And I was going to give everything I had to succeed.

The North Col: Beautiful, steep, dangerous, and today, hot again. The heat was going to zap us. We had done this before and knew what it would take: slow movement, lots of water, and suntan lotion. It was noon. Patrick, Martin, Dom, Grant, Magnus, Ang Pasang, and I had just made it to the first fixed rope on the wall. I stripped down to my softshell pants and a t-shirt. I wanted to avoid the overheating scenario and subsequent failure on the North Col that I experienced during the first round of acclimatization. Ready to climb, I clipped into the first of the more than 30 sections of rope fixed to the North Col.

Martin stayed right behind me which put me at ease. He was an excellent, experienced mountaineer, and was always looking to lend a helping hand. He was also about 200cm tall. If he stood next to me on flat ground, he made me look like a hobbit. As long as I stayed in front of him on the steep slopes,

I was at least at eye level. In front of us, Patrick, Grant, and Dom were leading the way. Dom was crushing it. He was usually at the back of the pack. Today he was way out front. Martin and I took our time. Like at the back of a school bus, we were having a blast taking pictures, telling stories, laughing, and goofing off.

It was 2:00 pm when we stopped at our usual lunch spot. The small angled plateau provided a small respite from the steepness of the North Col. What was unusual was the traffic coming down the mountain. The weather window had been open for a couple of days now. Summiters and non-summiters alike were making their way down the mountain. It was the busiest I had seen the route anywhere on the mountain.

David, Magnus and Ang Pasang had also caught up to us. David informed us that someone had stolen Franz's harness from the barrels at Crampon Point. Fortunately, David talked with the head of the Chinese team and he lent Franz his harness. Unfortunately, Patrick had lent Franz four brand new locking carabiners that were on that harness. They were gone too.

Our team looked great. We were all managing the wall extremely well. This was, for everybody, our third time at this point. I felt reborn. I was happy, strong, and had a clear head. I was thriving on the views, the steepness and even the burn in my legs.

There was a break in the bustle, and we decided to get moving. The two-way traffic on one rope proved to be troublesome. Several descending climbers and Sherpas were too tired to clip into the ropes. On one of the steeper sections two descending climbers let go of the rope to go around Patrick and I. As the second climber passed, I held out my hand to help him around me. He slipped. Still holding onto the rope and with a strong stance I braced his fall and he stopped.

"My bad," he said.

"No way," I said laughing. "I saved your life; you owe me a beer."

I was in a great mood. We circled around the large open crevasse before the last steep pitch of the North Col. Descending climbers were delirious from the combination of the lack of oxygen and exhaustion. Several climbers were being short roped to one or two Sherpas. The short rope technique is used when a climber is too unsteady to be trusted to make it down on their own, even if they are fixed to the safety line. It seemed ridiculous that climbers would rely on being leashed to a Sherpa to get themselves down.

We had that one last steep pitch on the North Col to get up to Camp 1. Grant was right above me. I had to stop and manipulate the fixed line, so I didn't pull Grant off the North Col. With a couple of heaves and hos I crested over the top. I was overjoyed. I was healthy, strong and full of energy. I just ate up the steepest face on the North Col. I was pumped.

I looked back down the North Col. Patrick was still working his way up. I could tell he was feeling rough. On the last steep section every move he made looked incredibly laborious: one more step. Patrick popped over the last bulbous block of snow and arrived at the top of the North Col. I congratulated him. We walked together through all of the other team's camps before we arrived at our tent. I was in such a good mood I stopped at the Chinese camp and spoke with them about their summit. Most of the guys were laying on the snow. They were scattered around the tents like a game of 52-card pickup. We laughed and I congratulated them. For how tired Patrick was, I'm sure I sounded annoyingly chipper, even if it was in Chinese. From there, it was only a ten-minute stroll to Summit Climb's cluster of tents. I picked out a beauty of a tent for Patrick and I. Patrick was not ready to have tent time. He was drained gave himself a time out. Alone, he sat on the northern edge of the North Col at 7,020 meters, looking down at ABC.

It was welcoming to finally see Patrick show that he was human.

I had strained myself chasing him up the Rongbuk Valley all the while, doubting my own strength and fortitude. Now I felt like a million bucks. He was having some quiet time to regain his composure. As he did for me when I was wrecked, I made sure I did the majority of the housekeeping. I know how much it helps.

I was incredibly sunburned and thirsty after the six-hour trip from ABC. I did savor having the energy to dig out a foyer for our tent and gather snow. It was pleasant and warm at Camp 1. There was no wind and I was walking around camp in a t-shirt. I was collecting snow by stuffing it into our boiling pot then dropping it off at our tent. Jon Lawrie saw me and asked if I wanted to have a large black plastic bag to collect snow in. He had an extra. I couldn't believe I had never seen this simple but effective tool used before. It was a genius idea. The bag was light, hardly took up any space, and would save tons of time and discomfort gathering snow. I could gather enough snow for the entire night. I thanked Jon and started stuffing snow.

Patrick had made his way into the tent and looked forward to chowing down on his Golden Shrimp Noodles that he had picked up in Tingri. I was sticking with my Mountain House meals. Tonight, was a classic. I had the beef stroganoff. After dinner I did a round of breathing. I got my SPO2 up from 71% to 83%. However, my heart rate was still high at 107 BPM.

The sun had gone down and it was getting dark. I felt fantastic. I took a quick stroll to take a pee. Fog socked in Camp 1 and made it eerily quiet. I saw Jangbu talking seriously with another Sherpa. I walked toward them but decided not to interrupt. It looked like Jangbu had just descended, from Camp 2 or higher.

Back in the tent, I tried to relax and lower my heartbeat. I closed my eyes, listening to the Sherpas having what sounded like a party in one of the nearby tents.

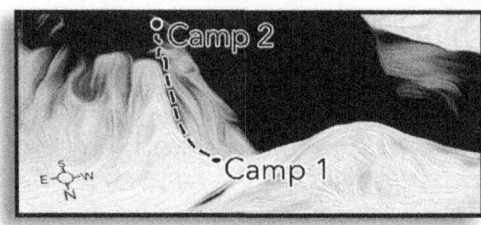

**May 17, 2018**
Day 35: Camp 1 (7,020m)
Ambient Oxygen: 7.0%
SPO2 63%
Heart Rate: 115 BPM

Camp 1 on the North Col is a horrible camp if you are looking for a good night's sleep. Actually, I take that back, it is not the place I would go if I want a good night's sleep. Evidently, Patrick slept fine. I had a rough night. I was comfortable, warm, and free of headaches. I just couldn't get to sleep. I was happy that the sun was up. We could finally start the preparations to leave this camp. Above us, the sky was dark blue. The sun was blazing over ABC. The melting glacier pools of the East Rongbuk glacier were glittering with the sun' rays. It was cold and crisp and another gorgeous day to be on the mountain. We started our slow mountaineer's morning.

We began the long process of boiling water. The black trash bag was still filled with fresh snow ready to be melted. It was great being able to stay in our sleeping bags while having a fresh supply. We lit the Primus stove which hung like a lantern from the center of the inside of our tent and loaded snow into the pot little by little. We wanted to start preparing for the day, but with equipment scattered all over the tent, wanting to stay warm in our sleeping bags, and an open flame dangling from some nylon, we decided to minimize movement. Frost from our breaths had frozen again to the inside of the tent. Now, with the stove pushing out some serious BTUs, the entire tent was dripping on us.

I had oatmeal. Patrick had some instant noodles. We both enjoyed tea that the Sherpas were graciously bringing around. My outfit for today would just be my summit suit, my Merino wool 1-piece long underwear, and SmartWool boxers. At the time it seemed to be sufficient. I again was cautious of wearing too much. I did not want to have a repeat of my overheating issue.

After eating it was time to get out of the tent. The wind had died down and it was warm enough outside to take it easy. We double checked to make sure we packed all the required gear for the successive camps and the summit. We also made sure to leave anything that we wouldn't be using. It was time to trim the fat. Energy bars seem to be the biggest waste carried up high. I find that at high altitudes they are hard to eat and often unappetizing. This trip I would leave all but two behind. Replacing the calories would be energy chews. These high calorie candies taste like gummy bears. I can always eat gummy bears. For my main meals, I decided to take two Mountain House meals. There were three servings in each bag. I figured that would be enough even if we got socked in for a day or two up high. I also packed a packet of oatmeal for breakfast. Patrick took one Mountain House meal and his now staple diet, Golden Stock Shrimp Instant Noodles. He also packed an assortment of energy goos, chews, and energy bars for summit night.

Camp 1 was buzzing with activity. Martin and Franz were clearing out their tent. Ang Pasang and Magnus were right next to us sorting their gear. Other Sherpas were preparing their own gear, gathering up fuel, and loading their packs with several oxygen bottles, sleeping bags, and sleeping mats. Patrick and I got ready and made our way to a clearing in front of the tents.

The goal of the day would be to make it up the snow slope to Camp 2. The rumor of the day was that our tents were actually just a bit farther than the snow slope, but no one knew exactly where. To be honest, we didn't really care. We were moving up the mountain and making progress on the big goal. From here on out, every step would be new. We were learning the details of Everest topography and I was stoked.

It was also the first time we would be climbing with oxygen. We all gathered out in front of our tents. David had us circle up to ensure everyone remembered the oxygen mask procedures that he had reviewed with us at ABC. He emphasized that if your exhale exit valves froze, as they often do, all it takes is one hard blow from the inside of the mask.

My oxygen was working fine, and I instantly felt a difference. I was awake, alert, and my mind was clear. I couldn't have asked for anything more. Everyone else was also about ready to go. The snow slope was intimidating but looked doable. I calculated how today's climb to Camp 2 would feel by comparing it to Mt. Baker Ski area, a mountain I knew well. The snow slope from Camp 1 to Camp 2 is 680 vertical meters; about 2,100 feet. Mt. Baker Ski Area is about 1,500 feet from the base lodge to the highest lift. The climb today would just be like climbing Mt. Baker ski area plus another 600 feet or so. That didn't sound too bad.

Scanning up the snow slope, it seemed way smaller than Mt. Baker Ski Area as well. However, I learned on Denali that on these big mountains, size is deceiving. As I scanned down the slope, my eyes met the team. We were all here. All in good spirits. It was warm and peaceful. The team looked tough in their oxygen masks and goggles, almost as if they were heading into the trenches of WWI. The Tibetan Plateau provided a mesmerizing backdrop. I slowly focused on each one of my team members. I gazed at each one of them for several seconds. I thought about what we had already been through to get to this point, the literal ups and downs. We had spent the last five weeks together and I considered all of them my friends. I couldn't help but be a bit apprehensive about what laid ahead. Would we all make it back?

At 10:00am, we left the North Col. Ten meters from camp there was a surprising and a seemingly insignificant downhill. Once at the bottom, we crossed an open crevasse that led to the beginning of the snow slope. We would be wrestling this steepness for the rest of the day. I wanted to take it slow. I wanted to be my own climber and not worry about the lightning pace that Jon or Patrick could potentially set. I decided to clip into the line right behind Dom. He had taken his time getting to every camp. If I set my pace behind him, I would be fine.

The view of Everest's North Face was just to our right. Like frozen roots branching down from the summit, the routes of daring climbers could easily be followed with the eye: the Hornbein Couloir, first ascended in 1963; American Direct route, first ascended in 1984; the White Limbo route, also first ascended in 1984; the Russian Direct route, first ascended in 2004; and the Japanese Super Couloir, first ascended in 1980, which leads into the Hornbein Couloir.[39]

The most recognizable feature on this face of the mountain was the Great Couloir/Norton Couloir. This morning it was catching the sun beautifully as it streaked down towards the Rongbuk Glacier. The wide U-shaped valley of the Great Couloir extends down from the 3rd Step and looks deceivingly welcoming. To summit from the Great Couloir would require steep technical climbing. However, once you were back in the couloir, the snow looked superb. Perfect as it might be; this couloir is notoriously prone to avalanches, rock falls, and crevasses. In 2001, Marco Siffredi, a French mountaineer climbed and snowboarded that very couloir. Tragically, in 2002 he went back to snowboard the Hornbein Couloir, just a few hundred meters west of the Norton Couloir, and was never heard from again.[40] His body was never found. His memorial at CBC is a stark reminder of how much more dangerous the "off-piste" slopes are than the fire escape I was on. The danger of a first descent is romantically enchanting though. I shook my head. I needed to stop daydreaming of first descents and focus on my first ascent up this snow slope.

After three hours of staring at Dom's backside, sidestepping, and front pointing, fatigue was starting to set in. The infinite wisdom of boxer Mike Tyson popped into my head, "Everybody has a plan until they get punched in the mouth."
Everest's jab caught me square in the face. The snow slope

---

39        "Elite Climbers to Blaze New Route up Everest." National Geographic News.

40        "The Disappearance of Marco Siffredi on Everest's Hornbein Couloir." Snowboarder Magazine.

was much steeper, longer, and more exposed than it appeared from Camp 1. While I had pushed to stay on the heels of Dom, one of the slower guys on the team, I was starting to fall behind.

"Damn," I thought as flashbacks of my failed North Col attempt raced through my mind.

A failed attempt on the snow slope would be a huge red flag that I should not continue higher on the mountain. Dom would turn around often and give me a thumbs up or shout unintelligible words of encouragement through his oxygen mask.

I started a conversation with myself: 'I have trained for this. I have been tired before. Focus. Go to your happy place. Get outside of this tired state of mind and just move your feet. There is no option for you to turn around. This is your shot. Enjoy the pain. Enjoy the suck.'

This was my shot. This was it. I just stayed on the heels of Dom. I cleared my head and focused on one step at a time.

We were ready for a break, but it seemed as if there was no good place to stop. The steep angle of the snow slope never let up. There was no place to just sit and relax. There were also no outcroppings that would give you cover from the increasing winds. You would either have to sit with your ice axe and crampons dug into the snow or stay attached to the safety line. We chose the first option. It was 1:30pm.

To my surprise, Patrick and Jon were behind me and just catching up. I had lost track of them as several teams and individuals were leapfrogging us and we were leapfrogging them. We all sat, unclipped, quietly staring out over this unassumingly monstrous snow slope. We gobbled down some snacks, commented on the strong and weak climbers coming up the fixed lines, and desperately sucked oxygen. Our oxygen bottles were set to deliver us a dose of half a liter a minute. We had control of this and were trusted to not run out before we made it to our tents at Camp 2.

Fifteen minutes later, we were back on the fixed line slowly approaching a steep section of layered rock that veers you to the looker's right. This was the welcome end to the snow slope. No snow on these rocks was a tell-tale sign that this wind was persistent. Dom, in his yellow suit, was still right in front of me. He continued his outward positive attitude which, at this point, was a challenge. The wind was increasing and now contained ice crystals that stung any exposed flesh. In front of Dom was a line of eight climbers. They were going slow. I did not mind their pace one bit.

We reached the first tent around 2:30pm. It did not belong to our team. I looked up and was shocked at what lay in front of us. Just as steep as the snow slope, Camp 2 snaked upwards on either side of the fixed ropes. Tents were battened down with multiple guy lines. They were placed anywhere there was a slab of rock or a patch of plateau. The real estate here was at a premium.

The steep path through the middle of Camp 2 zigzagged upwards like a poorly weighted bottle rocket. My crampons were slipping on the loose rock that covered the trail. The fixed lines followed the zig and the zag. Dom was sticking to the trail and I continued to follow him. The Sherpas made their own path here. They unclipped from the fixed ropes and scurried straight up the mountain. Dom and I tried this once but decided it would be better to take it slow and steady than try to keep up with the Sherpas.

We trudged past tent after tent. None belonged to Summit Climb. It was getting ridiculous. Dom and I often paused just to look around and see if we had missed it or if there was a Sherpa around that would be able to direct us to the right spot. No luck. We kept on.

It was 4:30pm, two whole hours since reaching the bottom of

Camp 2, when we finally saw the Summit Climb tents. There were several scattered over 10 vertical meters. I was the first to arrive at camp and I chose the top tent. It was set on the edge of a cliff with a four-meter drop. A portion of the tent footprint extended over the edge of the mini cliff. I zipped open the tent. It felt solid. The portion of the nylon tent floor that extended over the cliff was brighter than the rest of the tent floor. I chuckled to myself. I was surprised at the tent placement and relieved to have a home. I dropped my backpack and took a seat outside.

Too tired to do any organizing, I gazed out over the Himalayas. The winds from Nepal were raging between Everest and Changtse. Clouds whipped by directly below our camp. I was now at 7,700 meters, a new personal record. I was happy but tired. My SPO2 was down to 65%. This was not surprising as the ambient oxygen was one-third of what it was at sea level.

Patrick was making his way up through the scattered tents. I wanted him to see me so that he would also know that the end of today's climb was near. He gave me a wave from Dom's tent 10 meters below our tent. With that acknowledgement, I headed inside our room with a view. I was wrecked. That was my most challenging day yet. Six and a half hours of steep, mixed climbing. The most ridiculous aspect of the climb was that it was only 2.7km from start to finish, but it felt like a marathon.

Anyway, I was here. I could relax. Patrick pulled up to the front of the tent 15 minutes later. That's right, 15 minutes for 10 meters. He was too tired to move when he arrived. He sat outside in the wind, relieved, and checked his GPS. I was also exhausted but inside the tent with my boots off and my sleeping bag open. Before he entered the tent, I passed him our black plastic trash bag to collect snow. He was wasted but closer to the snow than I was. With a nod, he grabbed the bag and went to get snow.

The snow slope and subsequent climb through the entirety of Camp 2 had beat us both up. Patrick settled into the tent and we recounted the hardships of the day. We also immediately started melting snow for drinking water. Our mouths were dry, and our bodies dehydrated. Little by little, over a couple of hours we replenished the lost fluids in our body. Dinner time came quickly. Patrick had his shrimp noodles; I had my Mountain House rice and chicken. Eating was difficult. It was nauseating to remove my oxygen mask and forcefully gulp down a rehydrated piece of chicken. I knew I had to eat. I stuffed down spoonful after spoonful. Most bites I washed down with water from the snow that Patrick collected. I made the mistake of looking at the water in my Nalgene bottle. There were all sorts of weird floating pieces in it. I had heard stories of people getting toilet paper in their water at this camp. I now had to get that thought out of my head as it caused my nausea to spike. I repeated in my oxygen deprived brain,

"It's just paper, not toilet paper and the brown floaties, those are just dirt"

I ate two of the three portions of chicken and rice. My stomach was not having any more. Without the supplemental oxygen I was feeling a bit of a headache coming on. I closed up the top of my Mountain House meal, put it in the side pocket of the tent, and put my oxygen mask back on. I laid back in my sleeping bag. The oxygen was bringing back the good vibes and I instantly felt less nauseated.

We caught a sunset over Cho Oyu, the 5th highest mountain in the world. The peak of Changtse felt far below us. The wind whaled on the tent, but we were too tired to care.

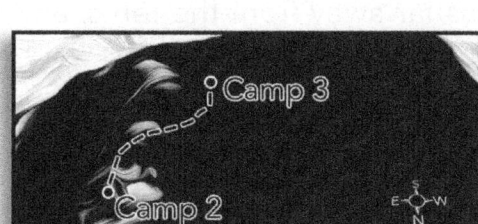

**May 18, 2018**
Day 36: Camp 2 (7,700m)
Ambient Oxygen: 7.6%
SPO2: 41%
Heart Rate: 84 BPM

The wind fought with our tent the entire night. The tent's flaps and fly cracked like a whip. This resulted in another sleepless night. Surprisingly, the tent was strapped down so well that the inside was remarkably still. The sherpas that set up this tent did an incredible job. It was solid. It was on the edge of a cliff, but solidly on that edge.

Patrick and I were on an oxygen slow drip throughout the night that had run out by predawn. Around that time the wind gave up its fight. Our heads were clear, free of aches, although my SP02 reading was 41%. We focused on the objective for the day: Camp 3 and, before midnight, the summit push. I felt surprisingly fresh considering how drained I was the night before when I plopped into the tent.

The tent was now warming up with the morning sun and it was time for a different type of plop. I put my summit suit back on and scooted to the side of the tent. Laboriously, I swung my feet outside of the tent and crammed my feet into my cold boots. I opened the vestibule and stood up outside. I was awestruck. Camp 2 was steep. In awe of its steepness, I continued looking down past the tents and onto the snow slope. To the right, way, way, way below us, I spotted ABC. Just then, the 'nearer' Camp 1 on the North Col caught my eye. I almost lost my balance. It was the first time I felt vertigo on any mountain. I was shocked with how far away Camp 1 was, how small it looked, and how it felt like we were directly above it. It looked as if we were atop a giant fishhook. Changtse was the barb and Camp 1 was the bend of the hook.

I still had to find a bathroom. At Camp 2 that bathroom is outside. The tricky part was to find a spot where I was secluded. I wanted to find a spot that was far away from the tents, and away from large swaths of accessible snow: our drinking water source. I also did not want to slide off the mountain never to be found. These constraints led me downslope to the backside of a cliff that was facing northeast. With years of squatting over squatty potties in China under my belt, it was quick and easy. Afterwards, I made my way back to the tents. Jon and Grant were just getting out of their tents to take pictures and Dom was also admiring the view. I thanked Dom for his hard work the day before. I told him that I did not think I could have made it to this camp without him setting the pace and encouraging me.

Looking up at our camp I had to laugh. The placement of our tent was absolutely incredible. I don't think it would have been possible to have the tent any closer to the ledge without it being a portaledge. The sherpas that put it there were definitely tent engineers. At the same time, it wasn't funny that I had to climb back up to the tent. At 7,700 meters without supplemental oxygen, it wasn't easy.

Back in the tent, we boiled water for breakfast and to fill our water bottles. David was making his rounds through the camp. He made sure everyone was in good physical condition and ready to push on to Camp 3. He wanted to leave Camp 2 as a team. When he came by our camp, he belted out his tag line, "Gooooooooood morning campers!" It was great to hear.

As a team, we lined up and clipped into the safety line that ran right through the middle of camp. Straight out of Camp 2 it was steep. Jon took the lead and made his way very slowly through the rest of Camp 2. I was directly behind him. Patrick, Grant, David, Magnus, Ang Pasang, and Martin followed me. It seemed that Dom, Franz, and a couple of the Sherpas were not quite ready to go yet. We were anxious to get moving, so we did.

At the very top of Camp 2, there was a plateau about as big as four ping-pong tables. Two Russian tents from Seven Summit Climb had climbers rustling, preparing for the day. David had us reconvene there. He gave us a little speech.

"The leader says, this is quite high, and the views are good," he said. "If you like views, then the next time you come here, bring your whole family."

We laughed. He was right on the views. From our current position we could see the summit, the top of Camp 2, Camp 1, ABC, IBC and the pinnacles, and the entire Rongbuk Valley all the way to Chinese Base Camp. We were excited, pumped, and ready to push through this climb. The day was gorgeous; warm, clear, and inviting.

I fist pumped with everyone on the team and we followed the one white snow path that veered looker's right. We left Camp 2 behind. The trail mellowed out considerably. The team stayed in clumps of climbers. There were no other teams on the ropes as we traveled up and traversed across the steep face. Jon, Patrick and I were up front. We were followed by Grant, Magnus, and Ang Pasang. The others dropped behind.

The climb was easy going. It was pleasurable, although I was still breathing quite heavily. At the end of the long traverse, you come around a steep cliff and then Everest brings the pain. A 300-meter snowfield at a 35-degree angle laid out in front of us. We hadn't pushed ourselves too hard this morning. Now was the time. We stepped up onto the snow slope with a cringe and a smile. It was going to be tough, but we were ready. Halfway through the snow slope Jon stopped. He took off his mask and turned to Patrick and I.

"I don't want to alarm you, but right here is 8,000 meters. Every step from here on up is in the Death Zone," he said.

We had officially entered the death zone: the area where humans cannot survive long without oxygen and where most of the deaths on Everest have occurred. In the Death Zone, oxygen is its most limited. Your body realizes this and starts to cull cells. Unfortunately, the cells in the brain start to go first and your judgement is impaired. You are also more likely to die of a stroke, heart attack, High Altitude Cerebral Edema (HACE), or High-Altitude Pulmonary Edema (HAPE). HACE is a reaction to not having enough oxygen which causes your brain to swell with fluid. Just as comforting, HAPE is also a reaction to not having enough oxygen which causes your lungs to fill with fluid. Both HACE and HAPE are results of severe altitude sickness. If a climber is afflicted with Acute Mountain Sickness, like I had on Denali and Kilimanjaro, and doesn't descend quickly, it can progress to HACE or HAPE.

Even though we were in the Death Zone, I felt better than I did climbing the North Col. It was supplemental oxygen to the rescue. My head was as clear as the dark blue skies above me. I was feeling great.

Just a year ago, Adrian Ballinger, the founder of AlpenGlow Expeditions, and an icon of high-altitude mountaineering, climbed Everest without oxygen. I would have been miserable at this point without any oxygen. Here I was at 8,000 meters, in the Death Zone, and I felt fantastic. I thought about my mental confusion at 6,000 meters on Denali and puking on Kilimanjaro. The supplemental oxygen is truly a game-changer. Experiencing the difference gave me the utmost respect for Adrian and any other climber that attempts this feat.

Camp 3 was coming up over the ridge. Camp 1 laid straight below us like if we tripped, we would land there. The summit was only a stone's throw away. This was the absolute best hiking day I have ever had in my life. I pictured summit night. I thought if the summit night was anything like this, it was going to be a breeze.

We knew we were close to Camp 3 when in the distance we spotted a gathering of yellow and orange tents over the lip of another incredibly steep section. I cautioned myself in saying that we had arrived. As ABC and Camp 2 proved, once you hit the first tent, it could be an hour or more of climbing before you get to your tent.

Cresting the lip, Patrick, Jon and I entered the beginning of Camp 3. It was noticeably smaller than Camp 2. This was a relief because it meant we would reach our tents sooner, begin drinking water, and, I hoped, get some sleep before the summit push later this evening. We made our way through the tents looking for our well-known Kailas tent labels or a Summit Climb logo. There were none in sight.

Twenty minutes later we arrived at the top of Camp 3.

We were all scratching our heads. None of the tent logos looked like the ones we had been using. We had also beat all the Sherpas up here. Not even David knew which tents were ours. All we could do was sit, wait, and take in the views. So that was what we did.

I was comfortable, content, and elated. My SPO2 was decent at 61%. The 5-hour journey from Camp 2 to the highest camp in the world, Camp 3, at 8,300m was exhilarating. Blue skies, a light breeze, breathtaking views, and a tank full of oxygen made the climb the best in my life.

It was 3:00pm. Patrick and I were sitting up against a large rock outcropping. My crampons were stomped solidly into the 30-degree slope. Jon was right below us. David was investigating every tent trying to determine which tents belonged to Summit Climb. Grant arrived at Camp 3 next. Through his body language, I could tell he was also looking for our Kailas tents. With no success in that endeavor, he continued until he sat down in front of us. David was still checking tents. When Jangbu, or any of the other Sherpas showed up, it would be a quick trot down the steep, slippery slope to shelter. Which shelter was the big question? We sat back and relaxed.

I enjoyed sitting there. Again, I was alone in my thoughts.

Mountaineering is a monotonous sport. Hours and hours are spent walking up inclined trails that are peppered with steep sections requiring some technical ability. The amount of time spent in threatening situations is dwarfed by the time putting one foot in front of the other. Other times spent on these adventures involve doing nothing at all. Nothing. It turns out, climbing this mountain was an endeavour and an escape. It is the freedom of the hills; that is, complete liberation. The months of intense training all while trying to live a normal life was hectic. Once I arrived on the mountain, I was away, unaccountable except to myself and my team. I was free from the intrusions of a connected world. All that was required of me was to labor uphill and not screw up. I spent most of the time alone in my own head. It became an intimately personal vacation.

Those of us who are extroverts, such as myself and Patrick, need this down time to regroup, reflect, and breathe. Especially the fact that we are both educators; a profession that requires you to be on stage, performing for others, the majority of the time. Maybe that's why we got along so well on the mountain. If he wanted to go lay down in his tent and chill out, that was fine with me. If I wanted to climb through a moraine pile by myself and stare at rocks for an hour, he was fine with it. There was no stress involved.

We all search for connections to others. In my experience, us mountaineers have found a way that we can form the deep connections we desire while maintaining a mutual respect for each other's independence. We spend time together without expectations and total freedom to be ourselves. Not saying a word, we both spent 30 minutes just sitting there watching the clouds, climbers, and the view over Tibet and Nepal. Doing nothing, as it turned out, was relaxing, recharging, and rewarding. Mountaineering was the perfect path to get there.

Cho Oyu, 8,188 meters, was below us. It was holding back clouds that were forming on its far north side. Clouds were also forming as the wind from the Nepali tropics pushed the water vapor up and over the wall of rock and snow between Pumori, 7,161 meters, and Everest's west ridge. CBC was a speck in the valley. The sun was still high in the sky. An hour had passed before we recognized some of Summit Climb's Sherpas climbing into camp.

We sat up. Still clipped into the safety line, we made our way down to the Sherpas. They surprised us. They had no idea which tents were ours. But not to fear, Jangbu would be up shortly. We sat back down. Twenty minutes later, Jangbu arrived. We all jumped up. If anyone knew which tents were ours, it was Jangbu.

Jangbu didn't know either. Now, it was worrisome. Of all the campsites in the world, Camp 3 on the north face of Everest is not where you want to be without a tent. All the possibilities were racing through our minds. Do we descend to Camp 2? How is this going to affect our summit bid? Would there be a summit bid? Do we try to scrape together a tent? Cuddle?

Negativity and doubt were creeping in. Camp 3 wasn't as inviting anymore. With all the beauty around us, suddenly the near details came into focus. Signs of disaster were abundant. Tents were shredded. Oxygen bottles were scattered. I was impressed with the lack of trash on the mountain so far, but as I looked closer, this camp was a mess. To my right a Sherpa was digging crazily through a pile of flattened tents, spent fuel canisters, freeze dried food wrappers, and other defunct climbing equipment. His motions were eerily repetitive. I couldn't imagine what he was digging for. What was in that pile that he felt was so valuable?

To my left, one tent pole stuck out of the snow. Remnants of guy lines were all that remained. Further down, I saw a climber drop a sleeping bag in a stuff sack. It raced off the mountain and down to the Rongbuk valley in seconds. That was a reminder to stay clipped in and ensure your footing was solid. The snow was dotted with rocks like chocolate chip ice cream, but it was also pocked with dark yellow and brown urination holes from dehydrated climbers. It was clear that at this camp, we climbers failed at keeping a sustainable human presence.

Jangbu, David, Ang Pasang, and Gelje scrambled to find us shelter. The majority of the team had arrived. It seemed that no one knew what was happening. Finally, Jangbu signaled us over to Gelje who was standing in front of a tent. He motioned and said this was our tent. Outside of the tent were food wrappers, a pile of poop, and a discarded oxygen bottle. We opened up the tent and it was full of climber's knickknacks: stuff sacks, unopened Mountain House freeze dried meals, lighters, batteries, earplugs, a sleeping bag, and sleeping mats.

We looked over our shoulders at Gelje and told him that this 2-person tent already had 2 people in it, or at least their personal effects. He said for the next 6 hours, that was our tent. Then we would be heading for the summit.

As it turns out, the Sherpas from different teams make deals with each other for tents at Camp 3. One Sherpa team will leave the tents up there for your team as long as your team carries them down. We were staying in other people's tents.

The previous tenants concerned us. Were they still up on the mountain? Did they have to retreat down to lower camps? Were they on their way back to the tent now? Would this two-person tent become a four-person tent in short order? Would we get kicked out? The tent had the mountain logo of Arun Treks & Expeditions. Could somebody radio to them to make sure it was OK? It didn't exactly make sense and it felt chaotic. At the time, we had no options. We needed shelter.

We removed our crampons, pushed the climbers' gear to the bottom of the tent, and crawled in. The slope of Camp 3 matched our tent floor: steep. We removed our boots, summit suits, and started organizing our own gear for the night. The tent quickly filled up with gear expanding from our stuff sacks. It was like swimming in a plastic ball pit as a kid. After 20 minutes of organizing we reclined as far back as the mountain would let us. It was time to chill.

Patrick and I, although friends for several years, had just found out on this trip that Phish was one of our shared favorite bands. Patrick turned on one of his favorite live shows: December 30, 2010 from Madison Square Garden. Too excited to sleep, we rocked out, nursed oxygen, and thought about what events the night would hold. Other Summit Climb members were also in borrowed tents scattered throughout Camp 3. Jangbu came by letting us know we would leave for the summit at 10:00pm. He also handed us cups of soup. Patrick started laughing hysterically.

"This is the cup," he chuckled, "This is the cup that I just saw Jangbu eating out of."

The laugh and the noodles gave us a bit of energy. I was relying on gummy chews for my calories. Gelje stopped by several times to fill our water bottles up with warm water. Since we were too excited to sleep, our goal was to rest, drink, and eat as much as we could. I did a round of Wim Hof breathing but skipped the breath hold. I was able to get my SPO2 up to 74%. We also rehearsed what we would say on the summit. We were ready.

David was outside orchestrating the team of Sherpas making their last preparations. He stopped by our tent and informed us that there was a new rule just implemented by the Chinese. Every climber going to the summit would have to be accompanied by a Sherpa. This Sherpa would be responsible for making sure we did not defect to Nepal. Jangbu was assigned to Patrick and Gelje was assigned to me. Having an assigned Sherpa wasn't something we necessarily wanted, but Jangbu and Gelje were such amazing people. We looked forward to them being with us. That, and if there was any danger, those two would know exactly what to do.

The sun went down over Cho Oyu. A quiet calmness consumed the camp. I peeked out of the left side of our tent and watched the last of the sun's rays illuminate the Kangshung Face just below the top of Everest. Soon it would be time to head for the summit.

# CHAPTER 13

# SUMMIT NIGHT

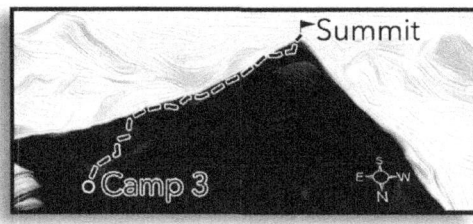

**May 18, 2018**
Day 36: Camp 3 (8,300m)
Ambient Oxygen: 7.0%
SPO2 65%
Heart Rate: 89 BPM

Gelje rattled our tent at 9:30pm. It was go time. Patrick unplugged his fully charged phone from his portable battery supply. The hiss of our oxygen masks filled the tent. Outside the tent we could hear David, Jangbu and the other sherpas preparing for the night. We got ready. The tent was crowded with gear. As soon as you found a piece of equipment you were looking for, another piece slipped away under a sleeping bag or mat eventually making its way down to the bottom of the sloped tent floor.

Footbeds went back in the boot liners. I doused my feet with Gold Bond Powder and put on a clean, unworn pair of socks. I slipped my summit suit over my one-piece Merino wool long underwear and Marmot polar fleece. I stuffed my Mammut Micro Puff in my backpack as a backup. Also in my backpack were my bulky Mountain Hardwear Men's Absolute Zero Gore-TEX Mitt (only for an emergency), three packs of GU chews, two packs of Cliff Double Espresso Shot Energy Gels, my oxygen bottle, extra batteries for my headlamp, a picture of my girlfriend, my brothers, and a flag from Qingdao Amerasia International School. In the front pockets of my summit suit I had two full Nalgene bottles that Gelje had just filled up. I was hoping the water would be piping hot, staving off their tendency to freeze. They were lukewarm but would have to do. I had my iPhone X, my Sony FDR-AX53 video camera and two spare camera batteries.

We put our goggles down and headlamps on. We were ready. I looked over at Patrick.

"Are you nervous at all," my voice shook a bit. It was nerves, a mix of being scared and of a deep emotional desire to make the summit without incident.

"Are you kidding me? I'm totally pumped," he replied.

That is why I climb with Patrick; the positive attitude. With that answer, I shrugged off my nervousness and focused on the objective.

At 10:00pm, in full summit regalia, I awkwardly clamored out of our borrowed tent. It was calm and we were surprisingly warm. Patrick's gloveless hands emerged from the tent. He gave me a fist pump. He was ready.

We strapped our crampons on, double checked our headlamps, cranked up our supplemental oxygen to 2 liters per minute. One quality I look for in climbing partners is being ready at the designated time. Nothing can zap your energy faster than being in the cold, exposed, and waiting for your climbing buddies to get ready. I make sure if there is a go-time, I am fully ready exactly at that time. Patrick was ready. Gelje and David were still herding cats. Jangbu told Patrick that they would climb at the back of the pack making sure everybody was in step. Patrick told him he would rather climb with me. Jangbu suggested that he just join Gelje and I. That was the last we saw of Jangbu for several hours.

After what seemed like 30 minutes of standing around, we clipped into the fixed rope that ran through the middle of Camp 3 and began the steep ascent to the summit. The steepness surprised me. There was no moon. It was pitch black. Looking down the slope I saw other headlamps zinging around the inside of tents, scrambling around outside of the tents, and lining up on our same fixed line. Ahead was darkness. I thought back to the early mountain pioneers. While they would have climbed during the day, it was incredible to imagine them negotiating these cliffs and cracks with even bulkier equipment and no indicators of if they were on the right trail or not.

John and Grant were right behind me. Patrick and Gelje were right in front of me. Other than them, I had no idea where the rest of the team was. Gelje was setting a relatively blazing pace. I would get close to him and Patrick as they were resting and then fall back when we were moving. It felt like I was being yo-yo-ed up the steep boot width passages known as the Exit Cracks. The narrow, often disappearing path went between, over, and around cliffs. It was proving more difficult and required more scrambling than I had planned for.

My nerves were settling, and my training kicked in: one foot in front of the other. Gelje's headlamp was extremely bright, which made it easy to follow. Patrick's headlamp started to fade. According to him:

> Gelje wasted no time. I stepped in each of his boot tracks noting that my headlamp didn't really light the way. Mistake 1: not checking how well my "new" batteries were functioning in my headlamp. After about an hour, I noticed that I couldn't see anything in front of me other than Gelje and his boot tracks. The rocks would come at me with each step and surprise me.

Patrick was sticking to Gelje for light and pace. I stayed behind him to give him a little extra light as well. We passed through the Yellow Band, named for the yellow sedimentary sandstone that gives it a distinct color.

It was often difficult to know where we were on the mountain.

This changed when a blast of jet stream welcomed us like an icy plunge pool. We had made it to the Northeast Ridge. The wind picked up and the temperature plummeted. We climbed up along the ridge. To the left was a cliff face and to the right some drop that our headlamps could not illuminate. As on the rest of the mountain, we were clipped in. However, at this altitude, moving your jumar and safety carabiner from one fixed rope to the next was exhausting and frustrating. I was falling behind Patrick and Gelje when Patrick had a humorous although strange encounter:

> We encountered several climbers about 2-3 hours into our ascent. As we approached them, I figured they were from the 7 Summits Russian team, but they were our teammates - Magnus, Ang Pasang (Magnus' personal Sherpa), and Franz. Magnus was hilarious! He said...."mountaineer Patrick....it is mountaineer Magnus" and then went on to tell me he was feeling confused. Magnus and Ang Pasang were sitting on a rock just to the side of the fixed rope. Ang Pasang seemed irritated, but Magnus was in high spirits. I asked him how he was doing, and he said his head felt funny. Immediately, I thought he had early signs of HACE because he complained about being disoriented. Later, I found out he was just confused about where he was on the mountain. I had no idea. When he said, "I don't know where I am" I immediately responded with sarcasm as in "well, you are on earth, on a mountain, on Everest...." and figured if he were OK then we could move on and let Ang Pasang sort out the details. Magnus turned out to be just fine. Franz was uncharacteristically animated - as if he were high or drunk. I didn't really make much of it, but he did seem odd; perhaps not as odd as Magnus but he acted strangely. Brendan and Gelje were not fond of standing around chatting much longer so we pushed on leaving them behind.
>
> Just before we ran into these guys, we passed by a

few bodies. I found the experience of seeing dead bodies rather odd. Death doesn't frighten me but seeing recently deceased bodies made me think of the stupidity of climbing high mountains. Yvon Chouinard said we were "conquerors of the useless" and just seeing those bodies reinforced the absurdity of it all. Still, I felt a strong kinship with these other conquerors and feel dedicated to alpinism. Death is part of life and big mountains just accelerate life both in intensity and duration. We all chose to be here. Dying in the pursuit of the absurd is what affected me. I thought for a moment, reflected on my life, and then took the next steps to pass by these bodies. Moving for me? Yes. I cannot explain it in words here other than it deeply affects me to see death in the pursuit of hobbies. Knowing many others who have died in various pursuits doesn't make these experiences any easier.

I don't remember this encounter. Nor did I see any dead bodies until I was on the way down. I was just focusing on keeping up with Gelje and Patrick as we trudged along the Northeast Ridge.

Along the Northeast Ridge, the fixed lines were always on our left. A gargantuan drop off was always on our right. The ropes were attached to boulders, snow pickets, and wound between rock fissures to keep us attached to the mountain. Everything was so cumbersome with the summit suit, my cow's tail, my jumar, goggles, mask, tube running from my oxygen tank to my backpack, my backpack straps, and the bulky mittens. It all was frustrating me. The operation of any equipment including using the jumar and carabiners on the ropes was like trying to load a Pez dispenser with oven mitts on. Several times I took off my outer mitts to make the rope transfer faster. It felt so good to operate the jumar with just the glove liners. With minimal effort my thumb would click back the smooth trigger, easily unhook the jumar from the rope, and carefully slip it back on. Taking off your gloves was asking for trouble. It was dangerous. Once your glove liners get wet, they freeze. At those temperatures, they freeze fast, stay frozen, and frostbite takes over. Even with the risk, I did it anyway because it was less stressful.

We had been on the move for three hours. The cold, wind, lack of oxygen, and my mitten frustration, took their toll on my nerves. I was so focused on my jumaring and bulky mittens that I almost ran into the back of Patrick's heels, which were at eye-level. His crampons were kicking out orange sparks as he was failing to gain purchase on the limestone face. Gelje's headlamp further up was my only indication of how steep this cliff was.

"Second step!" I yelled, trying to sound positive.

However, with the hats, hoods, and hisses from our oxygen tanks, I doubt they heard. None of our headlamps revealed what I was hoping to see: the ladders. They are the telltale sign that we had made it to the second step.

As I thought through everything I knew about the climb, I realized we had only reached the first step, one of a series of three cliffs above 8,500m that you must surmount to reach the summit of Mt. Everest.

I closed my eyes to maintain calm.

"You've got to be kidding me," I thought.

This meant we were at least another hour and a half just to get to the second step and a further 6 or more hours of struggling for the summit.

The reality of where I was, physically and mentally, sunk in. I chuckled to myself, a possible sign of dementia, about the foolishness of my being here. "Maybe I should have stayed in my cubicle?"

My back ached. My mitts were seriously pushing me off the

sanity spectrum. I started to doubt the point of this whole adventure.

"This is it," I thought.

The year of training, the nights sleeping in a fish tank, the money, the lost time with my friends, girlfriend, and family just so that I could have an adventure; an adventure so selfish that there was a risk that I might not even come back. People searched their entire lives for love and comfort. I was loved. I had comfort. And here I was letting them bounce around on the roulette wheel.

"Why can't I just be content?" The thought echoed in my head.

If my reason to climb a mountain was to come back, then rationally, I wouldn't climb it. But not climbing and taking those risks would not make me who I wanted to be. I needed to feel my time had meaning. And, right or wrong, my time on this mountain wouldn't have meaning unless I got to the summit. I wanted the full Everest experience. I wanted to know what the world looked like from the absolute highest spot. I had to push on.

I shook my head until I was out of my own thoughts and refocused on what I needed to do. To get up onto the first step, I had to thrust my jumar up the fixed rope, then with two hands, one on each boulder at shoulder level, jump, slam my crampons into the rocks, and desperately crawl with zero grace onto the top of the boulders. That was just the beginning. I continued scrambling, like an uncoordinated marshmallow man, for another five meters before the step leveled out.

The route continued to undulate. We worked our way around cliffs and passed two groups of climbers that were taking breaks on the side. Every 30 minutes or so, I would get us all to stop and take a drink of water. While this may seem like a responsible action to take, it was not altruistic. I needed to slow

Patrick and Gelje down, just a tad, to keep up.

Patrick had had enough of his headlamp not working. At one of the stops he tried to switch them out. My back was aching and welcomed the stop. None of his batteries worked. This is when my enjoyment of the stop ended. He asked if I had spare batteries. Ughhhh, I did. They were at the bottom of my pack. It seems silly to complain about it now, however, at the time, it was a monumental effort to carefully remove my backpack and ensure my oxygen mask and line to the tank stayed in the correct position. I also had to clip the backpack to the fixed line. Next, I had to secure my gloves to my backpack. Finally, I dug around my oxygen tank and spare jacket to find the batteries. I was afraid of one little thing going wrong in this process cascading into the whole ascent going wrong.

"Here you go," I smiled politely behind my oxygen mask as I untangled my cow's tail.

The headlamp didn't light. Patrick would have to carry on, sandwiched between me and Gelje.

Despite my disillusion and discomfort, I managed to follow Gelje and Patrick to the famed second step. I finally saw the alloy ladders and this time knew for certain where we were. The three ladders were intertwined with ropes securing them to the mountain. There were also numerous ropes that were left over from previous years. There were three climbers ahead of us. It was comforting seeing them struggle as it took the pressure off. It would be hard for any climber to make the ascent of these first two ladders look respectable. The first ladder cleared a slick 3-meter section of a cliff that seemed like it would be easier without the ladder at all. It led onto a steeply sloped plateau that could hold two climbers. On that plateau was a second ladder, about 1.5 meters long that was also more in the way than helpful. As I looked on, Gelje zoomed up the first ladder. Another climber was on the second ladder rattling the hell out of it. Patrick zoomed up the first ladder. Lines of headlamps, like bullies coming to take my lunch money before school, were arriving behind us. I knew Grant and the others were back there, but I didn't know where. The person in front of Gelje was still fumbling around on the second ladder.

Two thoughts entered my head:

1. "Seriously? Just grab the ropes and pull yourself up."
2. "God, I hope I don't cause a line when it's my turn."

This is what all Everest climbers are aware of but convince themselves that it won't happen to them: a bottleneck. The line was piling up behind me. Finally, the climber was off the second ladder. It was my time to start up the first ladder while Gelje and Patrick made quick work of the second ladder. I focused to stay calm as my metal crampons slipped on the aluminum rungs. It was ugly but I was fast up both ladders. I had caught up to Patrick and Gelje, just as they rounded the corner to the final ladder. We stood on the one-person-wide rock ramp that led around to the third ladder. The climbers in front of us were fumbling with their equipment and motioned us around. I looked back over my shoulder and Grant was standing right behind me. I nodded to him, took a deep breath, and took my turn on the ladder.

"Here we go," I thought, "Up this last ladder and we are over the crux. We can do this."

Gelje shot up the ladder then turned his headlamp looking down the 5-meter cliff giving Patrick and I had a full view of this Everest landmark. It was incredible. Patrick scurried on up. I followed right behind him. We crested the lip of the second step. Patrick and Gelje went ahead to find a stash of oxygen bottles. I looked back over the edge to give Grant some light on his way up.

Grant got to the top, his oxygen supply was low to zero. As he recalled in his blog, www.dingofishexpress.com:

Dragging myself bodily over the top (of the second step), I found a spot to get out of the way of the climbers coming up behind and sat for the first time in hours, trying to relax my breathing and checking my equipment. I have no idea how long I was there before Sherpa Geylje (Gelje) appeared with my spare bottle. At some point I noticed a climber in a brightly colored, down-filled summit suit sleeping not far behind me. He was on his side in a fetal position. I mentioned to the Sherpa that someone needed to wake that guy up. It was incredibly dangerous to fall asleep up high. The Sherpa commented that "that guy" had been asleep for about 8 years and wasn't ever going down.

Gelje returned from giving Grant his next bottle of oxygen. Patrick and I huddled around Gelje while he was sorting out a stash of 8 oxygen bottles. Patrick was ahead of him on the fixed line. The cold was starting to seep in through the zippers of my boots, the Velcro on my summit suit, and the threads of my gloves. I needed to move, or at least share with Patrick my misery and have a drink. I unclipped from the safety line so I could get around Gelje. Still focusing on Gelje down on his knees checking valves, I took care not to step on him with my crampons as I moved around him.

I misstepped. "Whoa," I said as my body instantly reacted to being off balance. My spine curved, my head jerked towards Gelje, and I reached out and grabbed the safety line. There was a berm on the path that I had stepped on the wrong side of. I looked over to see what was wrong about it. It was a drop that I could not see the bottom of. I carefully and quietly moved in between Patrick and Gelje. I clipped into the fixed rope, knelt securely down on one knee, and decided to just stay put until we were ready to move again. One more step to go.

At 8,710 m, the third step consists of vertical slabs of dolomite, split by a boots-width crack of ice and tangled ropes. Exhausted,

I made out through the dimness Patrick and Gelje nearing the top ridge of the third step. I just needed some time, a minute, 10 minutes preferably, to catch my breath. In the pre-twilight, I saw the headlamps of five badass mountaineers quickly gaining on me. Rest was not an option.

I hastily grabbed one of at least 10 ropes hanging in the crack. With my bulky left mit precariously holding my jumar, I lurched upward. With all my strength I pulled, crampons ineffectively scraping against the rock. I repeated that movement three times before being stuck, entangled in frayed climbing ropes. The climbers were nearing the bottom of the step. I was going to be in their way. It was the thing I didn't want to have happen. It took everything I had not to panic. I had failed once before on this climb. I couldn't let it happen again. At that moment, I told myself, "I belong here too."

Frantically, I fought off the web from my carabiners, from in between my boots, from the teeth of my crampons, and from the sharp corners of my oxygen mask and goggles. I stripped away the last strands stuck to the Velcro on my suit. I was completely zapped, but free. Still on the cliff, I bent over, hands on my knees, trying to breath. Gelje and Patrick were out of sight. The first of the approaching climbers attached his jumar to one of the ropes. It wasn't Grant. Whoever it was, I didn't want to be in their way. I sucked in a deep breath. With that, I was moving again. This time making sure to stay clear of the frayed ropes.

After the five hardest vertical meters of my life, I crested the third step. I found Patrick and Gelje catching their own breaths and adjusting their equipment. In front of us, the snowy white summit pyramid was emerging into view. I glanced back over my shoulder to look down at the third step. The climbers behind me were still at the bottom struggling to get past the first few meters. Beyond them, the view was stunning. Below the blackness of space, silhouetting the bluish black fins of nearby peaks, the curve of the Earth was outlined by a thin strip of bright orange and yellow light. We had made it through the night.

"You guys good?" I asked. Patrick and Gelje both nodded. With that, we headed for the summit.

Although every step was a challenge, the rising sun warmed our bodies and spirits. We trudged up to the bottom of the summit pyramid. The snow was 50cm deep, blown in from the constant Nepali wind. The path wound diagonally across the summit pyramid, below a false summit, and exited onto the top of the extremely exposed Kangshung Face. This is otherwise known as the Dihedral, where the north face of Everest meets the northeast ridge. The off-angle steep, slabby rock made the footholds here barely the width of your boot. Each step was treacherous. As Patrick or Gelje would take a step, the fixed rope would tug. It felt as if you were being pulled off the mountain. In the midst of terror, I looked up. Like a translucent black arrow pointing directly to the west, the shadow of Everest bisected the jungles of Nepal and the high plateau of Tibet. It was majestic. However, like all the thoughts, moments and experiences during this summit night, there was no time to dwell.

The awkward slope brought us to another false peak. Although we were finally back on snow, the crampons gripping like Velcro to frayed rope, I was starting to lose my patience. My shoulders dipped. My back was in full slouch. To my left was an enormous cornice and drop. I knew we were close and so pushed on. Only a few more steps.

Finally, we reached the summit ridge. I saw my first view of the prayer flags that indicated the true summit.

# CHAPTER 14

# HALFWAY THERE

**May 19, 2018**
Day 37: Summit (8,848m)
Ambient Oxygen: 6.8%
SPO2: 60%
Heart Rate: 110 BPM

At approximately 8:00am Patrick McKnight, Gelje Sherpa, and I summited the highest mountain in the world. About as large as a kitchen table, we remarkably had the summit to ourselves. In fact, we were quite possibly the first team on the summit that morning. But our private moment would not last. From the summit ridge on the Tibet side, that group of badass mountaineers who I saw on the third step were climbing fast. Their suits indicated that they were from the Russian-based Seven Summits Club. From Nepal, several teams were approaching too.

The 40mph wind gusts whipped icy bursts of snow on any exposed skin, notably between my goggles and oxygen mask. I quickly removed my gloves, felt the sting of the wind, pulled out my camera, replaced my gloves, and started filming.

I aimed the camera towards Patrick. Patrick sat still. I could not see his eyes through his mirrored goggles; however, I could tell he was staring off into space, exhausted, and somewhat confused on what to do next. I didn't know at the time, but he was having trouble with his oxygen mask and was on the latter side of loopy.

"OK," I said. "We are rolling."

Patrick hesitated, then took down his oxygen mask.

"Olivia, you and I made it!" Patrick gave a double thumbs up, turned around, and displayed the pink Olivia flag. Just as he did, the Russians arrived and took over the summit.

Patrick graciously scooted to the side so they could have their moment on the summit as well.

"I gotta get my flags out," Patrick said.

Then he sat there. And sat there. And sat there.

"Get out your flags." I yelled. "Let's go!"

The wind howled, further chilling the -40° degree temperature. The flags were not cooperating. We spent the majority of our precious time on top of the world trying to secure down four corners of a flag with two hands. It was a mess. We saw others on the summit with their flags, a dowel attached to the top and bottom. That would have made pictures a snap. Our world-changing speeches we prepared turned into a rushed jumbled mess as we tried to stay warm. We said what we could.

I turned the camera on myself and said a mini speech that began with my childhood bedtime prayer, my mantra.

"Thank you, Papa, Grandma, Nana, Pa, Mom, Dad, Julian, Stephen, thank you guys, cousins, counter cousin, all my friends from around the world, thank you guys. We gotta get down now. Thank you QAIS and Baishan for giving me this opportunity. And we gotta get outta here."

Pulling out my own flailing QAIS flag, Patrick snapped a picture for me. I snapped a quick shot of a photo of my brothers Julian and Stephen that I had with me. Also, I took one shot of a picture of my girlfriend, now wife, Tatiana. A picture of your girlfriend on top of the world can definitely work in one's favor.

Gazing north, Chinese Base Camp was a speck. To the south, a stream of brightly dressed climbers dotted the ridge down to the remnants of the Hillary Step. Beyond them rose Lhotse and sprawled the Indian subcontinent. Later, David told us that in his eight Everest summits he has never seen anybody cross the peak from Tibet to Nepal or Nepal into Tibet. The thought did not even cross our minds when we were there, however, I regret not jumping into Nepal for a minute. We were conscious of time, weather, oxygen, energy, and the descent ahead of us. It was time to move. Gelje Sherpa gave us a double thumbs up. I took one last look around. I had made it to the top.

We took the first of many downward steps, knowing that when you get to the top, you are only half the distance to survival.

We passed Grant, Jon, David, Martin, and Franz as they stepped onto the summit ridge. This was approximately 80 meters down from the summit. Through my oxygen mask, I shouted mumbled words of encouragement. Grant shouted back. At this altitude, neither of us had the patience or time to understand the other. We nodded and moved on. We descended off the snowy summit ridge and back onto the slippery, grey-brown limestone of the Kangshung face: The Dihedral. I looked at what lay ahead. Bunches of climbers, fixed to the ropes, zigzagged up the cracks in the rock face. Unfortunately, this was our exit route. Leapfrogging would be our only option.

Small rocks shuffled loose and accelerated down the face. According to Newton, the acceleration due to gravity on Earth is less at the summit of Everest than it is at sea level. Theoretically, if there was one misstep on this face, we would fall to our deaths a little more slowly than we would at sea level. That thought surprisingly comforted me.

The leapfrogging would have to be done with extreme care. We approached a group of climbers and unclipped from the fixed lines. With our pillow-like gloves, we gripped the line, secured our footing, and pulled ourselves around each ascending climber. Most climbers were accommodating and some even helpful. They would stay still or press their bodies against the cliff, and even give us a hand or grab our harness as we calmored around them. Some climbers were not in the mood for oncoming traffic and continued along regardless of our precarious position. From terrifying to frustrating, it took us approximately 20 minutes of death-defying acrobatics to exit onto the snow pyramid.

We reached the tip of the snow pyramid under the false summit. The wind died down. The sun was blazing. There wasn't a cloud to be seen.

"Let's stop here for a couple of minutes," I suggested, motioned, and pointed. "I want to take a minute to enjoy where we are before we leave."

Patrick and Gelje agreed.

Looking back at my most memorable adventures, I always wished I had taken the time to truly savor the moment. I was not going to miss it on this adventure. We stomped down the snow to create footholds as we moved away from the fixed line.

Struggling climbers were making their way up and across the summit pyramid. We watched a series of poor choices being made by several climbers. One stood out though. The climber, in a rush, tried to unclip and pass a group on the fixed rope. The 'unclipped life in the fast lane' quickly lost its appeal as the climber postholed every step. The person staggered, struggled, and slipped until exhaustion. Then the climber clipped back into the rope behind the same group. It felt good we were not a part of that fiasco. Out of the way, we gazed over the three steps, the Rongpu Valley, and Tibet.

It was peaceful, poetic, perfect. It felt like I was one with the universe: no endings, no beginnings, just being. My life up to that point flashed in front of my eyes. The meanderings of ups and downs, successes and failures, filled me with pride. This experience brought out the best in me.

I was enjoying the company of Patrick and Gelje, the pain in my legs, my tired eyes, and my parched mouth. Throughout the night I had been taking small sips of my water. I had finished one of my 1-liter bottles and knew I had a good amount left in my other bottle. I reached into my outside front pocket and pulled it out. I had a half-frozen Nalgene bottle of water. Undrinkable, I stuffed it deeper into my suit hoping a drop or two would thaw out. We were still around 8,750m and it was time to descend.

We scurried down to the third step with no major issues. I used the myriad of ropes to bound down the boulders. Each tarzaning step down was heavy on the legs but I was relaxed and having fun.

Several hundred meters later we neared the top of the second step. I recognized the section where I almost made a fatal mistake. Looking over the edge, the edge I almost fell off of in the night, I saw my first dead body. It was upright, covered in frost. It looked like a mannequin facing north towards Chinese Base Camp. I turned away trying not to dwell on it. After the climb Patrick said he saw several dead bodies both on the way up and on the way down. The only way I can account for me seeing only one the entire trip was my focus. When I was researching Everest climbs, I read several times on blogs of people's encounters with the dead on Everest. It caused a mind to tumble into self-doubt. I had my goal. I didn't want those distractions. I only saw one dead body. Was it my extreme focus? I don't know. Perhaps I am not very observant. Perhaps I was looking in the wrong direction every time. Perhaps I was trying too hard to keep up with Patrick and Gelje. Even now, trying to dig out more from my memory, the dead are not there.

Walking up to the edge of the second step was intimidating. I love rappelling, yet, looking down at 15 different multicolored ropes from years past, one being this year's rope, I had to choose wisely. Choosing wrong would be a potential death sentence. I was in front of Patrick and Gelje when we got to the step. I inched to the edge and fumbled through the different ropes, yanking, then dropping, yanking, then dropping. Does this one go all the way down? Was it secured at the bottom? Would it hold one more climber? It was insane how steep the Northeast Ridge dropped off. I was fortunate on our ascent that it was pitch black and I didn't see exactly how steep it was.

Patrick came up behind me. "Want me to go?" he said.

"Uh, yeah, go for it," I replied.

Just then, superhuman Sherpa Gelje stepped between us, grabbed the purple rope with red thread, hooked in and rappelled over the edge like Spiderman. He unclipped at the bottom, backed up to where we could see him, and signaled for us to do the same.

Patrick clipped in his rappel device and disappeared from sight. It was taking longer than Gelje but I knew Patrick was wasted. He eventually popped out below. I had no idea what had occurred, but Patrick later recounted it thusly:

> During my descent on the 2nd Step, I lost my footing while descending on one of the lower ladders, swung around (doing a "barn door"), and hanging over a huge drop. When I say huge, I mean huge - probably 5000m drop to the glacier way below. I knew I was roped in so nothing to fear; I just regained my footing and pulled myself back to firm ground. Once there, I felt embarrassed for the misstep.

Keeping an eye on Gelje's and Patrick's choice of rope, I slipped my rappel device on and had a blast rappelling down the second step. One of my biggest regrets to this day is not filming our descent, particularly this moment. It was a thrilling rappel on one of the most famous landmarks on the highest mountain in the world. I would love to be able to relive it through film. If I ever get back to Everest, my focus will be on filming the descent in the bright of day.

As I was relishing my rappel, Gelje was waiting for both of us. Patrick was running into more difficulties as he made his way off of the second step onto a narrow path of ice:

> Oh, but the calamity continued. Gelje said, "Watch out for that step...very slippery," and so what did I do? I slipped on it. Damn near fell to my death had it not been for being clipped into the fixed rope. Now, I really felt stupid. I couldn't keep my feet steady on these seemingly easy steps down. My oxygen mask now didn't work at all and often kept me from being able to breath. The lack of oxygen was really getting to me. I was slow and clumsy.

I had noticed that Patrick's legs were not as steady as they usually are but again, I had no idea that his oxygen mask was failing him. We stuck together as we navigated down the Northeast Ridge. There were a couple of steep boulder slopes that may have been the first step, but it was not notable. What was notable was that just before we left the ridge and headed down through the Exit Cracks we ran into Magnus. Patrick and I were both chuckling in disbelief. What the hell was Magnus doing here? He was asking himself the same question.

"Magnus!" I exclaimed. "What are you doing here buddy?"

He replied, in great spirits, something to the effect of, "Just taking in the view. I think I might check out that ridge over there," as he pointed off down the spine of the Northeast Ridge. This was a practically unexplored area. There were no fixed lines, no passing climbers, no chance anyone would be

able to find him if something went wrong.
"Are you sure?" we asked.

"Why don't you head back to Camp 3 with us," we urged.

Magnus was on his own trip. We couldn't convince him to come down with us. He did assure us he would head down soon. We took a sharp left down to the Exit Cracks, looked back up over our shoulders, shrugged, and started the stagger to Camp 3.

The Northeast Ridge was behind us. Gelje was cruising. I was feeling great -- tired, but great. My legs plunged ahead. Most of the time they could withstand the impact of their landing. Sometimes they did not. When they didn't, I would collapse forward, and catch myself on the fixed lines, a boulder, or a pile of snow. As I descended, it reminded me of skiing through cliff bands, but I was without skis. Dave Kellogg once said he would never climb another big mountain that he couldn't ski down. While it probably wouldn't be practical with the tightness of the Exit Cracks, I was thinking about his wise words.

Patrick was continuing to stumble and started falling behind Gelje and I.

> I told Gelje and Brendan to go ahead. It was clear to me that I would get down, but I had to go at my own pace. Those two were way faster and were waiting for me to descend the easiest snow slopes. I just couldn't catch my breath. My oxygen was running out but even if I had a new cylinder, the oxygen wasn't getting to my lungs or brain. I had to get down and I decided to just keep moving.

Patrick was a solid mountaineer, a great friend, and I trusted his call. I knew that if he said go ahead, he wasn't in any danger, he was just being polite. I kept him within sight as we navigated through the cracks. Once the tents from Camp 3 came into view, I knew he would be fine. As I exited the Exit Cracks, I saw

Ang Pasang, Magnus' personal Sherpa, climbing up with 3 oxygen bottles. Like most of the interactions above Camp 3 ours was brief, and relatively meaningless, until you see the bigger picture. Then you realize everything the Sherpas do above Camp 3 is of life-or-death importance.

The steepness of Camp 3 did not allow my quads a rest. I needed to find our tent and chill out for a bit. But something wasn't right. The tents where we left our sleeping bags, mats, spare food, and miscellaneous items were gone. I looked around, double checking the location. This was definitely it. In the place of our tents were scraps of discarded wrappers, a tube of Chapstick, and icicled human feces flush with the snow and rock.

For much of the descent I had been looking forward to laying down for a nap in the tent. I was at a loss. I dug my crampons into the snow and sat down. I was wiped, too tired to take out a camera, remove my summit suit (which was heating up fast), or immediately figure out the calamity unfolding around me. Gelje appeared out of nowhere and sat down next to me. I asked him about our missing gear. He was just as clueless as I was. We sat together quietly observing the camp. Gelje left to tend to a pile of oxygen bottles and then disappeared. Something wasn't right.

It turned out the majority of the Summit Climb Sherpa team was dealing with problems much more serious than missing equipment and not being able to take a nap.

As Jon recounted in his blog, www.sandtosummits.com:

> While descending the snow slope at 8,800m, fellow climber Franz, who had just celebrated becoming the first person from Paraguay to summit Everest, sat down in front of David citing exhaustion. At this altitude it is impossible to carry another human (hence the numerous bodies dotted along the route) and a helicopter rescue

is neither legal in Tibet nor possible from a capability standpoint. Franz, while focused on gaining a 'first', had clearly not left anywhere near enough in the tank for the descent and was now looking at a less-than-sympathetic David for answers. Along with two other fellow climbers, I moved onto another rope to continue descending with full expectation that that would be the last I'd see of our Paraguayan friend.

Meanwhile, ten meters below me, at a set of tents, I noticed some odd activity. Sherpas were piling up gear. There must have been 10 sleeping bags, several backpacks, and a stack of oxygen tanks.

Patrick arrived. Completely zapped, he sat down next to me. I explained to him what I thought was happening.

"Hey! That's my sleeping bag stuff sack!" Patrick shouted into his oxygen mask pointing at the camp below.

I spotted one of my stuff sacks as well. I was regaining a bit of energy. I trudged down to the Sherpas. I'm guessing they were from Arun Expeditions as they were huddled around those tents. I asked why they were stealing our stuff. They were very defensive saying that they were assigned the duty to clear the camps but chose to clear only what they deemed worthy. I grabbed what I recognized as our equipment and slowly walked back up to Patrick who was still sitting there with his backpack on. He was staring out over the Himalayas. I sat back down next to him. I agonized at the prospect of descending further down the mountain.

Then one of the Sherpas from the Arun Expeditions took out a knife. He grabbed the nylon of the tent he was standing next to and sunk it through the fabric. He proceeded to cut the tent. Patrick and I watched as they cut out the logo on the tent that said Arun Expeditions. Patrick later speculated:

...they cut out the labels to eliminate the climbing authorities from holding them accountable for littering the mountain with their tents. Well, Brendan and I saw them cut out the labels and would be more than happy to report them. They also stole some of my gear that I could easily estimate to exceed US$1,000.

They cut their company's names and logos out of the tents and left them there after they had pillaged the camp.

With a bitter, saliva-less taste in our mouths, we begrudgingly sat up and continued our descent. Our goal was to make it to Advanced Base Camp where we could crawl into our tents and have dinner and hot drinks made for us. This push from Summit to ABC in one day is a feat not unheard of but would be very difficult. We knew if we made it to ABC, we would be 100% safe and our expedition would be a complete success. And, more than any of that, we had also stashed two celebratory beers there. Haphazardly, we attached to our backpacks sleeping bags, water bottles, and anything else of ours that we could salvage from the scavengers. With shaky legs, we set off for Camp 2.

The ambient oxygen levels were increasing, which was helpful. Both of us had long since been out of oxygen in our tanks. Every 50 meters or so we would have to take a break. I thought about reshuffling my bag, taking off my oxygen mask and packing it away. Even digging out a snack sounded like a good idea. However, I did not have the willpower but to stumble downward. We were both out of water too and desperate for a drink.

We reached the top of Camp 2 together. Patrick was lagging a bit behind. I decided to skip stopping. I chose to push and get down as fast as possible. The dream of arriving at ABC was pulling me as much as gravity.

Scrambling through Camp 2 was difficult. Loose rock, boulders, and tents made the descent slower than I had wanted. The camp also seemed to extend much further vertically than I had remembered, and I had even remembered it being extremely long. I arrived at the spot where we had our tent perched on the cliff. It was gone. So was a spare water bottle and additional snacks we had stashed for ourselves. My initial thought was mountain scavengers from other teams must have stolen it. Just as likely, it could have been our Sherpas sensing the end of the season and clearing camps. I had no idea and no energy to track down answers. With a shake of my head, a deep breath, and a sigh, I kept moving.

It was around 1:00pm when I got to the top of the snow slope. I was now deadly thirsty, tired, and my legs were barely keeping me upright. I really wished I had skis now. Going down the snow slope was one of the hardest things I have ever had to do in my life. I would make it 10 to 20 meters and have to sit down. I would rest for a couple of minutes. Get up and repeat. It was a catch-22. If I sat down, I would feel better, but then getting back on my feet was a huge energy zap. It was unreal how long that snow slope felt. I had to just keep plugging away, rope length by rope length. I attempted a couple of times to slide on my butt in a zombie-like glissade. However, with the weight of my pack and the state I was in, it was not safe. Step by miserable step, I stumbled down.

Finally, through a wind-blown fog, the tents from Camp 1 came into view. As I approached, I realized there was a 10-meter uphill before reaching camp. Practically with tears in my eyes, I pushed myself up the hill and arrived at Camp 1.

At 2:00pm, after 18 hours of strenuous, continuous, high-altitude climbing and descending, I found our circle of Kalias tents. I laid face down in the snow and passed out.

What felt like minutes later, I was awoken by Patrick falling face down next to me and passing out. I slowly stood up. I wanted to push on and get down to ABC. I knew it was going to be a brutal downhill slog. My lips were dried and cracked. I was so thirsty. I tried waking Patrick so that we could go down the North Col. Just then Dom popped out of his tent.

"What are you guys doing?" he said. "It's 4pm. It is way too late to try to make it down to ABC. You guys are sleeping here."

I didn't have the energy to disagree nor the mental capacity to see his obvious wisdom. Dom offered water and a bit of food, which was what got my reptilian brain to obey. ABC would have to wait.

Dom helped us get into a tent. He was also incredibly tired but seemed put together; much more than Patrick and I. He told us that on his summit attempt his oxygen mask failed on the Northeast Ridge and he was forced to come down. Patrick and I nodded deliriously, and then shut down into dreamless oblivion.

# CHAPTER 15

# SAFETY AND CELEBRATION

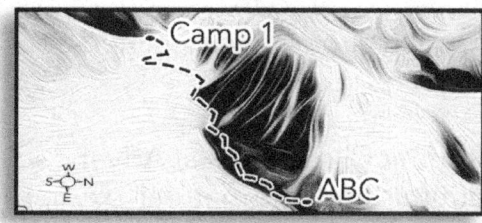

**May 20, 2018**
Day 37: Camp 1 (7,020m)
Ambient Oxygen: 8.4%
SPO2: 68%
Heart Rate: 84 BPM

The next morning, we woke up to a blindingly bright day. We were both so desperately dehydrated and tired that we could hardly move. Dom had a bit more water that he shared with us. We gathered our gear with substantial effort and descended to ABC. Dom led the way. Patrick and I slowly and carefully descended the icy face. We did not want to make any mistakes on this last obstacle. The gear that we had stashed at the North Col was also haphazardly added to the outside of our backpacks. We looked like walking trinket salesmen.

After a couple of hours, we were off the steep section of the North Col and wandering through a moraine debris field. I have never been so thirsty in my life. Eventually, the white Russian dome tent revealed itself behind a rocky berm. Still far away, it was an indication that we were getting tantalizingly close to our own camp and water.

"Maybe they have drinks there?" I whispered to Patrick, my throat being so dry I could barely get the humor out.

Dom had fallen back a bit. We were not going to slow down. We all knew the trail. We were all out of danger. We were all thirsty. At our current pace, Patrick and I were 30 minutes from our camp. Just then, we noticed Nobu, the kitchen boy, running up through the camps. He rushed up to us, a canvas bag in his hand. With "Tashi delek!" (hello in Tibetan), he opened the bag and we almost cried. He had two cold bottles of iced tea, two Cokes, and two waters. Dom showed up just in time to join in on the drinks. We were all so thankful.

Again, and again, the Summit Climb team went above and beyond our expectations. Nobu even offered to take our packs the rest of the way. As they were such a mess, we declined and walked on, following Nobu back to our camp.

We got back to the huddle of Summit Climb tents at Advanced Base Camp. It was warm, beautiful, and the natural oxygen level soothed our souls. All of the kitchen staff and porters were out to welcome and congratulate us. They grabbed our bags and ushered us into the mess tent. Inside they had hot water and a meal waiting for us. Dom decided to head back to his tent. Patrick and I sat down in the mess tent. I jumped up. Thirty seconds later I came back in with two of Tibet's finest in my hand: Lhasa Beer. The green aluminum cans were sparkling. We looked at each other's ragged, ugly, hairy faces and smiled. Our broken lips and leathered skin said it all. We shook our heads, cracked the beers and took a big chug. It was disgusting but we thoroughly enjoyed it.

Patrick and I discussed our highs and lows of the night before. It was the first time he had told me that his oxygen mask wasn't working. I finally understood his incoherence on the summit. I told him that his and Gelje's pace was so fast I felt like I was being dragged up the mountain. I joked saying that is when I made up my mind to make sure I dragged him down the mountain.

We both wondered about the rest of the team, namely Magnus. We didn't feel comfortable in the state and location that we had left him. Besides Dom, we had no idea where anyone else was. We passed several hours chatting, eating, drinking tea, and nursing the Lhasa Beers. Jon walked into the dining tent. He said that he had summited and then went into an explanation of what happened immediately below the summit. Patrick recorded this in his blog:

> Jon recounted the summit day with great clarity. He opened up a Lhasa "beer" (3.3% Alcohol by volume doesn't warrant an unqualified beer from me) and we talked about the events. The first thing he mentioned was some trouble with Franz. Apparently, Franz had little problem on the climb up but had no energy for the descent. Jon then went on to explain that he (Jon) developed a really bad cough and was coughing up green phlegm into his mask. The thought of that made me nauseous. Perhaps it was the Lhasa beer. I don't know but it was disturbing to say the least. Jon also said that with Franz not moving, he went on ahead - leaving David, Martin, Franz and their Sherpa behind. He had no idea what happened to them because he descended without others. It seemed like Jon was on his own or with his Sherpa for the rest of the descent.

Jon said he had not seen anyone else, and there was no sign of Magnus.

We continued to eat, chat, and try to understand what happened to the rest of the team. It was like putting the pieces together of who was where and when after a night at a raging, multistage music festival.

"Wait, you were where when you saw David last?"

"Really, because I thought I saw David on the 3rd step?"

"I don't think so, wait, no that was after I saw you, yeah?"

"Who?"

Grant came in a couple hours after Jon. He explained that after his summit he didn't have oxygen or energy to make it down past Camp 3. He ended up in another random tent with no

sleeping bag and no additional oxygen. He had no idea how long he was there. He just remembers a Sherpa coming by and telling him it was time he started making his way down. He went from Camp 3 to our dining tent at ABC. He was wiped but had also not seen Magnus, Martin, David, or Franz.

Before too long, Magnus showed up. As I said before, he was on his own trip. Magnus said that he really just wanted to experience the three steps. As he approached the Third Step on summit night, he was getting tired. He asked David what he should do. David told him that he was looking at another 2-3 hours up and 1-2 hours down to be back to the bottom of the Third Step. Magnus pondered life and decided he had made it high enough. He would savor where he was and slowly make it back down to Camp 3.

We swapped stories of summits and continued figuring out the previous night's events. We took naps, ate, and drank. The hours rolled by and still saw no sign of the rest of the team. In hindsight, it would have been comforting to have a radio at ABC for communication. Around 6:00pm, it was getting dark and we ate dinner. Chicken wings and mashed potatoes had never tasted so good. Although, it was hard to enjoy it completely as we worried about the remaining members. Just then, David and Martin came into the tent. They were both completely exhausted and extremely irritated from their efforts to save Franz's life high on the mountain.

The nylon door was pushed aside. Franz walked into the dining tent. He was wrecked. His lips were blistered and bleeding. The skin on his face was burnt. Everyone was quiet. Franz looked around at everybody and blurted out, "Who has my picture from the summit?"

The Summit Climb team was all accounted for.

**May 21, 2018**
Day 38: ABC (6,492m)
Ambient Oxygen: 9.1%
SPO2 87%
Heart Rate: 79 BPM

Good morning ABC! I felt rejuvenated, excited, and alive. The sun was shining, the birds were singing. I packed up my gear and would soon head down to Chinese Base Camp. I was surrounded by majestic snow capped peaks in all directions but Everest continued to steal my attention.

The wind on the summit was blowing and I felt sorry for anyone still up there. I could see climbers descending from Camp 2 to Camp 1. The snow slope that looked big on the way up and huge on the way down made people look like ants. The North Col was reflecting blinding beams of sun from its icy nooks. It would have been a scorcher for those descending around it's gaping crevasses.

We ate breakfast as a team. David said the plan would be to pack up ABC today and make it to CBC. Once there, we would have to wait a couple of days before we headed down to Kathmandu. The Sherpas needed time to strip down the mountain. For the Sherpas this was another chance for them to make extra cash. For every bottle of oxygen they brought down they received an extra $50 USD. That morning we saw several Sherpas coming down with up to eight oxygen bottles strapped and stacked on their packs. The Sherpas would also be taking down all the tents, bringing all the gear down to ABC, and loading up the yaks. A couple of them would head back up as high as Camp 3 (8,300m!) to make sure the camps were clear of gear.

Patrick, Martin, Magnus, Grant, and I took off for CBC first. On our way out, I said my goodbyes, to our Puja, to the North Col, and to my tent. We all walked with blisters on our feet but a spring in our step. The additional oxygen was filling our lungs and tickling our toes. It was warming up and we started dropping layers (but not as many layers as Martin prefers to drop). We strolled off the trail into the icy pinnacles. They were melting fast and had large pools of water at the bottom. Risking a crack through the ice into melt water, I aligned myself between the pinnacles and the sun. It was magical. We took pictures, explored their smooth surfaces and marveled at their beauty. We passed Martin's Rock, our lunch spot on the way up, and afterwards stopped often to turn around and get a peek of the peak. Tired, but excited, we made it to IBC for lunch. Dough-Che poked his head out of the tent.

"Noodles?" he asked.
"Absolutely," I replied.

Patrick and I giggled. Of course, we wanted noodles. This was to be our last bowl of yak poop noodles. Dough-Che came out with a big smile and several brimming bowls. We savored every granulated sip of the yak poop ramen.

After thanking Dough-Che, we headed for the final stretch down to CBC. As per his M.O. Patrick plugged in his tunes and blasted the trail. He was out of sight within minutes. I decided to take it as slow as I could. I turned around often to see the peaks. I sat down to examine the rocks and pocketing a couple of special ones. I continued down past the once frozen, now bursting, East Rongbuk River. Groups of other teams' Sherpas raced by me. It felt like spring and I didn't want it to end. I really slowed down once I was out of the East Rongbuk Valley and in the Rongbuk Valley. I found a rock that was perfect for sitting and had an unobstructed view of Everest.

I sat there reflecting on the experience. Franz's calamity kept coming to mind. It bothered me. According to David, Franz was fine on the ascent, although he kept taking his goggles off because they were fogging up. David reminded him over and over to keep them on to avoid snow blindness. A couple of hard-earned hours later, Franz became the first Paraguayan to summit Mt. Everest. Downhill from there, approximately 100 meters or so, Franz apparently sat down from exhaustion and snow blindness. David was put in an eerily familiar situation. In 2010, a climber on David's team became snowblind. Without the ability to see, the climber expended energy and oxygen until he was out. Despite David's and several Sherpas' best efforts they could not save the climber from death.[41] This time, David vowed to get Franz off the mountain. After extensive expletives, David held Franz up by his backpack and Jangbu picked up one foot, moved it, and put it down. He then repeated this with the other foot. Step by step, it took them 12 hours to get from the Summit to Camp 3. In comparison, Patrick and I went that distance in 3 hours.

Franz had shown signs of inexperience throughout the trip. However, he did complete every aspect of the acclimatization. He figured out how to use his jumar and figure 8. He made it to the North Col. He made it to Camp 2 and Camp 3 without any signs of trouble. It would have been hard for David to prohibit Franz from making a summit attempt. Like everyone else, Franz had spent a month on the mountain, reached every milestone, and paid $30,000.

Monetizing the mountain -- the very business of guiding high-altitude climbs and clients paying for those services -- creates a contradiction. The climbing companies need clients for their existence. The clients need their services to access these big mountains. Yet these companies and their clients have conflicting agendas. We were the Summit Climb Everest Tibet 2018 "team." However, we were not a team that would risk our own individual goals to make sure each member made it up and down safely. So, is that really a team? This is especially true above 8,000m where the expectations of companies and clients reach maximum tension. Up there, with the exception of company employees, it becomes every paying man/woman for themselves. Greed and self-preservation underlie the motives of paying climbers. When, not if, someone extends themselves

---

41      "Everest Team Forced to Leave Sick British Climber to Die." The Independent.

beyond their abilities, the paid guides and Sherpas are left to clean up. The lessons learned from a tragedy one season can often be forgotten when it proves bad for livelihoods or bad for opportunities to bag a summit.

Patrick and I were a team. But, coming off the Northeast Ridge, I left him. If something had happened, I would not have even known about it until it was too late. Even then, tramping downhill was a struggle for me. I would have been no help going back uphill. I truly believed that he was fine, and I could leave him. Perhaps simultaneously and subconsciously I thought if he did run into trouble one of our Sherpas would drag him off the mountain. In any way was such a mindset a best practice? No.

Signing up with a guiding company makes it easy to have the "not my problem" attitude. This attitude makes putting together a real team quite difficult. There is no way I would have left Patrick's side on Aconcagua. There is no way Paco, Dave, or I would have left any of the others' side on Denali. There is an expectation of mutual responsibility when a group is labeled a team.

And yet, throughout the Everest climb, there were instances when one of us was struggling and someone showed grace and compassion and helped out. Most notably for my own experience was Dom's encouragement on the way up the mountain and also him offering Patrick and I water and shelter when we returned to Camp 1 completely spent. True leadership can be found when one breaks free from the "not my problem" attitude that we can all fall into.

The rules of climbing Everest don't mention anything about how Franz went about his climb. Anyone can climb Everest how they want, as long as they pay the right people. Every year, many inexperienced climbers summit Everest and make the same mistakes Fraz did, or I did, or Patrick did. Most come down. Some don't. Most professionals come down, but some don't.

Staring at the Jetstream blowing snow like smoke off the Everest chimney, I imagined myself climbing all the way up there without any experience.

I could have done the same thing as Franz and to a degree I did. I went with my own set of rules based on what I value. I used oxygen. I used the fixed ropes. I used the help of Sherpas. Those were aids to my climb that I felt comfortable using. I would not have been able to climb Everest without those crutches.

There is no denying Everest is a checkbox. But in order for me to feel comfortable attempting Everest, it had to be at the bottom of a long list of smaller checkboxes. Meaning comes from purposeful pursuits, not goals. It was a slow build up over many years of enjoying life and increasing the risk incrementally on each adventure. There were small victories along the way. It was the "I don't want to take a cold shower, go to the gym, or sleep in a box" days that I overcame. It was traveling with and meeting amazing people on adventures to remote corners of the Earth where I learned to problem solve. It was waking up in the morning at Chinese Base Camp, zipping open my tent, and being completely in awe of this majestic mountain.  It was laughing with the members on the team, including Franz. It was interacting with the kitchen staff and the Sherpas. It was being woken up in the middle of the night from Patrick rolling over and pissing in his Nalgene Canteen. One of the most important checkboxes was the decision to leave the comfort of my cubicle. All of these fleeting moments were steps on my Everest climb. They are the stories of my life. Stories that I love.

I did a round of deep breathing to focus on the positive, continue my Wim Hof practice, and take in as much of the Himalayas as I could. The feeling was bliss. Wow. I did it. We did it. Gratitude overwhelmed me. Every setback and success in my life, and before my life, had led me to this moment. From my grandparents risking everything to come to America to Antarctica falling through, to all the ups and downs of training, this climb felt like the culmination of all of it.

Just seeing Everest would be a trip of a lifetime for most people. For me, a trip of a lifetime doesn't really exist. Each new trip or adventure extends the deeper meaning of my life. They push me to be the person I want to be. I value being in shape, being strong and healthy. I value an understanding of the world and its diverse cultures that have come from personal interactions while traveling. I value being able to create a plan and follow through, step by step, to reach the end goal. I value learning the skills and gaining the experience to accomplish those goals with expertise or at a minimum, competence. I value living outside of my comfort zone. I want to feel as comfortable walking through the jungles of Nicaragua, as I do climb the peaks in the Himalayas, as I navigate the subways in Tokyo. I value having deep connections with friends that I can trust in the most difficult situations.

For me to feel alive, to have a story, I will always be seeking the next adventure. I will not be stuck in a cubicle. For me, adventure travel and pushing my physical and mental limits extends my life's meaning.

If you undertake an Everest climb, make sure you are in the best shape of your life and believe it. Make sure you have enough energy to make it down from the summit. As the saying goes, climbing up is optional, climbing down is mandatory. Finally, enjoy every moment. It is an unparalleled experience that will be with you for the rest of your life.

*"Life should not be a journey to the grave with the intention of arriving safely in a pretty and well-preserved body, but rather to skid in broadside in a cloud of smoke, thoroughly used up, totally worn out, and loudly proclaiming, "Wow! What a Ride!"*

*- Hunter S. Thompson*

# PICTURES

Brendan Madden working for a civil engineering company in Kent, Washington, USA. 2005.

Dave Kellogg (left) and Brendan Madden skiing on the border of North Korea and China. 2007.

Dave Kellogg left and Brendan Madden road trip and ski Iran. 2009.

From left to right: Brendan Madden, Paco Monadero, Dave Kellogg.
Denali. 2011.

Brendan Madden at the summit. Kilimanjaro. 2013.

Left to right: Dave Williams, Brendan Madden, Patrick McKnight. Aconcagua. 2016.

Brendan Madden breaking in summit boots on Mt. Fushan, Qingdao, China. 2017.

Sleeping arrangements. Self-made hypoxic sleeping chamber, the fish tank. Qingdao, China. 2018.

Martin Szwed sorting out the medicine for the first-aid kit in Nepal. Photo: Patrick McKnight.

Brendan Madden and Patrick McKnight reunite and crash a formal dinner. Chinese Base Camp. Tibet.

Summit Climb tents at Chinese Base Camp.

Jangbu Sherpa. 20 Everest summits under his belt and serves hot apple pie with a smile. Chinese Base Camp.

Good morning Yak. Chinese Base Camp.

Dough-Che, the master Ramen chef at Intermediate Base Camp.

Gelje Sherpa. The sherpa assigned to Brendan Madden and Patrick McKnight for summit night.

View of the North Col from Summit Climb's camp at ABC.

Brendan Madden climbing through the penitentes on the way from
Intermediate Base Camp to Advanced Base Camp. Photo: Patrick McKnight.

Tashi, Brendan and Nobu. The kitchen staff at CBC and ABC.

The sprawl of Advanced Base Camp.

Grant Maughn leaving Crampon Point, headed for the North Col.

Preparing for the snow slope climb from Camp 1 to Camp 2.

Sherpas preparing for the snow slope climb from Camp 1 to Camp 2.

Summit Climb tents at Camp 1 on the North Col.

Brendan Madden and Patrick McKnight's tent (upper left) at Camp 2.

Sunset over Cho Oyu from Camp 3. Photo: Patrick McKnight.

The drop off of the highest camp in the world, Camp 3. David O'Brien (center). Photo: Patrick McKnight.

The second half of the 2nd Step in daylight. Tibet. 2018. Photo: Magnus Nerve.

Make sure you choose the right rope. Camp 3.

From the top of the 3rd Step looking down the Northeast Ridge. Photo: Martin Szwed.

From the top of the 3rd Step looking at the Summit Pyramid. Photo Martin Szwed.

Brendan Madden and Patrick McKnight on the summit of Mt. Everest. May 19, 2018.

Reflection of the summit and world in Brendan Madden's goggles.

Magnus Nerve safely down with Sherpas and kitchen staff.

Brendan Madden and Patrick McKnight share celebration beers upon arriving back to ABC after their summit.

The 2018 Summit Climb Everest-Tibet team from left to right: Grant Maughn, Magnus Nerve, David O'Brien (leader), Franz Rassel, Dominic Renshaw, Martin Swzed (co-leader), Jon Lawrie, Brendan Madden, Patrick McKnight, Heike.

# POSTSCRIPT

An Everest attempt has a huge impact on your life. Every aspect leading up to the climb, and the decisions you make after the climb are affected. As proof, after Everest, four members of our team, including Patrick and I got engaged, not to each other. Patrick and I both have babies now. Tatiana and I have a daughter named Kana. Patrick and his wife Simone have a son named Brendan.

For Patrick, he outlined the next chapter of his life with his wife Simone and baby Brendan as follows:

> We refinanced our house to give us some idea of timing in life. As such, our sights are firmly set on buying a sailboat in the next two years AFTER we have kid #2 (aka player to be named later). Seems so clinical that we plan these things, but we need to have some grasp on timing. Life and time keep marching on, so we feel compelled to keep step. OK, back to our plans. A sailboat purchase in the next two years once our kids are free of nappies. That boat allows us to sail up and down the eastern shores of the US. We plan to go up as far as possible (perhaps Iceland?) and as far south as possible (perhaps Columbia) given the constraints of a coastal cruiser. That dream ought to take us out about 8 years from now. Once Simone, the kids and I have enough coastal cruising together under our belts, we plan to purchase a more robust sailboat to sail around the world. Think of this voyage more as our intent to nudge a boat around this globe - one part of each ocean at a time. We both intend to continue working until…. well, we haven't gotten that far yet. Still, our 2, 5, and 10-year plans are to sail, climb, swim, ski, and flourish as a family.

My family is already planning on being a part of that journey. Although we may skip the ocean crossings and stick to the tropics where we can snorkel, scuba dive, surf and slowly sip sangrias in the sun.

For me, I will be trying to complete the seven summits by climbing Carstenz's Pyramid in Papua, Indonesia for my sixth of the seven summits. My final summit will be Mt. Vinson in Antarctica. This is now my focus, challenge, and goal. With a minimum price tag of $45,000, Antarctica is not a climb I want to pay for completely out of pocket. Like trying to figure out how to ski in Iraq, or survive in the jungle, I am a complete novice understanding how to make this financially possible. I need to learn about business, investing, sponsorship, sales, and self-promotion to afford this climb. I have realized that is where I need to grow most. It isn't going to be easy, but nothing in life worth doing, is.

While my published YouTube videos have hundreds of positive comments, I would like to address the most common negative comments. I believe climbing Everest can be done right in many ways. I believe that Patrick and I approached this climb with the best of intentions and completed it in a "right way."

## Preparation

**Dennis Tedder** 3 months ago

Dudes, just show up. This ain't rocket science. I saw your types in Kathmandu every day. Losers who want to do good when thousands of others have already done. it.

👍 👎 REPLY

We planned and trained. We had a range of background experiences that gave us technical mountaineering experience. Through other adventures we learned how to solve problems, deal with stressful situations, and overcome our fears. Climbing numerous peaks taught us how to push through situations where we thought we had no energy to take another step.

We have literally grown up with much of the equipment that we brought with us to Everest. We know how to use the equipment and how to not use that equipment. Much of our learning

came from trial and error. After packing for hundreds of trips, we have learned what to pack. It is not a universal list either. The decisions come down to what we need for the safest and most enjoyable experience in the mountains. We have learned how to travel in the snow, how to administer wilderness first aid, and how-to self-rescue in a crevasse. We have learned to read the weather of the mountains, especially nowadays with worldwide access to www.mountain-forecast.com.

Through past expeditions and adventures, we learned to "enjoy the suck." Mentally we understand that the hardest adventures give us the greatest meaning. We have made thousands of mistakes but on adventures where the consequences only affected us and the majority of the time the situations were not life and death. To make our adventures as successful as possible we have learned and continue to learn how to control all the controllables.

## Supplemental Oxygen

**Nylo** 5 months ago (edited)

People need to understand that climbing Everest (or any mountain) with supplemental oxygen is cheating and will not be taken serious among real mountaineers. Everybody who does that basically degrades the highest mountain in the world to a 7000m peak. Where's the accomplishment in that? Right, there is none. People dreaming of summiting Everest also need to control their fu**ing egos. Only because you summited the highest mountain on earth doesn't necessarily mean that you deserved or earned it. Using supplemental oxygen on Everest might be a safety measure for yourself, but it leads to so many problems that local people and also nature suffer from. In my opinion there should only be a handful of permits allowed each year and they should only be given to proven, accomplished mountaineers that do not use supplemental oxygen. Yes, it will hurt some people's feelings and might even destroy an entire industry in Nepal and Tibet, but it will also lead to proper respect towards nature and this holy place.

Why would anyone use supplemental oxygen on the highest mountains in the world? I just don't get the self-righteous mindset of those people. It's like doping. And for many good reasons, doping is not allowed in sports. It's like cheating in gaming. It's like cheating on your partner. It's like cheating in college. And who likes being cheated on? No one, because it's just a wrong and immoral thing to do. Not even on Mount Everest. Either do it by fair means or leave this beautiful place alone. Throughout the years and many expeditions I've seen so many dumb people on Everest myself that I can't stand this attitude anymore. And people cheering for rich people who let themselves carry to the top either aren't properly informed on how things work on Everest or are just plain dumb in my opinion.

Thanks for the video anyway, though.

We are not professional climbers and can't spend months and months every year training on high altitude mountains. Therefore, we cannot even get to the point where we would be comfortable attempting a summit without supplemental oxygen. Even if it was a possibility, the risk of dying increases tremendously and I don't know if I would take that risk. I understand firsthand how much of an outrageous advantage it is to climb with oxygen. Those that climb Everest without oxygen are incredible humans with drive, practice, patience and genetics that I most likely do not have. I have the utmost respect and admiration for these elite climbers. I do believe this makes me less of a high-altitude mountaineer than those athletes, however, I am still a mountaineer.

## Garbage

 **munnjean** 2 days ago
These macho boys and their ridiculous " expeditions " have managed over the years to take this natural beauty and turn it into the world's highest garbage dump. The individuals that lose their life on Everest, the majority of them with little mountaineering experience should never be there in the first place „ you want to risk your life attempting to climb Everest „ the rational is beyond me.

👍 2  👎  REPLY

Throughout the Everest climb I was amazed at how clean the mountains were. Chinese Base Camp was spotless. There was no litter to be found. The only litter that I saw from Chinese Base Camp to Advanced Base Camp was several Coke cans that had been discarded from the yak herders and porters. At ABC, the majority of the camp was also incredibly clean. There was one ravine that seemed to collect a bit of blown trash, but it was far from being a dump. From ABC to the North Col, there was a discarded Chinese satellite communication tower. This was not from climbers or Sherpas. Camp 1 on the North Col also lacked any noticeable trash. Camp 2 on the way up was also fairly clean. On the way down the camp was a disaster. As a small example of the abandoned items, there were boxes of unopened Snickers, broken tents, and all sorts of trash littering the camp.

Camp 3 was the biggest mess. Camp 3 had discarded tents, wrappers, poop piles, and more. It was embarrassing to see. People are literally on their deathbeds at this camp and taking down all their belongings is not the priority. Most of the time, I doubt it is even an option. My perspective is based on beautiful weather as well. If a group is caught in a storm at Camp 3 and needs to evacuate, it is an emergency situation and equipment gets left behind. However, besides the poop frozen to the mountain, it would not take more than one strong team of 10 climbers to completely clear the camp of all the trash.

With the fees that the Chinese Tibet Mountaineering Association are charging, they should be able to sponsor a team to go do a final clean up at the end of the season. I would love to be part of this solution. I agree that the climbers and Sherpas on Everest have a long way to go before becoming environmentally responsible. However, from what I have seen on the north side of Everest, the general public's opinions that Everest is a giant garbage dump are blown way out of proportion.

## Sherpas

**Ed McCaffrey** 5 months ago
No sherpas, no tourists on Everest. Most of the people climbing are not real mountaineers who dont belong there and shouldn't be there at all. No sherpas, no tourists, amusement park with long lines.

👍 3  👎  REPLY

Sherpas are the lifeblood of climbing in the Himalayas. There is not a high-altitude expedition that does not benefit from these superhuman climbers. They do everything from baking apple pies at base camp to saving lives at the summit. They are indispensable. Throughout the climb, I often thought to myself, "Why am I even here?" The Sherpas are carrying and ferrying massive amounts of gear and people. I'm just trying to get my butt up the hill using as little energy as possible. The Sherpas abilities, partly due to their genetics, make them incredible mountaineers. Yes, they do get paid well for their services. Yes, every expedition on Everest has required Sherpa assistance. Yes, they do die on the mountain and it is often because of a client. However, this is the Sherpa's decision to work on the mountain. Is the risk worth the reward? That decision is up to them. They also get a tip at the end of the trip and a large tip if you summit. I gladly tipped Gelje $1,500 USD.

## Money

**Beverley Lumb** 1 month ago

It's not though is it its for anyone who has enough money and that is not right

👍 👎 REPLY

Patrick and I, and the majority of the climbers on our team are far from being "rich." I am a teacher. My pay before taxes and living expenses has averaged around $50,000 USD/year over the last 15 years. In the eyes of people in developing countries, like Nepal, this may seem like I am "rich." However, having lived overseas for the past 15 years, I can say that from my vantage point it is all relative.

The total cost of my trip was around $30,000 USD. This is about the cheapest you can possibly get for an Everest expedition. Included in that was everything besides the tips to the guides and Sherpas. It actually felt strange after the climb when I pulled out my wallet to pay for something in Kathmandu. It was the first time in a month and a half that I needed money. In my opinion, the money is absolutely worth the experience and I believe it goes to supporting the local economies.

The negative YouTube comments were a great insight to a demographic that ultimately think Everest shouldn't be climbed at all. Or they are just internet trolls. It actually amazed me how many viewers with incredibly negative comments watched all seven episodes. Either way, it gave me an opportunity to reflect on my climb from a different perspective.

## Luck

One thing that none of the comments mentioned was luck. There is no doubt Patrick and I were lucky. Life on the edge requires a good deal of luck. I was talking with Patrick just the other day and said, "It's weird to think about us being so prepared and feeling that we did it so right but at the same time any little accidents from us or other people could have

made it a very different outcome."

What if I had been the one who's oxygen failed? Would I have turned around like Dom?  Would I have laid down for a nap and never gotten up? What if Patrick fell off the 2nd Step on his descent and tumbled to his death? There were so many ways that things could have gone wrong.

Patrick replied, "So true. It's a fine line between success and catastrophe."

# ABOUT THE AUTHOR

Brendan Madden is a high school biology and physics teacher with a thirst for adventure. He has ridden a mountain bike to Mt. Everest, ridden the longest mountain bike downhill in the world from Everest to Kathmandu, motorcycled across Thailand, scuba-dived all over Asia, bungee jumped in Macau, road-tripped Iran, walked across Nicaragua, climbed 5 of the 7 summits, skied in Kashmir, Japan, Turkey, Iraq, China, and Iran - the whole while making sure the camera was recording. His most notable film success was Everest for Mountaineers, a seven-part series in which Brendan chronicles his quest to reach the summit of Mt. Everest.

Originally from the United States, over the last 20 years he has lived and worked in Switzerland, China, and Japan. He currently lives in Amman, Jordan with his wife Tatiana and 1.5-year-old daughter Kana where they are planning their next adventure.

# APPENDIX

## Everest Videos and Reference Links

All footnote links and useful links below can be found at:
**http://www.indeepfilms.com/one-more-step.html**

Everest for Mountaineers: Episode 1
https://youtu.be/M0rBFWW4NAc
Everest for Mountaineers: Episode 2
https://youtu.be/sYpDnOctSJE
Everest for Mountaineers: Episode 3
https://youtu.be/RXl7fOHdZcs
Everest for Mountaineers: Episode 4
https://youtu.be/-yEZh7MZRT8
Everest for Mountaineers: Episode 5
https://youtu.be/z9fO2NO3h48
Everest for Mountaineers: Episode 6 Death Zone
https://youtu.be/C5KjFZ7rTHA
Everest for Mountaineers: Episode 7 Summit Night
https://youtu.be/RIXMa-4UzWY


In Deep Films - Experience the World from the Inside Out
indeepfilms.com/
Patrick's Everest Blog:
Climbing on Purpose climbingonpurpose.com/
Jon's Everest Blog:
Sand to Summits sandtosummits.com/
Grant's Blog
Dingofish Express dingofishexpress.com/
Brendan's Everest Training:
Madden 230 Day Training Document https://goo.gl/K4bwgc
Wim Hof Method:
wimhofmethod.com/
Summit Climb:
summitclimb.com

## Northeast Ridge Route: Timing and Distances

|  | Time (hrs.) rd1 : rd2:rd3 | Elevation (m) | Elevation Gain (m) | Distance (km) |
|---|---|---|---|---|
| CBC to IBC | 5.5 : 4.5 : 4 | 5,182 - 5,742 | 560 | 9.8 |
| IBC to ABC | 6 : 5 : 3 | 5,742 - 6,492 | 750 | 9.0 |
| ABC to C1 | n/a : 6 : 6 | 6,492 - 7,020 | 528 | 4.0 |
| C1 to C2 | 6.5 | 7,020 - 7,700 | 680 | 2.7 |
| C2 to C3 | 4.5 | 7,700 - 8,300 | 600 | 1.0 |
| C3 to Summit | 10 | 8,300 - 8,848 | 548 | 1.5 |
| Summit to C3 | 3 | 8,848 - 8,300 | -548 | 1.5 |
| C3 to C1 | 3 | 8,300 - 7,020 | -1,280 | 3.7 |
| C1 to ABC | 3 | 7,020 - 6,492 | -528 | 1.0 |
| ABC to CBC | 5 | 6,492 - 5,182 | -1,310 | 18.8 |

# Equipment List

|  | Item | Patrick | Brendan |
|---|---|---|---|
| Climbing | Binders | 3x lockers, 2x non-lockers | 3x lockers, 2x non-lockers |
| Climbing | Cows Tail | yup - made already (can make you one too) | yes please |
| Climbing | Figure 8 | BD | steel |
| Eating | Utensils? Mug? | 1x spork plastic | |
| Eating | Water Bottles | 4x Nalgene w/ 1 coarse filter | 4x Nalgene |
| Eating | Nalgene Cover | 2x | 2x |
| Electronics/ Comms | Phone | pixel 2 xl | iPhone X |
| Electronics/ Comms | Sat phone | Thuraya Satsleeve | |
| Electronics/ Comms | In Reach | Garmin InReach with unlimited texting | |
| Electronics/ Eating | Steri Pen | 1x with 6 replacement batteries | |
| Electronics/Entertainment | Kindle | Kindle in zip-lock bag | |
| Electronics/ PhotoVideo | Tripod | Small foldable and bendable one | Yuyintang (the best) |
| Electronics/ PhotoVideo | Camera | Sony Alpha 6000 | Sony 4k FDR-AX53 |
| Electronics/ PhotoVideo | Batteries | 5 batteries for Sony Alpha camera | Three 2hr, One 1 Hour |
| Electronics/ PhotoVideo | Accessories | Action camera accessories | GoPro Headband Mount, Pole Mount |
| Electronics/ PhotoVideo | Camera | Yi 4k action camera w/5 batteries | GoPro Hero 5 Session |
| Electronics/ PhotoVideo | Camera Stabilizer | | Feiyu GoPro Stabilizer |
| Electronics/ Support | Solar panel | LARGE 80W | Biolite 2200mAh |

| Electronics/ Support | Solar panel | Small foldable 20W - Anker | |
|---|---|---|---|
| Electronics/ Support | Charger | Goal 0 Sherpa 100 | |
| Electronics/ Support | Solar panel | Goal 0 light one for higher if needed | Solio Classic 2 3200mAh |
| Electronics/ Support | Cables | USB-C (2x) and USB-micro (3x) USB-mini (2x) | |
| Electronics/ Support | USB charger | 3x Anker 3000mAh bricks | 2x 6000mAh |
| Entertainment | Games | Chess | |
| Entertainment | Games | Cribbage board w/ cards | |
| Feet & Hands/ Hygiene | Nail clippers | yep, see above | |
| Feet/Climbing | Approach shoes | Adidas Terrex | Salomon Speed cross 4 9.5 |
| Feet/Climbing | Approach socks | 4x midweight short | 4x mid |
| Feet/Climbing | Mountain-eering | La Sportiva | La Sportiva Olympus Mons |
| Feet/Climbing | Boot Socks | 4x mid-weight wool | 3x Darn Tough, 1 ski sock, 2 compression |
| Feet/Climbing | Crampons | 2x with and for parts BD | Grivel |
| Feet/Climbing | Compression Socks | 2 pair | 2 pair |
| Feet/Climbing | Vapor Barrier socks | 6x bread bags | |
| Feet/Hygiene | Powder | heavy duty Gold Bond | Gold Bond |
| Feet/Leisure | Flip flops | of course, | of course, |
| Feet/Leisure | Tent Socks | 1x heavy weight | 1 heavy weight |
| Feet/Leisure | Down Booties | REI | REI |
| Full body/ Climbing | Summit Suit | MH Absolute Zero | MH Absolute Zero |

| | | | |
|---|---|---|---|
| Full body/ Climbing | Base Layer | farmer john longs | 1x ice breaker |
| Full body/Hygiene | Body wipes | 10 pack of wilderness wipes | Wet wipes |
| Full body/Hygiene | Body wash | 2x No rinse wash | |
| Hands/Climbing | Mitts | OR alti mitts & Norrona mitts | MH Absolute Zero & BD Mercury Mitt |
| Hands/Climbing | Gloves | Hestra & MH windstoppers | BD Guide & OR Sensor glove |
| Hands/Climbing | Ice Axe | 1x BD w/leash & padded head | Charlie Moser 60cm w/ leash and pad and pink duct tape |
| Hands/Hygiene | Antibacterial gel | 3x little bottles | 3x little bottles |
| Head/Climbing | Visor/Hat w/brim | visor | Camo hat |
| Head/Climbing | Goggles | 1x Oakley | 1x Oakley |
| Head/Climbing | Balaclava | | 1x light weight |
| Head/Climbing | Oxygen mask | TBD - will check & figure out options | |
| Head/Climbing | Warm hat | 2x beanies | 1x beanie |
| Head/Climbing | Sunglasses | 2x Nativ | 1x Julubo |
| Head/Climbing | Nose protection | Beako | No Geek Beak for me |
| Head/Climbing | Sunscreen | Neutragena | Neutrogena Clearface 30 + fluorescent zinc |
| Head/Climbing | Buff | 2x Buff (light/ midweight) | 1x midweight Santa Fe |
| Head/Climbing | Lip balm | 2x sticks | Carmex x2 |
| Head/Climbing | Headlamp | 2x with 3 full battery changes | Petzl Tikkina 2 & Black Diamond Spot |
| Head/Entertainment | Headphones | 2x wired | 1 wired |
| Head/Entertainment | Headphones | 2x wireless | 1 Beats |
| Head/Entertainment | Tunes | 3x Sansa clip with 2x SD cards | iPhone |

| | | | |
|---|---|---|---|
| Head/Hygiene | Tooth-paste | tom's 2 x 4oz | Japanese Toothpaste |
| Head/Hygiene | Floss | 2x Glide | 1x Glide |
| Legs/Leisure | Puff pants | 1x primaloft pants | 1 MH black |
| Legs/Climbing | Compres-sion | 1 pair for lower legs | Mammut Soft Shell |
| Legs/Climbing | Hard shell | 1x hardshell bot-toms | 1 x hardshell patagonia black |
| Legs/Climbing | Harness | 1x BD light | Petzl Altitude Harness |
| Legs/Climbing | Base Layer | 1x med & 1x hw bottoms merino wool | 1x uniqlo black 1x mari-no cabelas |
| Legs/Climbing | Under-wear | 8x ex-officio poly | 3 smart wool 5 normal |
| Legs/Hygiene | Butt wipes | Preparation H wipes (don't freeze) | Wet wipes |
| Legs/Leisure | Shorts | 3 pair - 2 stay in KTM and 1 to CBC | 1 Nike Running |
| Medical | stomach/diarrhea | Imodium AD - nev-er know | |
| Medical | Diamox | yep - usually don't use | awesome |
| Medical | Dexa-metha-sone | yep - usually don't use | awesome |
| Medical | Epineph-rine | yep - usually don't use | awesome |
| Medical | Antibiot-ics | used prophylacti-cally for sinus and stomach | |
| Sleeping | Thick pad | Basecamp - pur-chased in KTM | Basecamp - purchased in KTM |
| Sleeping | Sleeping bag liner | SeaToSummit reactor | SeatoSummit Reactor |
| Sleeping | Pad | Z-lite for higher camps x 2 | Z-lite for higher camps |
| Sleeping | Down Bag | -40 REI (might bring a light one for high camp) | -30 MH Lamina |
| Sleeping | Pillow | sea 2 summit | |

| | | | |
|---|---|---|---|
| Sleeping | Pee bottle | 1x Nalgene Cantene 96oz | 1x Nalgene Canteen 96ox |
| Sleeping | Earplugs/ Eyeshade | 3x ear plugs pairs & light eyeshades | Green Ear plugs |
| Torso/Climbing | Parka | MH w/hood | MH Puffy |
| Torso/Climbing | Light puff | 1x Marmot no hood | ------- |
| Torso/Climbing | Tech shirt | 2x long sleeves (white) | Black Uniqlo |
| Torso/Climbing | Hard shell | 1x hardshell top | Blue Patagonia |
| Torso/Climbing | Pack for rounds | McHale 120L | |
| Torso/Climbing | Pack for summit | GoLite 50L | MH Absolute Zero |
| Torso/Climbing | Base Layer | 2x top BL | |
| Torso/Climbing | Mid Layer | 2x fleece tops | Marmot Black ski fleece |
| Torso/Climbing | Tech shirt | 4x short sleeves | NB run, Kaleen |
| Torso/Hygiene | Deodorant | 1x | 1x |
| Utility | Multitool | Gerber | Gerber |
| Utility | Journal | Write in the Rain journal w/pen | |
| Hands/Climbing | Ascender | Petzl L&R ascenders (only use one though) | |
| Feet/Climbing | Traction cleats | Yaktrax for approach if icy | Yaktrax for approach if icy |
| Hands/Climbing | Trekking poles | BD telescoping | |
| Travel | Plug adapters | A/B to C,D,M x3 | |

Made in the USA
Monee, IL
07 July 2026

56552285R00152